GROUPS AND GROUPINGS

Life and Work in Day and Residential Centres

Edited by

ALLAN BROWN

and

ROGER CLOUGH

TAVISTOCK/ROUTLEDGE

London and New York

D0264400

First published in 1989 by Routledge
11 New Fetter Lane, London EC4P 4EE

©1989 Allan Brown and Roger Clough

Typeset by LaserScript Ltd., Mitcham, Surrey
Printed and bound in Great Britain by
Biddles Ltd, Guildford and King's Lynn

British Library Cataloguing in Publication Data

Groups and groupings: life and work in day
and residential centres
1. Welfare work: group work
I. Brown, Allan, *1935–* II. Clough, Roger
361.4

ISBN 0-415-01080-2

CONTENTS

THE EDITORS

Allan Brown is Senior Lecturer in Social Work at the University of Bristol, having worked previously in community work in Kenya and probation work in England. He has contributed to the development of the theory and practice of groupwork, as author, practitioner, consultant, and trainer. His book *Groupwork* (2nd edn 1986) is a student text, and (with Brian Caddick) he has made a video training package, *Developing Your Groupwork Skills* (Bristol University 1985). He is co-editor (with Andrew Kerslake) of the new refereed journal *Groupwork* (Whiting & Birch 1988) which is committed to improving the quality of groupwork practice. He has also published a book on *Consultation* (Heinemann 1984). His current interests include 'race' and gender in groups and groupwork, and the development of anti-discriminatory groupwork practice.

Roger Clough is Lecturer in Social Work at the University of Bristol. Before this he worked at Bristol Polytechnic. His experience of residential work comes from being a teacher and housemaster at approved schools for older boys, and from a year's study on a CCETSW Fellowship at an old people's home. He has written widely on residential practice including *Old Age Homes* (1981), *Residential Work* (1982), *Living Away From Home* (1988), and stresses the link between the details of daily life and theoretical frameworks. He has just completed eight years as a County Councillor on a social services committee, and a new book which draws on these experiences – *Local Government, Politics and Social Work* – will be published in 1990. His current research examines the hallmarks of good and bad practice in residential centres.

THE CONTRIBUTORS

Dorothy Atkinson is a Lecturer in the Health and Social Welfare Department, Open University. Her background is in social work and social work education, and includes several years' experience of working with people with mental handicap and their families. She publishes widely in this field.

Lucy Ball and Theo Sowa have both worked with young people and as trainers and consultants for the last ten years. They are the authors of *Groupwork and IT : A Practical Handbook* (London: Intermediate Treatment Association 1985). Theo currently works as a freelance consultant and TV researcher/presenter. Lucy is Director of Youthaid.

Ben Bano is a Community Mental Health Service Manager with Kent Social Services Department. He was manager of Bedford House Mental Health Day Centre in Southampton from 1981–7.

John Burton has long and varied experience in residential work. Now, as an independent consultant, he is struggling to assist deep change in policy, management, and practice. He writes regularly for the social work press.

Brian Cairns and Kate Cairns have cared for children within the Children's Family Trust (CFT) since 1975. Brian is also a fieldworker with Gloucestershire Social Services Department. Kate has a training role in CFT and is currently studying social work education at the National Institute for Social Work.

Peter Hawkins is a psychotherapist and trainer, and also an organisational consultant with Bath Associates. Previously, he spent eight years working in and with mental health communities. He is co-author (with Robin Shohet) of *Supervision in the Helping Professions* (Open University Press 1989).

Carol Sapsed is a Senior Probation Officer in Bristol. Following eight years as a project worker, she obtained the CQSW at Bristol University in 1980. She then worked as a field probation officer, and from 1986–9 as Warden of the Brigstocke Road Probation Hostel in Bristol.

Christine Stones is the Project Leader of the (Barnardos) Fulford Family Centre, Bristol. She has previously worked as a Local Authority Social Worker and Senior Training Officer in Avon, and as Senior Social Worker with the Bristol Council for Voluntary Service.

PREFACE

ALLAN BROWN AND ROGER CLOUGH

The idea of trying to produce a book on this topic first occurred to the two of us several years ago. We were both involved in teaching practitioners and managers from day and residential settings, on courses in the university and in agencies. Many of them were eager to learn more about working with people in groups, because this was so much a part of their daily task. 'They' and 'we' became increasingly frustrated at the inadequacy of the existing groupwork literature as a guide to practitioners in these 'group living' settings. For about two years we kept saying to each other at intervals, 'We must do something about it; let's encourage people to write about how they tackle the group perspective in their centres, and let's try to conceptualise the notion of "groupwork" in these settings'. Eventually, the process started which culminates in this book.

We joined together for this enterprise in a mood of excitement mixed with some apprehension: excitement at the prospect of working with each other and with colleagues from these settings *and* possibly breaking some new ground, and apprehension about trying to bring together our respective specialisms in residential work and groupwork. On this latter point, there have been tensions at times as we have tended to approach the task from our different orientations, but these tensions have, we believe, been a creative and necessary 'mix' in the development of the book, and in particular the writing of our own three chapters. A further 'sub-plot' in our partnership has been our different amounts of experience in large and small group contexts respectively. This is significant because it illustrates the point we make in the final chapter that we are all different people with different experiences, work-styles and strengths; and that this needs to be recognised and taken into account in making the most of the different resources of individual users and staff.

We are delighted to have gathered together ten contributors (to eight chapters), all of whom have past or current experience of working in these settings *and* who have also given special consideration to a 'group perspective' in their work. Some are still working in the settings about which they write, others have moved on to other roles and settings. This distinction (between the current and the retrospective) has inevitably been an important differential in the approach to what is written. On two occasions we met for a day with most of the contributors (as a group!) to share ideas and attitudes to the writing of the book, and this has been helpful in bringing some cohesion (but certainly not uniformity) to our collective contribution.

With only seven centre-based chapters (the eighth being one that looks across settings) there are inevitably big gaps in the coverage of both settings and user groups. We have not included anything for example on centres for people with physical disabilities; children's homes (although three are about centres for children/adolescents); prisons or schools; or private sector establishments. There is no logical reason or justification for this, the explanation being the constraints of finding authors and the limitations of space. However, the span of contributions is wide, much of the material is innovative, and the accounts from the contrasting centres which are included, plus the four general chapters, provide transferable ideas, concepts and experiences for those readers who work in other contexts.

There are eleven chapters, the first two of which set the scene by considering the nature of day and residential centres, the centrality of groups and groupings (these terms are defined), and the need for clarification of relevant theoretical concepts. The eight contributed chapters then follow, three on day settings, four on residential, and one on the 'social learning' approach to work in day and residential settings. The final chapter, drawing from the rest of the book, attempts to synthesise the key theoretical and practice strands into a framework for thinking about strategies, action, and skills from a group perspective. Inevitably this final chapter, particularly in its emphasis on values and 'climate', goes well beyond the group approach into more general principles about practice in these settings. It provides a first step towards the kind of integrated approach which so many practitioners are seeking when thinking about working with 'groups and groupings in day and residential settings'.

ACKNOWLEDGEMENTS

We would like to express our thanks to the many people who have contributed to our understanding of the subject of this book. We are grateful to former students on post-qualifying courses in day and residential work with whom we have discussed some of our ideas; to the other authors, working with whom has been a stimulating and most enjoyable experience; and to our colleagues, Brian Caddick and Phyllida Parsloe, for reading drafts of chapters one and two, and making helpful comments.

Allan Brown and Roger Clough
Dept. of Social Work,
School of Applied Studies,
University of Bristol,
April 1989.

Chapter One

LIFE IN DAY AND RESIDENTIAL CENTRES

ALLAN BROWN AND ROGER CLOUGH

PEOPLE IN GROUPS

In day and residential centres people spend much of their time in the company of others. We are using the term 'centre' as short-hand to describe the range of day and residential establishments which are sometimes termed 'homes', sometimes 'day or family centres', occasionally 'therapeutic communities'. Similarly, the word 'user' will be used as a general term to describe those who attend or live in such centres. The two vignettes which follow illustrate the complexity of interaction in such centres. Both are snapshots at lunch-time.

It is 1.15 in an adult training centre, a large day centre for a hundred people with a mental handicap. On this particular day there are eighty eight of the total membership present. Some people have given messages to say that they cannot come because they are not well; others have not arrived. One staff member has phoned in to say that he cannot get in because of illness; the deputy is away on a training course and a relief member of staff is covering for her. There are other people around who are neither staff nor members: first a party of eight day visitors (police cadets and pre-nursing students); two volunteers who come on a regular basis for one day a week and do many jobs which otherwise would be done by staff; a social worker has called to meet one of the members and to discuss, with her and staff, how she is getting on; finally the mother of one man has arrived, following a phone call to tell her that her son has been behaving in a withdrawn manner, sitting on the edge of the group and not speaking to anyone.

Some people have already eaten their lunch. It is served in a cafeteria style, starting at 12.45. People collect their food from a serving hatch, sit where they want and are expected to return the trays to another hatch. When they have finished they are asked to leave promptly so that there is plenty of room for others. Some of the staff and all of the visitors eat at the same tables with members, though there are often two or three non-handicapped people sitting and talking together.

After lunch members are free until two o'clock when the afternoon programme starts. Today it is raining hard which has meant that those who would have liked to walk or sit outside have had to stay in. Some people are drinking tea or coffee at tables at the far end of the hall. Others are trying to hurry up those finishing lunch at half a dozen particular tables so that the tables can be pushed back and a table-tennis table put out.

From down the corridor comes the noise of loud music. One of the classrooms has an annexe with comfortable chairs and sag bags; this is used as a common room during breaks in the day and fifteen people are in there. The building is one of many which, inappropriately, are termed '*purpose*-built'. In this case the lack of purposive thinking is demonstrated by the fact that there are few alcoves and little space that is not predetermined. The result is that some people chat and smoke in the lavatories. One couple is sitting in a van outside which has been left unlocked; another is in the greenhouse. One or two of the members walk backwards and forwards along the main corridor; a man is standing outside the staff-room door, where he has been waiting for a quarter of an hour to catch the woodwork instructor; a further dozen people are in a room where there are darts and snooker, some playing, some watching.

Of the staff who are not eating in the main hall, there are people who are cooking and washing up; there are those who are in the staff-room eating sandwiches or having a drink; someone is preparing material for the afternoon in the room being used for snooker and darts; the manager is on the phone to headquarters, seeking clarification of a circular on users' access to files; one person is wandering around the building, stopping to chat on the way.

The second example is set, not far away, on the edge of a council estate where life is very different in a small residential centre for children and young people.

This is another example of 'purpose building', this time from the mid 1960s. It is intended to look like the buildings around and is, in effect, two large council houses knocked together. It now provides a base for eight young people, most of whom are adolescents. It is intended to be a short-stay unit, but the reality is that, for a variety of reasons, the young people stay for longer than had been planned.

> At present there are six young people who are living in the centre. Two are at school, while a third is attending a special centre. One of the young people is in bed upstairs. She has refused to get up this morning in spite of attempts by staff to get her moving. The other two young people are sitting at lunch with the two members of staff: salad and cheese on toast, followed by fresh fruit. It has been prepared by one of the young people. The cheese on toast is a little dry, having been overcooked while a tape was being changed on a cassette. There are grumbles about this from the other resident. The staff ignore this and talk about the circular on user access to files which they too have received. Not surprisingly this proves of more interest to the young people. 'Can I read what my foster mother wrote about me?' one of them wants to know, while the other contends that nothing will change because staff will keep secret notes. Before long the conversation turns towards the girl who has not come down for lunch. 'Is she all right?' 'I bet there's nothing wrong with her.' 'It's not fair, the rest of us have to get up.' 'What are you going to do?' 'Have you told her social worker?' 'Did she have anything to eat?' 'It's because you had a go at her last night.' All are fired off in rapid succession as they move between concern and notions of fairness, jealousy, and blame.

GROUPS AND GROUPINGS

Centres are places where, inevitably, people find themselves with others in groups and groupings. ('Groups and groupings', our term for the range of occasions when people are with others, is defined and discussed in Chapter 2.) Individuals, whether users or staff, *may* have some private, individual space: residents perhaps will have their own bedroom, while staff may have an office. Nevertheless for much of the day they are in the presence of other people in a whole range of contexts: formal and informal, inside and outside, voluntary and coerced, large and small, structured and unstructured, talking and doing things together, eating meals and playing games, interacting energetically or sitting silently side by side. The list is endless. What is clear is that working and being with others in a group ('groupwork' in the widest possible use of that term) is at the core of every day and residential centre and all that happens there. Whatever the context, being with others in groups presents both an opportunity and a constraint.

It is important to acknowledge the constraints at the beginning of the book. Many of the chapters which follow demonstrate the positive opportunities for users arising from groups and groupings; the balancing of individual choice with collective opportunities is a recurrent theme and poses structural and ethical issues.

People who live in or attend centres may have had little influence on the process by which they have come to be there. Usually they have not come to the centre to be with friends, nor because they wish to associate together nor even because *they* consider that they have attributes in common. It must be remembered that people may not want to be with or have responsibility for others. Fisher *et al.* (1986) found that young people in residential establishments 'felt extremely angry about any attempt to mimic family life . . . . Teenagers in particular worked hard to avoid the feeling of being obliged to help their fellows in the way siblings would have (sometimes) helped one another' (p.91).

Sometimes what is apparent is that people do not make friends as readily as outsiders expect them to (Clough 1981: 103). On other occasions, it is noticeable that residents regard their peers as antagonistic to them, as Whitaker *et al.* (1984: 15) describe. The majority of children 'reported personally experienced physical abuse, verbal tormenting, feelings of intense aggravation with other children'. Not surprisingly 'there was little indication of strong, positive and mutual bonds between unrelated peers'. Residents in some group schemes for older people have said that they do not want to have to work out with other people who should be doing the chores.

VALUES

Power is central to daily activities in all types of centres. Whose place is it? Who decides what people will do, what people will eat, the times of bathing and similar arrangements? Who is involved in drawing up individual care plans? How far can one group of people decide what is good for others and act on their conclusions? It is in the consideration and resolution of issues like these that the quality of daily life in the centre becomes apparent. An understanding of the value system of a centre is crucial to an understanding of practice.

People who come into day or residential centres have low status simply because they are the sort of people who have to rely on the facilities of centres. However, many have lived with other disadvantages, oppressions and prejudices held about them for part or all of their lives. These are people who are disadvantaged and discriminated against because of their race, class, age, gender, sexual orientation, or disability. They may find their disadvantage perpetuated or even exacerbated in the centre. For example, black care staff in older people's homes may suffer racial abuse or stereotyping. While this racism is most likely to come from residents or their relatives (as instanced in the report on Nye Bevan Lodge, Southwark, 1987), as well as from some white care staff, the structures of the organisation may leave untouched the power of an existing dominant group. In many agencies there are a disproportionately large number of black people employed at manual grades compared to those at officer grade. The prejudice and racism of staff may be far harder to manage than that of residents or relatives.

The examples could be multiplied for any group. Why are women overwhelmingly the people who provide the physical care of others, whether in their own homes or in centres? Further, why is such work paid at such low scales? In addition, it is essential to find out whether the day-to-day practice within centres reinforces existing stereotypes. The contributors to this book have no doubt of the importance of the concept of *empowering*. In some chapters this is an explicit theme; in others it is the backcloth to practice. For all of us there is an awareness that life in the centre must actively confront oppression and prejudice (whether of self, colleagues, users, or other people) and must play a part in the transfer of power from the provider of the service to the user. If words such as 'partnership' are to have any relevance, they must relate to the detail of daily living.

THE NATURE OF DAY AND RESIDENTIAL WORK

Life in day and residential centres is multi-layered and complex; in addition, it differs from setting to setting. There are, of course, huge variations between establishments in terms of purpose and style. In some places the objectives will be specific (e.g. to rehabilitate drug misusers or to provide day care for under-fives); in others, they are more general (e.g. a place where older people live or a day centre where what happens is determined by what users negotiate with workers).

Conceptually it is hard to distinguish a residential centre from many other styles of living which would not be termed 'residential living'. Some examples are clear cut: an older people's home is a residential centre, whereas the private houses of older people who live on their own or with one or two others are not. However, there are an increasing number of places which are at the boundary between 'ordinary housing' and 'residential centres'. One type of *group home,* for people with a mental handicap, is discussed in a later chapter. In such places residents and outsiders as well as workers are involved in the structure and management both of the premises and of the life-style. Centres like these are not 'fluid' groupings; they do not necessarily have an identifiable staff group; they may not be subject to environmental interventions.

In a similar way the boundary between residential and day centres is also less clearly defined. It has become more commmon for people to spend the day in a residential unit and sleep in their own homes; occasionally they will stay overnight in the centre or combine day care with blocks of residence, often known as respite care. There are also centres which are resource units for the community, as well as the place where a small group of people live. Nevertheless, the key distinction remains that some people sleep in a residential centre and none do in a day centre.

The boundaries of day centres are also shifting. There are a growing number of examples where users do not attend every day but are allocated a set number of sessions per week. There are some agencies which are developing the idea of a *day service* : little activity with users happens on the premises; the site is a reference point for the provision of services elsewhere. We are not referring to such developments.

Nevertheless there are factors which are common to many day or residential centres :

Status of person

By and large people are stigmatised before moving into a day or residential establishment, and further stigmatised as a consequence of moving in. Going to a centre is often taken in itself as an indication of inadequacy. In some places, like day nurseries, provision may be limited to parents who are defined as problematic (e.g. unable to cope, liable to abuse their children). Indeed, some parents may not want a nursery place because they do not want such a label attached to them. Some people purchase care simply to avoid the process of having to be assessed for local authority or, perhaps, voluntary provision.

Common criteria

Most centres are designated for people who are thought to have certain sets of needs or characteristics in common (age, gender, race, religious denomination, common attributes). Only a few establishments are open to anyone.

Size

Centres have been much larger than ordinary houses. This has been because there are thought to be economies of scale. Sizes have been steadily reduced until it is now possible to envisage many units being little more than large houses.

Communal facilities

Residents have been expected to share facilities with more people than in an average household – for example, baths, lavatories, dining and sitting rooms. In day centres such sharing takes place for only a part of daily life.

7

Thus, life in centres differs from family life and from the conventional picture of groupwork. In centres people move from one grouping to another; in doing so they take knowledge with them of how people have acted in other places. But even this complex network misses a key element, that of the context in which the centre exists. The way in which people act towards others is influenced not only by practices within a centre, but by the structures within which that centre has to operate. The following questions may highlight some key structures in relation both to the organisational system and practices within the centre.

What control do those who live and work in the centre have over the planning and organisation? Do staff or users have a say in the level of the budget, the ways in which money is spent or the systems which operate within the centre? Can the 'insiders' buy goods where they wish, decorate the place as they like, hire and fire staff? King *et al.* (1971) contend that the more control centre staff have over matters like these, the better will be the quality of care of users.

What control do users have? Many users of centres have only minimal influence on the decision whether or not to attend. It is a far cry from the *positive choice* advocated so fervently by the Wagner Committee (1988). Do users have any say concerning the people with whom they are to live or work? Within the centre they are likely to give up control both of large parts of the arrangements for the routines of daily living and of their lives.

What are the roles and responsibilities of staff? To what extent do they manage the buildings, provide physical care for users, influence the decisions of users? Are they available twenty four hours per day? Do users expect to do things (or 'live') without staff intervention? Do staff expect to share any of their lives with users?

Who owns the centre? Some small units for older people or those with a mental handicap are being purchased by housing associations or by the individuals with mortgages. In this case residents have a different type of stake in the property. Can an establishment still be called a 'centre' if it is owned by the users?

8

Who manages the centre? Users rarely manage either the staff or the premises. Staff are not employed by users although there are some examples where residents have begun to exert more say (see Miller and Gwynne 1972).

How long do people stay? Do people stay for the rest of their lives (in the case of residential centres for older people), for the whole of their adult life up to retirement (as with an adult training centre), or for brief and perhaps intermittent spells?

How permeable is the boundary? Is the membership defined (and thus limited), or are there many functions being carried out in the one place?

What services and facilities are provided? This allows consideration of the quality of the physical resources (access for wheelchairs, numbers of single rooms, ratios of lavatories to users) and of the services which are provided (physical care such as bathing or dressing, hairdressing, nursing).

Mention has already been made of the fact that the boundaries around centres have changed with many people being in the centre for shorter spells. In part what has changed is the perception of the centre as a base. For example, day nurseries, increasingly calling themselves family centres, may provide fewer children with full care on each day of the week. Instead they may concentrate on supporting more children on a part-time basis and working with parents so that the parents can offer better care. While there are sound reasons for making such a move – the wish to see the child as part of the system in which it lives, the importance of helping people learn parenting skills, the shortage of resources for expansion – there are attendant dangers. First, there is the likelihood that it is the new work which is regarded as the most skilled. Thus the aspects which are most like that of the higher status field social work – counselling and training parents, not direct care – will be thought the most important. Second, more may be expected of parents: the idea that it is reasonable to share the care of children with others may recede.

It is essential that day and residential centres should not be isolated from what happens outside them. However, it is equally important that the core task of providing a base, by day or overnight, should neither be underrated nor wither away. In those establishments where the provision of a base is still the central task, staff will be well aware of the stress and demands that this creates. They have to share and live with the sadness, pain, uncertainty, and anger of others *and* try to create a climate which will be beneficial to consumers. It is not surprising that working away from the centre is attractive to many staff.

Our contention is that the provision of a base can itself be healing and therapeutic. Thus in a day nursery it is possible to think carefully about the activities, the regime, and the environment for the group of children, including their need for attention or love. But it is also possible to plan for the specific needs of an individual child who may overcome fear and hurt by safe play with adults. In the same way in a residential establishment, adults or young people may lead a fuller life than they did before.

We take this task, which we have termed the provision of a base, to be the core work of a residential or day centre. By this we mean that the creation of the climate (or the environment) appropriate to the function of the centre is the essential task. Thus the nature of the base in a place where people expect to stay for the rest of their lives will be different from that where people drop in when they wish. Nevertheless, they will only *want* to drop in, if the establishment appears safe and welcoming.

There are some features which, to a greater or lesser extent, are common to the types of places which we are considering. In day and residential centres a range of tasks are carried out, with or without staff involvement:

Maintenance of premises.

Negotiations with outsiders (e.g. neighbours, other professionals, line managers).

Direct physical care of users (e.g. bathing, feeding, toileting).

Preparation for the physical care of users (i.e. tasks which may be carried out separately from users – e.g. cooking, cleaning, washing clothes).

Other direct work with users (e.g. talking, which may be described as interviewing or counselling, joining in activities such as walks, games, going out for a drive, accompanying people on their appointments outside, perhaps to hospital or court).

Planning and recording concerning individuals (e.g. contracts, checking on what has happened, writing reports); reviewing life-style within the centre.

Administration concerned with users (e.g. money, visitors), budgeting and ordering, planning menus, together with reading reports and instructions from managers and compiling information for them, such as occupancy figures.

The core task in any centre is to manage these activities (and any others) in ways which help to create the type of environment that is wanted. There are important differences in emphasis from groupwork. In groupwork, the group itself is regarded variously as the context, the means, or the focus for achieving desired ends. In centres, working with people in groups in these ways frequently contributes to the core task, but is not the overall task itself. In addition, the buildings and their environment are far more significant in day and residential work than in fieldwork. Indeed, *the place*, which becomes *a base* for users, is a key element of what is special. One of our central themes is that an understanding of group behaviour, and development of skills in groupwork, should be used to improve the quality of that base. Workers require both a knowledge of group dynamics and skills in practice in groups.

DIFFERENCES FROM GROUPWORK IN THE FIELDWORK SETTING

Nevertheless there are substantial differences from conventional groupwork. An example will illustrate the complexity of the subject. During the lunch-time breaks at the day centre for people with a mental handicap described earlier, someone becomes the centre of attention. It seems that she is being isolated; nobody sits with her; comments are passed about her fussiness and poor manners and the length of time she takes to eat when some people want to start playing table-tennis; she looks unhappy. What are staff to do?

An individual perspective would be seeking out explanations focused on a particular person: does the problem arise from depression, a consequence of previous loss and bereavement, an inability to fit in, lack of sociability or her own troublesome behaviour? *A systemic analysis* would seek explanations in the group living patterns: how are others (staff and users) contributing to this behaviour? what group processes are occurring that may be driving her into this position? how may it be functional for others to have her in this role? is she isolated on account of stigma? how may the group composition be affecting her isolation, loneliness and powerlessness? For example, is she the only one of her race, gender, age or class? *Structurally*, questions would be asked about the whole organisation and management of the unit, and the principles and policies governing both how people get there and what happens within it. Are there explicit values and practices concerning user participation, rights and anti-discrimination?

Thus people's understanding, their explanation of why things are as they are, will vary. However, the worker at the centre also has a variety of options as to what should be done, and these are different from those available to the conventional groupworker in a fieldwork setting. First, the staff in the centre have a responsibility not only for the group at the meal time, but also for the environment in which that group exists. The staff could intervene directly in the external system. For example, they could alter what happens *before* the meal, if this was thought to be influential in the process. They could change: the timing of the meal (so that it does not clash with some other activity); the food; the system for serving the food; the system by which people decide where they will sit; the staffing arrangements (it might be decided that more staff should eat with users and that someone will eat with this particular person, trying to attract others to join them).

Second, staff are able also to influence people outside the meal. It would be possible to discuss the problems with a small group or with the whole community; some people might be asked to befriend the individual and take her in with them to the meal; the person might be taught skills concerning eating habits; the status of the individual might be enhanced by helping her in activities which she does well. In addition, staff may choose to intervene during the meal to make clear that such nasty comments will not be allowed.

Working in centres has other differences from groupwork. While these will be developed later it is useful to list them here:

Staff directly intervene in the lives of users both because they have a prime responsibility for the way in which the place runs and because they provide some of the care; in groupwork, staff do not have this dual responsibility.

In settings where people meet each other frequently through the day and where some of the work involves heavy and perhaps unpleasant physical care, feelings of worker and user are much nearer the surface and are more intense.

The boundaries around the groupings and activities of people are different (people move in and out of groups, there may be no fixed membership, group members may meet frequently outside a particular activity, staff may provide direct physical care for users or meet them informally through the day, for example at meals).

For staff, the opportunity and challenge posed by this different 'group reality' is one that cannot be avoided. It is central to their task, and demands both detailed *understanding* of how people (including themselves) behave in groups, and *group practice skills* appropriate for the settings in which they work. The understanding should extend beyond small group processes to the significance of *context* (whether physical, organisational, agency, or community) and to the study of inter-group relations. Similarly, group skills are needed at many levels of which two have particular significance.

The *first* is the 'macro' level of the centre itself and the skills of creating a culture, climate, and living environment which facilitates groups and groupings which are mutually enhancing of both people's general and specific needs and wants *and* the purposes of the centre. The *second* level is the skills of working face-to-face with people in a whole range of small groupings, formal and informal, planned and spontaneous.

This 'two-level' focus is a recurrent theme in the practice-based chapters which form the major part of this book. The complexity of the dynamics in which workers have responsibility for structuring the environment and acting within those structures is one of the themes in the final chapter. Staff are themselves trying to behave or live in ways which they are hoping users may discover to be useful; they may want users to take more control of their own lives but, in most places, the staff retain responsibility for the life of the place.

LITERATURE REVIEW (UK AND USA)

It will be apparent from the discussion in this chapter that in day and residential centres there is an ebb and flow of people in various groups and groupings. There are three main strands of writing which have some bearing on this theme: literature on groupwork, residential work, and, to the extent that it exists, day centre work. Each of these is considered in turn. In addition, there is a brief reference to community work.

Groupwork

Until recently nearly all the 'classical' groupwork literature on both sides of the Atlantic has been based on formed groups in the fieldwork setting. The emphasis has been on closed membership groups, with an assumption of structured meetings at regular intervals, usually weekly. There are however some indications of the 'rediscovery' of the open group and of self-help groups, which in their ethos, unpredictability, and context-based emphasis broaden the parameters of social groupwork practice in directions more akin to centres, although still fundamentally distinct from them.[1]

It has been difficult for day and residential workers to use this literature on formed groups in their settings where the interaction is more complex. Indeed, this 'gap' in the groupwork litera-ture leaves them in one of three positions: ignoring the tradi-tional groupwork texts as mostly irrelevant (and reverting to 'common-sense' and 'experience'); using fieldwork theory uncritically, crudely, and inappropriately; or trying to work out for themselves what is relevant and what can be adapted, with virtually nothing to guide them in the process.

Residential centres

It is surprising that the disciplines of groupwork and of residential work have remained so distinct. Much of the writing on residential centres scarcely mentions 'groups' and virtually nothing links groupwork to daily life. Some people (e.g. Polsky 1965), particularly in America, have written about the use of structured groups in residential units. More recently, the current vogue title 'group-care' has been used to describe residential work (e.g. Ainsworth and Fulcher 1981). The dilemma contained in this new generic title is that, as in any other setting, life is a mix of being separate and being with others, of privacy and community. Residential living is more complex than the phrase 'group care' allows: there are times when it is neither in a 'group' nor is it 'care'.

Much of the writing which captures the reality of life in residential establishments is pervaded by awareness of groupings of people. Yet, as already said, specific references to groups and groupwork are minimal. Pick's (1981) lovely descriptive and analytic study of one residential centre for young people is an example of this:

> Meals, when there was a cosy feeling of being full up was a
> good time, and we often lingered a little longer and talked.
> Conversations would pass from table to table, from person to
> person, like a ball game. Some took part, others listened.
> Some found it understandable, others out of their depth.
> Sometimes it revolved mostly around the grown up,
> sometimes mostly around the younger ones. But talking went
> on everywhere ... These were fields of expression, discovery,
> sharing, discussion, disagreement, tolerance, vehemence.
> They were important, because they helped to allow new and
> changed attitudes to take shape.
>
> (Pick 1981: 82)

Writers who do address the group dimension are to be found in the specialist literature where several strands can be identified.

The therapeutic community literature. This is discussed more fully by Hawkins (Chapter 3). These highly specialised settings have always depended on carefully selected staff and clientele and sophisticated 'therapeutic' regimes, traditionally based on psychodynamic/psychoanalytic concepts and more recently drawing on humanistic psychology and systems theory.

The positive peer culture/guided group interaction literature (mostly USA, e.g. Vorrath and Brendtro 1984, Stephenson and Scarpitti, 1974). These methods aim at major changes in behaviour and values (e.g. of offenders and substance abusers), and highly intensive peer confrontation and support methods are used, often with a distinct, value-laden, philosophical underpinning.

15

The group psychotherapy literature (e.g.Yalom 1975). Much of this refers to out-patient groups, but where it does apply to in-patient groups the emphasis is clinical with little or no regard for the impact of the institutional context of the hospital. (Maxwell Jones 1952 and 1968, in his work at the Henderson Hospital is a notable exception to this). It is interesting to note that the importance of informal self-help groupings of patients (whether in the hospital ward, villa, or day-room) is seldom addressed by authors.

A variation on this theme is the use of psychotherapeutic approaches in non-medical residential settings, as described by Lennox (1982). She selects three group psychotherapy approaches (behaviour modification, encounter groups, and transactional analysis) and describes, in useful detail, group sessions based on each of these methods. What she does not do to any significant degree is relate this 'group treatment' to the group living environment and all the other groups and groupings to which members belong, inevitably 'importing' knowledge and experience into each therapeutic group meeting.

The literature on residential staff groups and teams. When 'groups' are mentioned in writing on residential work, they are often *staff* groups.[2] There has been an increasing and much needed interest in this topic in recent years. What tends to happen, however, is that the staff group gets discussed in isolation from the residents' groupings, inter-group relations and the total group living environment. There also tends to be a heavy emphasis on supervision, management and support.[3] Many years ago Dockar-Drysdale (1968), from her psychoanalytic background, had stressed the effects on staff of working with young people who, at times, tried to swallow them up or annihilate them. More recently Fulcher and Ainsworth (1985) examined the consequences of working with disturbed adolescents, not only for individual staff but for *staff group dynamics.* Some writers emphasise the significance of the interaction in the staff team for the daily life of the residents: if you want to understand what is happening amongst the residents, you must look first at what is happening amongst the staff, the argument would run.

Other relevant existing sources on groupwork in residential settings include two useful but rather outdated texts (Maier 1965, Konopka 1970) and a chapter by Payne in McCaughan (1978).

Probably the most useful book to date for an analysis of group processes and dynamics in residential group living contexts is Douglas's recent book, *Group Living* (1986). We regard the theoretical background provided by Douglas as complementary to this book, which gives some attention to theoretical concepts about group processes (see Chapter 2) but which is mainly concerned with the development of group approaches and group skills in centres.

Day centres

The literature on day centres is much sparser than that for residential centres, and it mostly comprises booklets, tracts and articles on establishments or specific user groups. A review of some of this literature confirms the self-evident fact that much of what takes place in the centres occurs in many different kinds of groups and groupings. The implications of this for worker and user actions and skills are, however, rarely considered. We are thus in relatively uncharted territory.

One of the very few general books on day centres is Carter's (1981) *Day Services for Adults*. In a survey of centres for a range of different adult users, she makes the interesting observation that many users valued the day centre experience more for the informal opportunity to meet and talk with other people than for the organised events and groups.

Family centres. A perusal of this literature confirms both how much happens in groups and groupings, and how little emphasis is placed on a 'group living' perspective.[4] There are references to tensions between different kinds of groups; self-help group issues; the importance of 'drop-in'; the mix of social, activity, therapeutic, and action groups; staff groups ; and informal groupings. But there is very little on the 'community', process, and skill implications.

Mental-health day centres. A MIND (1980) publication, *New Directions for Psychiatric Day Services*, has a number of contributions which talk about different kinds of groups from 'drop-in' to therapy groups and there is some discussion of group issues, for example whether capacity to use a group should be a criterion for membership. Moos's (1974) seminal contribution on 'treatment environments' emphasises the importance of the 'social climate' of a centre, and Mounsey (1983) takes Yalom's (1975) eleven curative factors in groups as a basis for establishing a conducive climate in a mental-health day centre.

Day centres for older people. Fennel *et al.* (1981) carried out a study of centres in East Anglia in which they mention various group activities, but the process of group interaction is not addressed. General books on social work with older people (e.g. Marshall 1983, Mortimer 1982, Rowlings 1981) mention the potential of groupwork, but do not relate this to day centres.

Day centres for people with a mental handicap. A sparse literature has recently been enriched by Carter's (1988) account of a week in the life of a 'creative' day centre. The mosaic is viewed through the daily experience of individual users and staff, giving a vivid picture of the consumer's view of moving in and out of different activities and experiences both inside and outside the centre. Although the group perspective is not addressed *per se,* the importance of group experience and learning how to develop peer relationship skills is a recurring theme throughout the book.

Day centres for offenders. In the last decade there has been a significant increase in the use of day centres by the probation service, and these centres have extensive groupwork programmes. The full significance of the 'group living' and groupings aspects has not perhaps been fully grasped. There are two accounts (Hil or Vanstone, both in Pointing 1986) of small-scale consumer research into two very different centres and their groupwork programmes. Several points emerge: how much life in a centre can offer when compared with the set-piece office interview; the users' appreciation of contact with centre staff in informal groupings and individually; and their preference for groups which are practical rather than personal in their orientation.

Community work

Dharamsi *et al.* (1979) write about a rare example of an attempt to incorporate a residential home as part of a community project. Many residential places have developed various types of outreach work; in the Harlesden Project described by Dharamsi (1979), workers formed a community work team and took on the responsibility of a residential home for young people. The literature illustrates a central difference, though not one made explicit in the text, between day and residential centre work on the one hand, and community work on the other. Community workers set out to enable or empower local people; they may provide expertise in, for example, analysis of need, presenting information, or lobbying, but do not take on to run groups or activities on a permanent basis. By contrast, the workers in a day or residential centre expect to do things for other people and to have the responsibility for the management of the centre. This oversimplifies: there are examples of centre workers, as in group homes, who have neither management responsibility nor provide the physical care of others. Nevertheless for the majority of staff this holds true.

However, community work literature has an important bearing on an understanding of task and process in some aspects of centre work. For example, emphasis is given to identifying issues and the use of a community profile. (How many staff have a 'community profile' of their centre?) Twelvetrees (1982: 46) suggests that community workers, in addition to possessing analytical and organisational skills, must also have 'the skill or ability to form relationships with other people in such a way that they will listen and take action on your advice'. The worker has to notice emotions and feelings. He argues also that workers have to consider the role they will adopt, and plan for their withdrawal (pp. 50–65), and contends that trying to counsel an individual and to act as community worker leads to role confusion (p.87). Staff in centres have to manage exactly this uncertainty as to where is the appropriate boundary between indifference and interference, and have to manage the complexity of relationships with individuals and with the life of the centre.

However, the theme which is strongest in community work, and weakest in day and residential work, is that of empowering. At the heart of community work is the notion that people can have more say in what happens to them: 'Have you ever thought that you might be able to do something about that?', the worker might ask.

Many groups seek greater control over the decisions that affect their lives.

'Allowing genuine participation in decision making –
including shared control of financial decisions – is sometimes
the most effective form of support that can be given, yet local
authorities . . . have found it difficult to relinquish control
over even small decisions. Even where there has been some
achievement of genuine participation, unless it is at the same
time firmly tied to the principle of positive discrimination, it
will tend to benefit the stronger, better organised interests in
the better off areas who least need local government support.

(Harlesden 1979: p.386)

NOTES

1 An examination of standard American texts (e.g. Hartford 1971,
   Konopka, 1983, Glasser *et al*, 1974, Garvin 1981) or British ones (e.g.
   Douglas 1976,1978, Brown 1986, Heap 1985, Whitaker 1985) confirms
   this emphasis on closed membership groups, as does an analysis of
   articles published in the journal *Social Work with Groups*, during the
   first decade of publication (1978–87). Schopler and Galinsky, (1984),
   and Galinsky and Schopler (1985) write about open groups while
   self-help groups are discussed, for example, by Silverman, (1980) and
   Lindenfield and Adams (1984).
2 Concerning staff groups, Beedell (1970) writes about 'the unit as
   worker', Wolins (1982) stresses the importance of shared values
   amongst the staff team; Ainsworth and Fulcher (1981) have a chapter
   entitled 'Team functioning in group care' and Clough (1982)
   similarly focuses in one chapter on 'Working in a team'. 'Teamwork
   in community work and residential care', is a chapter in Harlesden
   (1979). The authors also discuss accountability and support, and refer
   to their style of leaderless group (p.323).
3 Literature on supervision and management includes Evans and
   Galloway 1980 and Collins and Bruce, 1984).
4 See Adamson and Warren (1983), De'Ath (1985), Willmott and
   Mayne (1983), Hasler (1984), Phelan (1983)

Chapter Two

THE MOSAIC OF GROUPS AND GROUPINGS:

Some Theoretical Concepts

ALLAN BROWN AND ROGER CLOUGH

In Chapter 1 we have tried to paint a contextual picture of the complex mosaic of groups and groupings which occur in day and residential settings. The theoretical frameworks which are normally offered to social groupworkers rely substantially on small group theory and a fieldwork-based, structured, closed group model. This provides an inadequate and incomplete basis for a group analysis of centre life. We begin this chapter by considering definitions of different kinds of gatherings of people; we then suggest a typology of the different 'groups' which actually occur in centres; and, finally, we explore the relevance of group theory to an understanding of processes in day and residential life.

DEFINITIONS

Social groupwork practice-theory is based on a general notion of what constitutes a group. Lang (1981,1986) has made an important contribution in identifying a continuum from 'aggregate' through 'collectivity' to 'group', and she has explored the practice significance of these different social forms. The distinction between these entities is clarified in the following definitions (quoted by Lang (1986) from Theodorson and Theodorson 1969):

An AGGREGATE is 'a gathering of persons in physical proximity who have come together temporarily and lack any organisation or lasting pattern of interrelationships'.

A COLLECTIVITY, as a small social form, is 'a plurality of persons having a degree of social structure, collective consciousness, and interaction that would be classified as intermediate between an aggregate (having no such structure) and a group'.

A GROUP is 'a plurality of persons who have a common identity, at least some feeling of unity, and certain common goals and shared norms. A group is further characterised by direct or indirect communication among its members, standardised patterns of interaction based on a system of interrelated roles, and some degree of interdependence among its members. According to this usage, a group is a more developed type of collectivity with a distinct sense of identity, and definite social structure, based on direct or indirect interaction among its members'.

In her analysis, Lang goes on to distinguish collectivity from group according to several kinds of variables, 'related to *time*, *context*, the *constituents*, the functioning of the *entity*, the *worker*', and by identifying various conditions which generate collectivities. For example, taking the *time* variable, if there are either very few meetings, or the meetings are very short and/or they are only very infrequent, the potential for group cohesion, continuity, and development will be seriously restricted. The member (or *constituent*) variable provides an illustration of the distinction Lang is making, which has perhaps more direct application to day and residential settings. She says, 'The nature of the personnel, their problems, their development level, their degree of competence in the skills of relationship construction, and the skills of group membership, may influence whether the entity becomes a group or a collectivity, or may affect the speed with which "groupness" can be achieved' (Lang 1986: 18). The 'functioning of the entity' refers to core group factors like group composition, shared goals, regularity of attendance, and quality of group interaction. The context variable refers to the suitability of the physical environment for group interaction. The *worker* variable includes the degree of control over content and process which is exercised by the worker. In the same publication, Sulman identifies high levels of worker control as a key feature of worker role in certain types of collectivity (Lang 1986: 62).

Lang also describes several paradigms for change (e.g. learning, relational, social compliance) which are typically employed in collectivities and which have the effect of limiting the potential for group interaction and mutual aid to a residual level, below that expected in a developed group. A learning paradigm places the emphasis on the content to be learned, rather than group process (e.g. as in an alcohol education 'group' and some social skills 'groups'). A relational paradigm stresses the dyadic relationship between each individual member and the worker (a sort of casework or individual therapy in a group arena), whilst a social compliance paradigm is one where participants are socialised into a learned procedure to which they submit and then adapt (with a high level of worker control). In each of these examples it can be seen that the scope for spontaneous group interaction is severely restricted, making the entity more a 'collectivity' than a 'group'.

These distinctions are important for practitioners. A different range of skills is required when working with people in different kinds of 'grouped' circumstances, many of them of a transient nature, yet part of the continuing social system and 'community' life of the centre. The worker has to understand the significance of the differences in 'groupness' both for users and for her or his work. Thus the nature of the contact between users and workers differs in a drop-in 'group', where the participants are always changing, from a settled group of parents, in the same centre, which has been meeting regularly for several months.

For the purposes of this text we shall use *group* to describe the more strictly defined entity, and *grouping* to correspond to Lang's 'collectivity'; that is, looser collections of people sharing some things in common but without the cohesion, stability, and 'togetherness' of a group. We are not entirely consistent in our terminology, especially in the more ambiguous contexts, but we shall try to make it clear when we are referring inclusively to both groups and groupings.

As a practical example of the distinction, consider the not unusual situation of twelve older people sitting around in an open space in a residential home, with no obvious group purpose and very little overt communication amongst themselves. They can be regarded as a grouping. They are more than an aggregate because there are a whole range of shared group living factors which contribute to their interrelatedness.

They would be termed a 'group' if it were arranged that every Thursday morning they would have a reminiscence session when they would be joined by a member of staff who encouraged them to share experiences from their younger years and discuss them together. In such a group, efforts are made to reduce interruptions to a minimum, and the group boundary is protected by establishing that if any other resident wants to join in they do so only on the understanding that for one hour all the people are there for a shared purpose. This group is not, however, a closed system because the other residents (and staff) will have feelings about the fact that some people are sharing something in which they do not have a part. This will have consequences (not necessarily adverse) for everyone living and working together in that residential home, for example in how they relate to one another, following the group, in their various groupings over lunch.

A TYPOLOGY OF GROUPS AND GROUPINGS IN DAY AND RESIDENTIAL SETTINGS

We now propose a typology of the different kinds of groups and groupings which may be found in these settings. The distinguishing variables include purpose, membership, roles, type of interaction and context. The distinctions are not always clearcut, due in part to the numerous different kinds of centres and 'mosaics', but also because groups and groupings are interacting, dynamic systems, many of them constantly changing their form and nature. It should also be noted that the existence or otherwise of some types of group and grouping depends on prevailing conditions in the centre, and in particular on the extent to which users and staff are subject to internal and external constraints and agency policies. This typology provides a framework for a group perspective and for thinking about practice strategies and skills for work in these centres.

The 'whole community'

This refers to the total membership of staff and users at the centre. In some places people will have little sense of being part of such a totality, but, nevertheless, the whole community exists. In other establishments there will be a sense of identity, sometimes captured by the existence of community norms. For example, someone might say, 'In this place we do/do not behave in this sort of way.' There are some centres where all the members meet together in regular community meetings, and have a real sense of being part of a single large group or grouping. Criteria for membership of the 'whole community' may not always be clear, particularly in centres with very permeable boundaries. For example, what about staff who are taken on a temporary basis for a few hours per week, and users who only turn up very occasionally to the drop-in centre?

Living together 'groups'

These are the groups and groupings in which people are together because they share a group living context. Examples include mealtime groups and bedroom groups. The appropriate placing on the aggregate . . . grouping . . . group continuum will vary according to the nature of each centre, and in centres for very small numbers of people (see chapters by Atkinson and Cairns and Cairns) there will be a single living together group. The mealtime arrangements in different centres illustrate the variations. They may range from users being required always to sit with the same people, to being able to choose where to sit, to choosing to be with one's friends, to something much more random and characteristic of the aggregate.

People may be in the same room together because they want to read the paper or use the chairs in the entrance hall. Staff are rarely part of such groupings (though they are not specifically excluded from them) and, similarly, staff are hardly ever leaders or facilitators of such groupings. One of the few occasions when they become so is when they are present at an event such as a meal and, although having no formally invested leadership role, are ascribed such a role when something happens.

Informal friendship/affinity groups and groupings

These are groups of people who affiliate together 'naturally' when they are not grouped together by others or by set programmes. The reasons for their affinity may stem from some shared characteristic, common interest, spontaneous friendship, or many other factors. They are different from many of the other groups and groupings because *they* (the members) have chosen whom they want to be with – or been chosen or pressured by their peers!

These friendship/affinity groups are thus not the same as the 'living together' groupings of people who happen to share the same space, say a sitting room, not because they particularly want the company of the others but because the place is congenial for sitting around, reading, writing, or chatting. Yet even these looser groupings are likely to have developed some kind of informal group structure.

Groups to discuss group living issues

These groups are for staff and/or users. They may be called house meetings, tenants' meetings, centre meetings, group meetings, or any other title. Their purpose is to discuss matters of shared concern arising from group living, whether residential or non-residential. Examples of agenda items might be meals, money, rules, membership, sanctions, responsibilities, activities, centre events, and other matters arising from shared living. They are not the same as community meetings because they will often be small groups or groupings from only one section of a centre, and their focus is likely to be more on practicalities.

Organised groups

These are groups similar in format and purpose to social groupwork groups in fieldwork settings. They will have some stability of membership, will give attention to group interaction and process, and will focus on issues relevant to members' lives outside the centre, or inside the centre if it is their long-term home. The aims and content of these groups will vary over the whole social groupwork range, typical examples being social skills, reminiscence, counselling, art therapy, behaviour modification, problem-solving, psychodrama, parenting skills and assertiveness training.

Organised groupings

These groupings occur because people come together for some activity, for example, educational classes, clubs, music, games, domestic tasks, and other regular centre activities. Unlike the previous category of groups, these groupings do not necessarily give much attention to interaction between members, group cohesion, mutual aid and other group characteristics.

These groupings-for-activities will often be initiated and organised by staff, but in some centres for some activities they will be initiated by users (or jointly) and may include for example, running a shop, providing coffee, organising an event, representing the user group on various committees, negotiating with staff. They are similar to affinity groups in being user initiated, but different in being consciously and visibly structured for a definite task or purpose.

A further variation are *groupings for special 'one-off' events*. These fall into two broad categories:

Inside the establishment, e.g. plays, assemblies, parties, visiting speakers or entertainers, religious services.
Outside the establishment, e.g.outings, trips, expeditions, camps, educational visits.

Many of these are likely to be staff initiated, but again some may be organised either by users alone or on a joint basis. If the membership of several of these events is the same or similar, then it may well develop the characteristics of a cohesive group.

Staff groups and groupings

These fall into three broad categories. The first is formal groups like staff meetings for running and managing the centre. The size and number of these will vary according to the size of the centre and how it is organised. The second is groupings of staff responsible for particular activities of the many different kinds already referred to. The third is the informal, self-generated 'affinity' subgroupings of staff which may be based on shared characteristics such as age, race, gender and roles; shared values, attitudes and political views; or the mutual attraction of people who like being together.

Groups and groupings whose membership crosses the boundary of the centre

Examples of these kinds of groups, which contain both 'insiders' and 'outsiders', are family groups, case conferences, teams of field and day/residential staff, and groups including both residents/ users and members of the local community. The groups may be formal or informal, and a significant factor will be whether they are held on the centre premises or on some other territory. '*Drop-in'groupings* which do not fit neatly into any of the above categories, can be considered as falling into this category inasmuch as there is by definition no restriction on membership and they are intended to bridge the boundary between the centre and the community. Mention should also be made of groups which are entirely composed of 'outsiders' but meet on the premises of the day or residential centre. Examples of these 'imported' groups and the kinds of issues they may raise for the centre appear elsewhere in the book (see the chapters by Burton and Stones). They may be groups whose function is quite independent of the centre and which simply want accommodation. Some may have official or semi-official status; managers provide an example of the former, 'Friends' of the centre, perhaps with user representation, illustrate the latter.

Users are likely to have membership of groups and groupings in several of these categories, and this makes for complex relationship patterns. People move from one group to another but take with them all that comes from membership of other different groupings and a knowledge of how they and others have acted in different settings. They also take with them information about personal events which have happened to themselves and other people. One of the main differences between many groups in centres and the 'fieldwork' groups described in much of the literature on formal groups, lies here. In centres, people often happen to be with others because they are in the same place but they may not have come to that room for the purpose of meeting those other people (it is not like calling round on friends for a chat or a cup of tea); nor has that group of people necessarily come together for a common purpose. Individuals happen to be in the same sitting room but while they are there they get to know many intimate details about others primarily by observation, though there may be occasions when they are told directly.

Residents might feel that other people were listening to all that was going on. Mrs Loosely was talking to me in the sitting room. Several times she said 'You see, there's no privacy' and followed that later with 'They're talking about us' . . . . A few days later as I talked with her she asked: 'Are they talking about us? That's the trouble here – all your business is known.' There was no doubt that all your business was known. Most of it was transacted in front of other people and the rest they would hear commented upon . . . .(Two residents commented about a third) . . . 'There you are, you see. She's picked up that letter again. Watch her, look. There, holding it again.' While there may be much that people are willing to share, there are episodes that they want to keep private. Goffman points out how the normal pattern is to move out from home, to work, to yet another base for leisure or club activities. With each move parts can be left behind that one does not want to share in the new situation. Residential living exposes the individual in all areas. In particular the indignities suffered by residents are witnessed by others. 'You should have gone before lunch' said a staff member to a resident as he went to the lavatory during the meal. Everybody around him would see him slightly demeaned.

(Clough 1981: 97-8)

In addition anyone, staff member or consumer, may pass information about one event on to another group. 'Do you know what has just happened?' people will say and proceed to tell everyone about it. The more that all of one's life takes place in one environment, the more that people will attach significance to small events.

KEY GROUP VARIABLES

The classification outlined above is based on identifiable and distinguishable kinds of groups and groupings in centres. However, as is very apparent from the practice accounts in this book, these groups and groupings occur in a vast range of very different kinds of places which are included under the umbrella term 'day and residential settings'. We do not attempt any classification of types of centre, but need to preface this section on group processes with a recognition that there is a great difference between being in a centre permanently or temporarily; being resident or non-resident; being there voluntarily or without choice; going there for a specific limited purpose or living there as your home; being with or without regular staffing; and so on. The common feature of all the centres, as identified in Chapter 1, is nevertheless that of being a shared physical base.

In this section we have selected some key aspects of group theory which are of particular significance in day and residential settings, so that their relevance to different kinds of groups and groupings in a wide range of centres can be examined. This examination (both here and in readers' own interpretations) involves both the translation of theory from one arena to another, and, particularly where this is found wanting, the development of new concepts and analyses to fit the reality of day and residential settings. For example, on group composition, one of us has written, 'The key decisions in group composition are concerned with homogeneity and heterogeneity, balance and compatibility' (Brown 1986: 37). How far is this true in day and residential centres? And if it is in part, what are the implications for practice? The concepts which follow indicate processes and directions which may illuminate what is going on in centres, but not always and not inevitably. The ultimate test of theories and skills is 'what actually happens, and what really works?'

Purpose

The purposes or aims of groups and groupings are manifold, and each groupwork author tends to produce his or her own list (e.g. Heap 1977). In centres, purposes (both of individual members and of groupings) may have many levels, conscious and unconscious, and people may join a grouping for many different reasons. For example, in a prison, a man may join a music group to avoid a work duty, to get away from a cell-mate or a prison officer, to have a change, to get a better cup of coffee, to be with his friends, to have female company, as well as to enjoy the music. He may not be consciously aware of all his reasons.

Douglas (1986) emphasises the importance in group living groups of the connections between purposes at all levels from the individual user to the umbrella agency of which the particular centre may be a very small sub-system. A constant source of difficulties in centres is the conflict which can arise between purposes at all these different levels. Because people spend so much time in the place and 'know each other's business' the existence or otherwise of a shared overall purpose, an integrating ethos, will have particular significance for the dynamics of the many discrete groups and groupings which may be part of the daily experience of staff and users.

Membership – entry criteria

Four aspects of group/grouping membership are particularly significant: entry criteria, composition, size, and open/closed format. Each of these will now be considered in turn, beginning with entry criteria.

In day and residential centres the first consideration is entry criteria for the centre as a whole: what do you have to do or be to gain entry in the first place? The purpose of a centre sets membership boundaries, but such boundaries are not as clear cut as they may appear. For example, how young can you be to qualify for admission to an older people's home? Is it a matter of chronological age or does it depend on some assessment criteria about social and physical need? How much choice does the person herself have? To what extent, if any, is the overall composition and balance of the centre population taken into account? Who finally decides, and do existing users have a say in that decision?, and so on. Other centres, for example community centres, may not set any restriction on membership. Some centres admit people compulsorily, for example, a secure unit for adolescents. Other places may have exclusion criteria based on gender (e.g. women's aid refuges) or race (e.g. day centres for Asian people). Whatever the entry criteria are, they will influence the kind of groups and groupings which are formed and those that form spontaneously from within the centre membership.

Membership – group composition

Small group theory provides us with some useful indicators of the likely group and individual consequences of any particular composition of a small group. Bertcher and Maple (1977) distinguish descriptive characteristics (e.g. age, ethnicity, handicap, social class) from behavioural characteristics (e.g. 'personality', style, attitude, behaviour), drawing on research to suggest that, as a general guideline, the most productive groups will be those composed of a combination of homogeneous descriptive attributes and heterogeneous behavioural attributes. They also stress the likely negative consequences, for the individual *and* the group, of having any one person who is the only one of their kind (on any fundamental attribute). For example, to be the only woman (or man), or the only black (or white) person in a group is to experience many additional pressures resulting from being the only one of your kind in the group. Additionally (and a point not made by Bertcher and Maple), all groups and groupings are social microcosms of the wider society. They reflect, at least initially, the deference accorded to people of higher status, and the prejudices and discriminations against people on the basis of their gender, skin colour, disability or other attributes.

In day and residential centres these general principles will apply, but the context is more complex because of the interplay between all the different groups and groupings, some of which may be quite transitory, between which members may move during the course of a day. The composition of each group and grouping will therefore result in group dynamics influenced by the centre environment as well as the group itself. For example, in a centre where anti-racist and anti-sexist policy and practice have been successfully established, the consequence should be that women and black people experience less sexism and racism in any formal and informal groupings to which they may belong, than they would if such a culture was not prevalent. It may well be that in places where people have similar attitudes or beliefs to others, and therefore want to be with them (such as a residential centre for a particular religious group), users are happier and make more friends.

In some centres (for example, a community-orientated family centre as described in Stones' chapter) the membership is constantly changing and so one of the worker's core skills is adapting to the group composition as she or he finds it, and as it changes.

Membership – size of group and the large group

Size is a crucial variable in all groups and there is a high level of predictability about how some aspects of group process and interaction will be affected by size (Bales and Borgatta 1955). We know, for example, that small groups change their nature when they get as large as eight or more members: subgroupings tend to proliferate, verbally dominant members become more so, and the quieter members are increasingly likely to become silent. Groups in the range of five to seven members are a particularly good size for many interpersonal and task purposes. In medium sized groups, of say ten to sixteen members, face-to-face communication is still possible but becoming more difficult as there is a decreasing amount of 'group space' for each individual and an increasing chance of getting stuck in a particular role and getting labelled or marginalised within the group. In large groups, say over twenty, people can no longer be aware simultaneously of all the other members and, particularly if the group is not structured, the process can become extremely difficult, with individuals feeling very alone and uncertain where they stand in relation to others, and especially those in positions of power. Communications can be very confusing and dicussion may not follow a logical progression.

Large group meetings, often rather euphemistically known as 'community meetings', are quite common practice in centre settings, and yet are notoriously difficult to run productively. Large group theory (Kreeger 1975) throws some light on why this is so. The individual in a large group faces difficult dilemmas about how to participate. If he or she remains silent, anxiety and frustration can build up with the feeling of being submerged in the whole or being peripheral and unable to participate or exert any influence over what is happening. On the other hand, if they speak out there are considerable risks of being ignored or attacked with no indication of the degree of support from other group members. It can be a very isolating experience, especially for someone with low self-esteem and emotional difficulties. Another phenomenon that occurs is the attributing, often unconsciously, to others (particularly those in positions of authority) of feelings, behaviour, and attitudes which may be mostly fantasy. There can be a temptation for senior staff to collude with a powerful 'prima donna' role, thus making other group members, perhaps including other staff, feel even more impotent in the large group.

Reality-testing through effective communication with other individuals becomes problematic, as the group member anxiously searches out some kind of contact with others with whom they feel some shared identity, be it of gender, race, age, affinity group, or other reference group outside the large group meeting. There is some comfort in arranging to sit next to your friends, if you have any. Often as soon as a community meeting is over people congregate in twos or threes exchanging experience and checking out perceptions, quite likely critical, of what happened in the meeting. This is not just gossip; it is an essential process of trying to put together something which may have been very fragmented and confusing.

Large groups also have some positive features. By bringing together everyone in a centre, they can not only be a useful arena for sharing information, but can also be a way of developing collective morale, feelings of togetherness, and shared identity. In the type of living–learning community described by Hawkins in this book, the large group can also be a context for shared learning and decision-making. The 'flip-side' of these positives is the potential for instilling a crowd effect which may obliterate the integrity of individuals.

It is surprising how often large community-type meetings are held in institutional settings with those responsible not taking into account these large group phenomena. In the final chapter we suggest some steps that can be taken to try to reduce the more destructive aspects, and make large meetings more productive, notwithstanding Shands' comment (1960) that 'it is impossible to be skilful in a truly novel situation'!

Membership – open/closed format

Open groups are distinguished from closed groups by a changing membership. A closed group is planned to have a fixed membership for the duration of the group's life, and if people leave prematurely they are not replaced. The group also has a fixed end-point. The term 'open group' encompasses a vast range of entities from groups in which membership change is very tightly controlled (and group process is quite similar to that in a closed group) to a 'drop-in' type of grouping in which the membership may change substantially or even completely on every occasion the group convenes. In day and residential centres there are some closed groups such as a house-meeting or a contracted social skills group; there are also a whole range of open groupings from say a dinner-table grouping (for which you may or may not be free to sit where you like), to a voluntary carpentry class, to gatherings where people happen to be together watching a particular TV programme. One complication is that some groups that are ostensibly 'open' are in fact 'closed' because everyone knows who belongs, and that it is not possible to join. An example of this would be in a community home, when an affinity group of adolescents always congregates together under the same tree in the evening.

When we consider the process of an open group, one of the core features is the cycle of *re*-forming which occurs every time the membership changes. This does not necessarily mean 'going back to the beginning' because a combination of a few core members and the known history, tradition and culture of the grouping, can produce an overall progress through more 'advanced' stages of development. This of course applies to the 'whole community' of a centre as well as to any particular small groupings within it. In groupings with a frequently changing and unpredictable membership the role of staff members becomes particularly critical (and potentially very powerful) because they are the 'carriers' of continuity and tradition.

One issue is particularly important. What are the effects on different groups of people in a centre of some being there during the day while others live there? This pattern is becoming increasingly common as agencies set up 'multi-purpose' centres. Allen (1983), raising a related point, argues that it is better to have specialist centres for short-stay residents. At the Harlesden Community project (1979) staff found that they could not keep to their plan to open the residential centre to all the young people in the area because they could not cope with the demand; in addition they began to think that there were times when too easy access to the centre meant that young people did not have to face tensions in their own homes. Conversely it can be very unsettling for residents to have streams of day attenders, particularly when public and private spaces in the centre are not clearly separated.

Time

Groupworkers are becoming increasingly interested in the time variable and how it affects group process and task achievement

(Alissi and Casper 1985). Conventional assumptions that a minimum amount of time is necessary for a group to be productive are reviewed in favour of a more flexible approach which analyses for example the potential of the 'single-session group'. By contrast, Lang (1986) considers the 'temporal' variable as one of the key variables which determines the distinction between 'collectivity' and 'group'.

It is perhaps more significant to observe that residential and some day-centre settings (like those that users attend several days per week) experience a completely different time pattern from fieldwork. Members of a group in the residential setting may spend more time together in a week than their fieldwork equivalent do in a year. This affects the whole pace at which things can happen but not necessarily in a straightforward arithmetical way. For example, it would be simplistic in the extreme to assume that a group meeting in a single day for eight hours would accomplish the same as a group meeting for one hour per week for eight weeks! The former group would have favourable conditions for building up group cohesion in an intensive way, but unlike the 'spread-out' group there would be no developmental or reflective space, nor time to try out and practice new behaviours, all of which require a span of time.

In centres there is also the pattern of seeing people briefly in passing, but regularly. This, coupled with sporadic shared events such as meals, work groups, house meetings, provides a strong combination of contact time episodes which can be mutually reinforcing opportunities to check out how other people are.

One interesting way of thinking about the time/grouping equation in centres is to trace an individual's group/time path for a day or a week. Or better still to trace this for all members of the establishment (staff and users) over a given time period.

Role of the worker

Another key factor distinguishing different kinds of groups and groupings is the role of the worker in relation to any gathering of people in a centre. Lang (1972) in her 'Broad-range model of groups' focuses on the way power and responsibility are shared between worker(s) and members in any particular group. She develops a continuum stretching from what she calls 'allonomous' (worker-controlled) through a mid-point termed 'allon-autonomous' (shared control) to the other extreme 'autonomous' (self-governed). Any group can be located at any point on this continuum which can also be used to track changes in the role of the worker over the life of the group, For example, a 'facilitated self-help group' may begin with the worker and members sharing responsibility for the group, but with a clear expectation that the worker will gradually take a more peripheral role, eventually withdrawing, leaving the group fully autonomous.

In day and residential centres the picture is again more complex. The role of staff in relation to any gathering of users, formal or informal, cannot be considered in isolation because it will be influenced by the model of staff–user relations in the whole 'community'. The degree of power that staff hold over users, and the sanctions available to exercise that power, will permeate the interactions in every grouping whether or not staff are physically present. Residential staff often hold extensive power over other peoples' lives and an ever present issue is how much freedom and responsibility is devolved to residents/members. Also, within the informal self-generated groupings of users, power and control hierarchies soon develop with massive impact on individuals. This raises a fundamental question: to what extent is it part of the responsibility of staff to try to influence informal groupings which emerge, particularly when such affiliations are seen as destructive or antagonistic to the purpose of the centre and the centre community ? (We return to this issue in Chapter 11.)

Intergroup relations

Relationships between groups and groupings are a very significant feature of life in day and residential centres settings. Some groups are distinguished organisationally as, for example, the staff group and the users group, different house groups, different activity groups, and so on. Others are identifiable visibly ,for example, by race, age and gender, but may not be thought of, or acknowledged, as groups or groupings. Others form informally and spontaneously as friendship/affinity groupings which may be at least as significant to their members as their 'ascribed' group memberships.

Many readers will be able to recall being put temporarily into one of two or more groups for the purpose of a training exercise or a game like charades, and having experienced just how quickly and intensely group loyalty can build up, with the associated rivalry and fantasies about the other group and what they are thinking and feeling! Little surprise therefore that intergroup conflict occurs so readily in group living contexts, particularly when one group holds much more power than another, e.g. staff vs. users, 'old' members vs. 'new' members.

Studies of intergroup relations (e.g. Rice 1965, Sherif and Sherif 1969, Tajfel 1978) indicate some of these processes. One is the tendency to idealise the group to which one belongs, denying the less attractive features, whilst emphasising the negative characteristics and underplaying the positive features of the 'rival' group. This process reveals the tendency to 'export' intra-group tension and conflict by blaming another group and attributing all the problems to them. (But see Tajfel 1978, for another explanation.) There is nothing like an external 'enemy' to build group cohesion in one's own group! Another point made in inter-group relations theory is the importance of good communication patterns across the boundary between the different groups. Groups may communicate in a number of ways. They can write to each other, they can arrange for representatives to meet, or the entire membership of the two or more groups can meet together (as, for example, in a therapeutic community meeting). Another method is when members from each group meet informally and exchange information and views.

These choices, and they are not of course mutually exclusive, are exemplified in centres by the methods used for communication between staff and users. Boundaries are necessary to distinguish role, function and task; yet when inter-group communication is poor, for whatever reason, boundaries can rapidly become barriers exacerbating inter-group tensions and almost certainly obstructing the purposes of the centre. This can happen between groups of users, and commonly occurs between different staff teams. This is particularly the case if people rarely work with members of other teams.

Other groups and groupings will cross the boundary of the centre, with some centre members facing potential conflicting loyalties; e.g. officers-in-charge who belong to a managers group with their peers and their line manager; users of a family centre who are members of a local tenants' group; Asian users of a day centre who also belong to the local Indian Association. This 'cross-group' membership, which can also occur for people who are in two or more different groups within the centre, complicates the pattern of inter-group relations and may lead to role-conflict; e.g. for the only black member of staff responding to black users' complaints about racist behaviour by her white staff colleague; for the officer-in-charge asked to carry out management group policy to which her staff are strongly opposed.

Task and maintenance: functions and interplay

In every centre, whether viewed at the level of the whole centre or when considering sub-groupings, there will be a group task and there will be a need for group maintenance. The former refers to the purposes of the group and what it can achieve for the members, the latter to the relationships of the members and what they feel about the experience of being in the group. It is the interplay between these two group functions that will determine the success or otherwise of the group. It was Bion (1968) who drew attention to the unconscious life of the group and members' need for psychological security. He suggested that effective groups are those in which the group's need to maintain itself is compatible with, and reinforcing of, the group task. In any segment of life in a residential or day centre, people will be together for a purpose. Even in a loosely grouped gathering of people sitting around for a rest, interaction will be occurring which will be either consistent or obstructive to the purpose of resting.

Stages of group development

'Linear' models of group development (Tuckman 1965, Garland *et al.* 1965) are those which suggest groups move smoothly through predetermined stages from formation to termination. In real life this is rarely the case because unlike the 'laboratory' group there are usually many extraneous factors affecting group development. Some closed membership groups which meet regularly over a period of time come closest to the classical linear model. Most other groups, including many of those in the mosaic of day and residential centres, are much more 'untidy' and are characterised by cyclical and spiralling movements as identified by Schutz (1958) and other theoreticians. Some of the groups in day and residential centres, like settled staff groups and long-term user groups with relatively slowly changing membership, may follow a discernible linear pattern. Indeed at one end of a continuum are places where staff are making a long-term commitment to the people who come to live there and where bonds between people develop to the extent that 'residents' become part of the 'family'. They will develop the same expectations as family members of being able to return after they have left and of joining with others in times of joy and sadness. At the other end of the continuum would be a drop-in centre with a constantly changing membership of both users and staff.

Most of the groups and groupings in shorter term establishments will however be characterised by a complex pattern of some discernible linear development with regular cyclical features, such as frequent re-formings to cope with changes of membership and shifting patterns of groupings. One of the distinguishing features of Lang's 'collectivity' (our 'grouping'), is that it does not reach the more sophisticated stages of group cohesion and maturation characteristic of the 'group' (Lang 1986).

The individual and the group – the group as a system, and allocation of roles

An understanding of group systems and the ways in which individual roles get 'allocated' as part of the group process is essential for those working with groups and groupings in day and residential centres. Individuals will attract particular stereotypical roles which they will carry into all the different groupings to which they belong. This may make change more difficult than, say, in a once-weekly stranger group because the role or label can be reinforced in every grouping to which the person belongs; but it can also make it more possible, as membership of a range of groupings and groups offers the opportunity for different kinds of role-taking in the different contexts. This issue of the choice of 'response options' offered by a group living context is returned to in the final chapter.

40

Physical space

The physical characteristics of a centre, and the physical location of any particular group within it, are known to have profound effects on group relationships and the whole feel of a place. Not that we all have similar preferences in this matter! For example, some people like to meet in crowded conditions because this, they say, develops group intimacy and cohesion more quickly. Others find this very oppressive and like plenty of space for their meetings. There is also the question of how the room is furnished and laid out for the participants, and indeed who decides. Certain formations, e.g. a circle, are much more conducive to interaction between all the members than others such as a long narrow room.

These characteristics have immense influence on the life of people within centres. In nearly all circumstances more people are grouped together than is the case in a typical household, without a consequent increase in either facilities or space. Thus the tendency in large establishments is to have three or four lounges, perhaps for seventy people. The only way for those in the room to watch the television is then to place the chairs in rows facing the screen. The consequence for interaction is obvious.

Control is a central element in relation to space whether concerning one's immediate environment (Willcocks *et al.* (1987) have shown the importance of being able to open and close windows or adjust the heating) or in relation to access to parts of the building – are kitchens and laundries 'out of bounds' for users? Do staff have areas from which residents are excluded? How private are residents' rooms? Slater and Lipman (1980) contend that, in residential centres for older people, the balance between public and private space has undesired results. Residents tend to live most of their lives in public space and yet they develop few friends in the establishment. They suggest that there should be more private space, reducing the public space available and thus positively encouraging people to make more use of private space.

'Group living' schemes, in which people are grouped in small satellite units or small independent group homes (see Atkinson, Chapter 9), each with its own facilities, do lead to more informal life-styles and more independence for the residents. However, one unintended consequence may be that some people get left doing more than their share of the work. Individual flatlets in a small community where services for washing clothes or providing meals are available on the premises may provide a better answer. Staff would bath people or supply other services as wanted *to people in their own rooms.*

MOVING FROM THEORY TO PRACTICE

This chapter has provided a brief introduction to a vast field. After establishing the significance of groupings in day and residential centres, a typology of the range of groups and groupings in these settings has been outlined. The relevance and limitations of some group concepts for understanding the complex mosaic of groups and groupings in centres has then been discussed. Practice-based contributions now follow from other authors who describe and analyse life and work in centres from a group perspective. Many of the concepts and actions emerging from their experience are incorporated in the final chapter, which attempts to provide a framework for translating understanding into action.

Chapter Three

THE SOCIAL LEARNING APPROACH TO RESIDENTIAL AND DAY CARE

PETER HAWKINS

The way we interact with others is affected by the values and beliefs contained within our models of the world. These models or paradigms are often absorbed unconsciously from our culture and can be very resilient to change, surviving for many generations beyond their appropriateness. Theory is important to the extent that it frees us from these limiting models and ways of viewing the world.

If we look at how group work is written and talked about we find that the models that are used to think about what is happening are often drawn from other areas of life in a way that inappropriately constrains the operation of the group. The two most common archetypal models that are fallen back on in the absence of a useful theory are *teaching* and *healing*. These models have ancient roots in our history and are experienced by all of us in childhood, when we are most open to absorbing perspectives on our world.

The archetypal model of teaching leads us to arrive in a group setting expecting to be instructed, not only in the imparting of information but also in how to behave in the present setting.

The archetypal model of healing creates expectations of a doctor or other healer diagnosing our ills and applying some treatment or remedy.

Illich (1975, 1977) has written widely on how such models, in time, create many problems, including decreasing the ability of individuals to learn and heal themselves – as they acquire more learnt passivity. Many writers have tried to address this problem by taking both words back to their roots. Originally the word healing meant a co-operative and holistic process and was linked to the words whole and holy. Healing did not mean just eradicating symptoms. At its root education comes from 'e-duco', meaning to draw out from learners what they already know, through dialogue.

What is needed is a unitary paradigm that unifies group work whether it is done with closed therapeutic groups, informal groupings in a residential home, or community work groups trying to bring about social change. We must create our own models and maps through which to view the world or be constrained by those of others. 'I must create a System, or be enslaved by another Man's', wrote William Blake in *Jerusalem.*

In residential homes and day centres there is often a variety of models in operation. Some homes still operate as if they were a family. Others see themselves as teaching life skills, and some as providing therapy. Within the same centre several models may operate. There may be leisure activities such as games and crafts; therapeutic groups and talks or skill learning sessions. In the leisure activities the staff may be thinking in an entertainment mode (the social worker as Butlin 'red-coat'); in the therapy group the staff may operate within a medical model of providing therapy for problems; and in other sessions the staff may be acting in the role of teachers.

Rather than this plethora of models, with the inevitable role conflicts that it creates, it is possible to have a unitary model that is consistent throughout all these activities – this is the model of *social learning.* This model has been developed from the experience of therapeutic communities and also from humanistic psychology. It provides a unified understanding of how individuals learn about themselves, through engaging with others interpersonally or in groups; through activities of daily living, leisure pursuits, or through co-managing their centre or community activities.

It also provides a perspective that links processes on the micro-level of the individual person or event, with the macro processes of understanding what is happening at the collective level either of the whole centre or of the organisational level of the department. As an approach, social learning offers a way of understanding the diversity and complexity of the groups and groupings of people in day and residential centres; furthermore, it suggests ways in which the daily experiences within those groupings can become life-enhancing.

Before going on to show how I apply the social learning

perspective to residential and day care establishments, I will first share a little of the history of how it emerged in the development of therapeutic communities and the approaches of humanistic psychology.

THE DEVELOPMENT OF THE SOCIAL LEARNING MODEL

The social learning model has been greatly influenced by the experience and development of therapeutic communities which in turn had their unlikely beginnings in the British Army in the Second World War. It was in this war that the realisation that social environments of army units contributed, not only to the morale of soldiers but also their health and personal well-being. This was discovered by realising that army units which had very high rates of shell shock also had high incidents of physical illness, discipline problems and soldiers going absent without leave. It was then discovered that these high rates of problems could not be correlated with the stress that the unit was under but could only be explained by the state of 'morale' of the unit, what has later been termed the extent to which a unit has a healthy culture.

In the famous experiments at Northfields Mental Hospital the army medical staff tried to see if they could reverse the process of unhealthy organisations bringing out people's unhealthy sides, by working with the patients to create a healthy hospital organisation in the hope it would draw out people's healthy attributes. (see Main 1980)

These realisations were combined with the development that was taking place in group therapy by psychoanalysts such as Foulkes and Bion, to develop a mental hospital regime that was an experimental living–learning environment.

The experiment was aimed at creating together a social system based not on a medical model of a healthy knowledgeable staff and sick obedient patients, but upon the joint recognition of each individual's capacity and limitations for performing essential tasks, and with participation by all in arranging that these be carried out. Where problems arose and failures occurred these would be subjects not for discipline but for investigation as failures of interpersonal art (Main 1975: 53) At the same time Maxwell Jones was working not with neurosis, but heart disease, but he too found that the social change thrown up by the turmoil of war facilitated a new approach to illness.

> The Second World War acted as a stimulus, and in 1940 I was put in charge of a 100-bed unit to study and treat effort syndrome. Working with cardiac neurosis in armed forces personnel, we started out on a 'scientific' study of the physiology of exercise fatigue, but circumstances almost forced my colleagues and myself to depart from traditional psychiatric practice. To have a unit of 100 soldiers all with a similar syndrome seemed to demand that we discuss their problems with all 100 men at the same time. Was this innovative or merely common sense?
>
> (Jones 1979: 1)

Like many social experiments, therapeutic communities soon became absorbed into the main stream of mental health and its approaches institutionalised. Some of the aspects of the experimental living-learning environments became adopted as treatment methods, or as ways of organising mental hospital wards. Although this in many cases had a beneficial and humanising effect, it was a retreat from a social learning approach, to a treatment approach. (For a fuller critique of this change see Hawkins 1979.) Only a few hospitals carried on and developed the original tradition (Clark 1965). Tom Main continued his work at the Cassel Hospital in Richmond, Surrey. Maxwell Jones pioneered the now famous Henderson hospital, which was then known as the Belmont in Sutton, Surrey. Newer communities were developed at Fulbourn Hospital, Cambridge, Littlemore Hospital in Oxford; Claybury Hospital in East London and elsewhere.

David Clark (1965) looked at the difference between those that used the full *therapeutic community proper* and those that used an adapted *therapeutic community approach*. The six key factors of the approach which he outlined can be summarised as follows:

Freeing of communication. It has been said that a therapeutic community is a place where everyone gets listened to and where communication is person to person and not just professional to patient.

Analysis of all events. Traditional hospitals focused only on symptoms and what happened in the sessions with the doctors. In the same way traditional social work establishments focused on problem behaviour and what happened in formal groups or sessions. In the therapeutic community approach one focuses on all aspects of behaviour and the whole of the twenty-four hours and seven days of the week.

Provision of learning experiences. This approach uses a learning perspective that looks to not just providing physical and mental well-being but also to the potential of all its members and how this can be developed. It aims to provide opportunities for members to try out new forms of behaviour in a safe environment where they will not be punished for failing.

Flattening the authority pyramid. Therapeutic communities are often thought of as places that try to be democratic with no distinctions between staff and clients, but the approach does not necessarily lead to less control and authority. Rather, it advocates that authority should be personalised and owned; all members should know who has authority about what, and be able to question and challenge those who have authority in any situation; authority should be exercised in a direct manner, face-to-face.

Role examination. Many patients in hospitals would take different parts of themselves to different staff: their physical self to the doctor, their social needs to the social worker, their need for caring to the nurse, their need for creative and productive outlet to the occupational therapist. In social work establishments as well one can often see clients sharing different fragmented parts of themselves with different staff. Therapeutic communities were instrumental in developing a team work approach that cut across professional boundaries and allowed staff to use all of their personal as well as their professional skills.

Community meetings. The realisation that communities and groups could be healthy and life enhancing or sick and demoralising, meant that it was important to attend to the health of the whole group not just the individuals within it. Thus the community meeting is a place where everybody comes together to reflect on the state of the community and to co-manage it. It is also held that by being part of a healthy group managing itself, we each increase our abilities in attending to our own individual health and in managing ourselves.

In the late 1950s and early 1960s the therapeutic community approach began to be adopted outside of the health service. The Richmond Fellowship developed a whole number of half-way house therapeutic communities for the mentally ill. Places like the Cotswold Community, the Mulberry Bush School and Peper Harow used the approach to work with children and adolescents. Grendon Underwood used the approach inside the prison service and there were numerous other applications.

In the 1970s the approach was expanded into day care, such as in the range of day centres established by Kensington and Chelsea Social Services. Also by this time the ideas had been so disseminated that many were using parts of the approach without realising that they derived from therapeutic communities.

The danger has always been that the therapeutic community approach can become a method providing answers that must be slavishly applied, rather than a perspective that provides the questions with which to challenge and reflect on what is happening. Both Main and Jones have argued against therapeutic communities becoming an ancillary treatment method, used to assist in the cure of certain individualised pathologies, rather than a 'particular type of social organization'; 'an open system'. Tom Main (1980) writes:

> if the term [therapeutic communities] is to retain any distinct meaning, it should define not techniques or procedure but a particular type of social organisation. It involves the total community in a culture of enquiry into the nature of the social processes within, and how these truly succeed or fail in caring for the specific individuals in it, both patients and staff. I mention staff, not only because they too are human beings, but because culture spreads from the top in any hierarchy, and as staff are or are not cared for, so they will care or not care for their charges. (p. 55)

Maxwell Jones (1979: 7), has, in more recent years, argued against the whole approach of treatment and diagnostic labels: 'except for mental "illnesses" which are organically determined e.g. brain damage, or genetically determined (e.g. Huntington's Chorea).' He suggests that the rest of what is referred to as mental illness should be approached in a way that tries to bring about a renewal, or at least an adjustment, of the social forces which resulted in the aberrant behaviour in the first place.

What is needed is not medical treatment, but 'social learning'. Jones (1979: 7) continues.

> I would like to suggest that, as all 'therapy' is clearly part of a process of learning, we should use a term such as 'social learning', which would include what is at present called psychotherapy, or extended to include the social matrix, psycho-social systems of therapy, and now add learning techniques extended to problems of living and prevention. By social learning, I mean two-way communication in a group, interaction motivated by some inner need or stress, leading to overt or covert expression of feeling, and involving cognitive processes and change. The term implies a change in the individual's attitude and/or beliefs as a result of the experience. These changes are incorporated and modify his personality and self-image.

Maxwell Jones took the ideas of social learning beyond the hospital context and into schools, prisons, and community organisations. His vision is of a social ecology built on continuous learning throughout all of life's activities.

At the same time as the ideas of social learning were being developed in therapeutic communities, humanistic psychology was developing similar approaches. Kurt Lewin (see Smith 1980) and others developed the concept of 'T' or training groups which researched how people could best learn from each other. Moreno (1972), the founder of psychodrama, developed many techniques for increasing learning from doing and enacting and Maslow (1972) studied how the most healthy and creative people continued to learn and develop.

The most developed theories of social learning have been integrated by a humanistic psychologist Charles Hampden-Turner (1970). In my own research I have linked Hampden-Turner's 'psycho-social learning' cycle to the theories of Gregory Bateson, who elucidated the way in which all learning proceeds through living experimentation, trial and error and provides greater levels of choice to the individual (Bateson 1976, Hawkins 1986)

Although social learning and many forms of humanistic group work had their early history in hospitals and other systems for treating the mentally ill, the ideas have gradually spread and become more prevalent in working in all types of residential and day centre. Whether one is working with young children who are emotionally deprived, adults who are handicapped, or old people who are isolated and fearing death there is much to be gained by providing a community where the members are co-responsible for creating the structure and activities. In such a community the whole effort should be geared to all those involved, learning from each other and from their experiences together, in order to increase their individual abilities and life options.

APPLYING SOCIAL LEARNING TO DAY CENTRES, RESIDENTIAL CENTRES AND SOCIAL WORK ORGANISATIONS

I now want to look at the ways in which the social learning approach can be applied to residential and day centres. The examples I draw on are taken from my own experience: first as head of a residential home for twenty-four mentally ill adults; second as a middle manager supervising a variety of residential and day facilities for mentally ill adults, children, and adolescents; then as a consultant to a wide variety of projects from intermediate treatment centres right through to old people's homes; and finally as an organisational consultant to a number of social work departments and voluntary organisations.

Social learning can be used to give a coherent explanation of the total operation of the centre – to link the various activities of the centre into a meaningful whole. A residential community for the adult mentally ill described in its brochure its principal aim as 'to provide a supportive learning environment for residents where adjustment and growth can take place.'

A later leaflet that was written jointly by staff and residents for new members stated that:

First and foremost [the community] is a learning environment where there are many opportunities to learn from experience about ourselves, our ways of relating to others, the roles we get into playing and the patterns of relationships we set up for ourselves.
Most situations, be they misunderstandings, arguments over

the cooking, or more positive events, can be used as possible sources of learning. This learning does not just take place on an intellectual level, but involves the emotions and the whole person; nor does it stop with the realisation of what is going on but it involves trying out new roles and making personal changes.

Everybody in the community, that is, staff, students, trainees, and residents, are all involved in their different ways in the learning, and all are seen as resources for each other's learning. The staff role is significantly different in that they have the responsibility for maintaining the overall structure, but within this structure, everyone has some measure of responsibility for their own learning and that of others.

This framework provided a perspective for viewing issues raised by the staff or by members of the community whether they were about individuals, or organisational matters. It provided a value base from which to make decisions, by asking what would help maximise the learning for all of those involved in this situation.

The second advantage of this approach is that it gives value to all aspects of the life within the centre or residential home. There is a danger within many projects of giving higher status to therapeutic groups and to see other activities as filling in time. I have seen homes where the counsellors and group workers have claimed much higher status than the care workers, who were described as 'just looking after the residents'.

A Home Office probation-run day training centre, where people went as an alternative to prison, provides another example. Here there were many well-run groups and community meetings helping members look at how they related to each other. But the members had little relationship to the physical centre. The place was institutionalised by a whole army of gardeners, cooks, cleaners, and secretaries. An important area that can provide learning and development opportunities was being ignored.

When the residents of an old people's home became involved in preparing and planning the meals, there was a radical improvement in the quality, not only of the food but also of the meal times. It should be the aim of every form of social work facility to help the users to increase their own control over their own lives. Involving users in planning and carrying out the everyday tasks of cooking, cleaning, decorating and generally creating their own physical environment has an important effect in increasing a sense of one's own worth and decreasing institutionalisation. It also provides social learning, not only in the area of practical life skills, but also through working together, since there is great potential for increased self-awareness and interpersonal skills.

A social learning approach provides a different orientation to conflict and crises within the centre. In traditional homes and day centres, staff try and avoid conflict and crisis. When it happens it is resolved as quickly and privately as possible so that 'life can continue as normal'. The old person who dies is carried out by the back door and their chair mysteriously disappears from the lounge. The adolescent girl who starts crying about how her father attacks her is taken off by a staff member to the privacy of the office, to talk through her problems in private.

In the social learning model the crisis is seen as providing the heat in which new learning can be forged. Organising a group to share the news that one of the residents has died not only gives the opportunity for the other residents to support each other in sharing the variety of feelings this invokes for them – loss, grief, anger, guilt, fear – but also provides the residents with another chance to deal with the feelings and preparation for their own dying. The girl in the adolescent project who breaks down in tears about her father can discover that other project members have parallel problems at home. They can learn from each other ways of handling these situations and find they are not alone or abnormal with the feelings they have. This situation also provides an important learning opportunity, for all those sharing the crisis, in how to relate to the feelings of others: what are appropriate ways of expressing feelings and appropriate and helpful ways of responding?

Staff conflict can also be seen from a different perspective, for it is important to bear in mind that staff dynamics reflect community dynamics and vice-versa. The mirror metaphor can help staff realise that part of their job is constantly to explore both how what is happening in the community is being mirrored within the staff team and also how whatever is happening in and among the staff will be consciously or unconsciously played out within the community. Staff conflicts sometimes need to be understood in terms of what aspect of the community the conflictual staff members are representing. Also community behaviour must sometimes be understood in terms of acted out, unresolved tensions in the staff group.

Any social work centre is importing distress, fragmentation and conflict, in as far as the clients carry these inside themselves. In relating closely to the clients the staff will absorb some of the distress and dis-ease of the clients. Some of this they will be able to contain and transform in their work, but some of this dis-ease and conflict is inevitably carried into the staff team and needs to be contained and worked through in that context. A staff team where there is little or no conflict is nearly always one where there are institutional defences against getting close to the pain of the clients (see Menzies 1960).

However, a team that is so full of conflict that the distress of the staff is being acted out against each other becomes mal-functional and has failed to act as an effective container.

The social learning model calls for a high degree of team work, where individuals are not role-bound but regularly meet and share and explore what they are each carrying, in terms of feelings, concerns and responsibilities. I believe that any centre that is trying to operate a social learning ethos needs to have, not only regular staff meetings, but also regular opportunities for staff to recognise and work through the psychological dynamics they are immersed in. Many centres have introduced regular staff dynamics meetings and quarterly or twice yearly 'away-days' where the whole staff team can stand back and learn from what they have been intimately engaged with, within the work (Brown 1984).

Regular work on group dynamics also increases the ability of staff groups to contain and respond to crisis situations when they emerge. I was once working in a residential home where a resident managed to kill herself. The staff immediately went into manic activity trying to deal with everything and calm everyone else down without attending to their obvious distress. I called a staff group and encouraged each staff member to focus on his or her own feelings. It soon became clear that one staff member was carrying the anger for the group, another the guilt that we should have done more, and a third the grief at this tragic loss. It was only when these feelings could be shared and collectively owned, rather than deposited within the individuals with the most valency for carrying them, that the staff were able to help the community of residents to work through the same process in a special community meeting.

This whole event became an experience through which the residential home matured and in which there was a great deal of emotional and interpersonal sharing and learning.

The social learning model applies theories of group behaviour to all the living–learning processes within a centre, not just what happens in groups. One of the key concepts in understanding group behaviour developed by Bion (1968) is this notion that individuals carry and express feelings, not only for themselves, but also for the group, family, or centre in which they function. It is important that we see the whole centre as a system. Pathology does not lie solely within individuals, neither are clients the victims of society. In understanding the deviant behaviour of any individual within the community, it is inadequate to just look for causes within the psycho-social history of the individual. It is also important to understand the event from the perspective of seeing it as a symptom of the present group and of community pathology. It is essential to constantly attend to the level of the health of the whole system.

This tendency to see collective problems as residing within individuals is not confined to groups and families or even to residential and day centres. In my consultancy work with whole social services organisations, I have been in senior management meetings where one home is seen as being the problem child of the department. Phrases are used like: 'If we could only close that home' or 'If only we could get a new strong leader to run that centre'. The home or the centre head has become the 'identified patient' for the whole department, and the belief is that if only this problem part could be exorcised or otherwise removed, then everything would be running smoothly. If only it was that easy! When this scapegoating is acted out and 'the problem home' is closed so often this is followed by another home occupying the now vacant role of the department's 'problem child'. The social learning approach does not mean that homes are not closed or staff sacked, but it does ensure that certain questions are asked as part of understanding the problem:

'What is this home or staff member expressing for the whole department?'

'What can we learn from the experience of this home?'

'How is this home a symptom of an illness that the department must collectively own?'

This social learning approach uses not only an understanding of group dynamics and of ways of viewing systems, but also an understanding of organisational culture. The culture of an organisation is the collective unconscious of the social system – the beliefs, attitudes, and assumptions that are so much part of how the members of the system view what happens that they are taken for granted and disappear from consciousness. There is an old Chinese proverb: 'The last person to know about the sea is a fish.'

Likewise the last people to be able to see the culture of a social work centre are the staff and members within it. A social learning approach needs to find ways of helping staff and members get access to their own culture, to bring into awareness the collective unconscious of the centre. There are a number of approaches that help to access the underlying culture, which my colleague Adrian Mclean refers to as *enactment, estrangement* and *exemplification* (Mclean and Marshall 1988).

I have used the *enactment* technique of group sculpting, taken from psychodrama, with a number of residential homes and day centres. The staff and members of the centre are asked to find objects, or draw images that symbolically represent what is at the heart or core of the centre and to place these in the middle of the room. Having done this, people are asked to place themselves both in relation to the centre and to each other:

Are they central or on the periphery?
Who are they connected or close to?
Who are they distant from?
Which way are they facing and who are they looking at?

They then are asked to adopt a position that characterises their basic way of being in the total group of the centre. Then each person has the opportunity to say: 'In this position in the group I feel . . . ' After this round is complete I provide an opportunity for any members who wish to explore how they would like to change their position and the role they are in within the whole centre group.

This community sculpting approach is a way of enacting the underlying dynamics and culture of the centre. It shows up not only the way certain people have been elected to play certain roles for the whole group, but also the sub-grouping within the centre and what is central stage and what is marginalised within the centre.

Estrangement can be used to explore the centre culture by asking the group to look at the group sculpt they have created as if it was part of a different system. For example, asking them: 'If this group was a family, what sort of family would it be?' or 'If this group was a country what sort of country would it be, what would its government be, what sort of trade would it have, what way of dressing, speaking or making art would it have?'

This is called 'reframing' and one can also use many different frames depending on what sort of dynamics are emerging. I asked a holistic medical centre, if they were a body, who would be which organs and what illness the centre would be suffering.

One residential home for the mentally ill that did a group sculpt, looked at their sculpt through the frame of a family. They created a family that had many children, a mother, and a grandmother. They were asked what had happened to Dad and this led to a spontaneous discovery that the centre was still dominated by the ghost of an ex-staff member. This led on to an open exploration of unfinished feelings about this staff member and how he or she left, after which the ghost could be finally put to rest, over a year after the person had left.

Accessing the culture of a centre through the approach of *exemplification* can be done by looking at what people, events, rituals, phrases, or words exemplify the centre. Mclean and Marshall (1988) ask who are the heroes/heroines, villains and fools in the stories that are told within the organisation. Residential homes and day centres also develop their own folklore, stories that are repeatedly told to newcomers about past events, jokes that often re-occur.

Working as consultant to the Simon Community, a large charity working with the down-and-outs of London, I paid particular attention to the rituals which were such a central part of the communities way of life. However, the rituals that had been developed by the charismatic founder, Anton Wallich-Clifford, no longer exemplified the living culture. The rituals survived as the community could not free itself from the ghost of their founder. There were two cultures, the one that was kept going in memory of 'how it used to be' which was exemplified in the formal rituals and, second, a sub-culture of how the members of the community now operated, which was exemplified in the informal ways of operating within the community.

These methods of helping a centre, home, or whole organisation look at its culture are important as they provide a way of a collective group learning about itself. A social learning approach to residential social work cannot be limited to providing opportunities for clients and staff to learn about themselves, but must also provide an approach for communities and organisations to learn about themselves collectively. Organisations need to learn as well as individual people.

It is also important that organisations develop a framework that links processes at the micro-level, such as the individual client, group meeting, or single event, with processes at an organisational level, such as the whole centre, department, or social services organisation. In the social learning approach all forms of change, whether they be the rehabilitation of one client or the reorganisation of a whole social services department, are looked at from a consistent perspective. This is a perspective that does not try to change behaviour or structure, without first understanding the underlying culture of what is already happening and why. To try to bring about change without first working with all those involved to learn more about the present situation is to run the risk of creating more resistance to change by not being aware of the threat to the underlying culture.

Organisational change at any level must attend to *what is* before it tries to create *what should be* and the most helpful order of approaching change is:

Learn more about what is happening with all those involved: what are its strengths and weaknesses? what causes it to stay happening the way it does?

Discover from those involved what is their vision of how it could be;

Work with this vision on helping bring about change in the culture;

Only then work to bring about a change in behaviour or organisational strategy;

Then find the appropriate structure to carry out this strategy.

CONCLUSION

In this chapter I have tried to give some flavour of how a social learning approach can help link what happens in groups and groupings, and see this work in the context of the system or macro-group within which it exists. It is important that staff develop the 'helicoptering ability' to move levels from observing the dynamics of individual groups to understanding the dynamics of the whole home or centre. The home can be seen as a continuous twenty-four hour, seven days a week, group; the day centre is equivalent to a work group, a five-days-a-week, eight hours per day group. This perspective can help staff pay attention to the learning possibilities of all aspects of the residents' lives, not just when they are in formal groups, and to see the inter-relation of the various events.

A social learning perspective also links an understanding of the dynamics of the home with that of the wider organisation. So often workers in centres complain that senior managers do not understand what they are doing, nor the principles by which they operate. Senior managers also complain that staff in day centres or homes fail to see or understand the pressures and the problems of the wider dynamics. *Social learning* provides a language which can link the group and groupings dynamics within a home to an understanding of the total system of the home as a whole and to the dynamics of the organisation or department which manages it.

Chapter Four

INSTITUTIONAL CHANGE AND GROUP ACTION:

The significance and influence of groups in developing new residential services for older people

JOHN BURTON

This chapter focuses on change in a large residential institution. It uncovers the intricate group formations and processes which both help and hinder the development of convivial and purposeful life and work.

Residential workers and their managers need to understand the significance of groups and groupings at a time of change. Above all, they need to grasp the meanings and consequences of their own positions and actions within the constantly shifting and richly varied communities of residential centres.

The chapter also illustrates and discusses the inevitable tensions and contradictions between flourishing groups and groupings and the organisations which seek to control them.

THE 'LOBBY'

It is a cold January evening: fifteen people of ages ranging from 20 to 95 turn up at the Town Hall where a meeting of the Social Services Committee is about to take place. They have travelled by bus and car from an old people's home in the south of the borough, and as they arrive they arrange themselves either side of the committee room door. Some of the older people find chairs to sit on. They have brought information sheets to hand out, and friends who neither work nor live at the old people's home join them. As senior officers, councillors and members of the public begin to arrive for the meeting, the 'lobby' from Inglewood (the old people's home) approach them and ask for their support.

They see a lot of people they know and generally get a sympathetic response.

Although, in this borough, this sort of democracy in action is quite common, especially from user groups and is officially encouraged by policies of 'open government', most of those being lobbied are surprised this time, partly because some of the old people are actually there taking an active role alongside the workers.

At issue and on the agenda of the meeting was the proposal to annex a large and important part of Inglewood for another purpose. The residents did not want to lose their old dining room, which was now used as a hall and luncheon club, and was soon to be opened up for day care as well. The staff didn't want another and altogether different establishment set up in the middle of, but quite separate from, the centre for older people which was developing at Inglewood.

The lobby group sat through most of the committee which that evening discussed and made decisions on many issues which were important to the running of their residential home.

A few weeks later a further meeting was called by the Chair of the Social Services Committee in the old dining hall at Inglewood, for councillors and senior managers only, to discuss the plan 'on site'. Residents and staff at Inglewood were not invited but a group was there, and residents, in particular, very forcefully restated the objections they had to part of their building being annexed without their consent, and to their exclusion from the process of consultation and negotiation, which almost any other group, whose neighbourhood or environment was to be so drastically affected, could have expected.

The protesting group learned a few weeks later that the council had pulled out and had found a much cheaper and more suitable site for their project.

Why were councillors and senior managers so disconcerted by the forceful group action of the tenants and workers at Inglewood? After all, even at that committee meeting there were other groups present, one of which was being much more vociferous and had stopped the meeting for a long period while they harangued the committee members. Why was the manager of Inglewood upbraided by the Director of Social Services who could not accept that older people, users of the service he managed, had not been manipulated into attending the meetings or that they had genuine objections to the plan being put forward?

Well, groups can be powerful and dangerous, and can change things. Older people are one of the last sections of the population in our society which is expected to take power and to use the almost universally practised, but much less acknowledged, process of collective action on their own behalf – especially older people living in local authority residential homes.

A DIFFERENT SORT OF INSTITUTION?

So what was different about Inglewood which challenged these assumptions and expectations? How was it that such a group resp-onse was forthcoming and active? To get to the roots of the answer we have to go back from that committee meeting about three years to the beginnings of major changes in the home and trace some of the development and growth of a new social life in the place.

In 1982 Inglewood was a large, traditional, run-down, over-crowded, under-staffed institution. There were ambitious plans to convert it to a very different place, plans drawn around a vague but professionally popular notion of *group living*. It was relatively easy for the planners to be specific about the physical alterations which they proposed: self-contained, long-stay, smaller units with their own kitchens and dining rooms, a hall, day-centre, luncheon club, a shop, a social club, a reception area, etc. But, as with many plans for converting or even building social services centres, the most problematic area of development was not designing or even achieving the physical result; realising a successful *social* result, making it actually work for users, was (and always will be) the difficult bit.

Most institutions which undergo extensive remodelling remain essentially the same; they may *look* different and the newly printed brochures about them may proclaim that they *are* different, but to the practised observer or to the user of the service, it is often evident that social relations have not altered.

The proposed changes at Inglewood were all designed to produce a state of 'Group Living' which no one knew quite how

61

to define, let alone achieve, but its opposite was seen to be the existing 'Block Treatment', and one did not have to live or work there very long to know exactly what that was. The consideration of groups and groupings in residential centres has made me re-evaluate the meaning of 'Group Living' and search for its essence in relationship to the development of Inglewood over a five year period.

EATING TOGETHER

A description and analysis of mealtimes will serve as an important and illustrative starting point. Meals are certainly some of the most significant events in any residential setting, and I include private households, hotels, hostels, hospitals, indeed wherever people live and eat together. So much can be observed of social relationships and so many inferences drawn about the quality of everyday life.

In the old Inglewood, as in most institutions, mealtimes were the highlights of an empty day, even though they were such monstrous occasions. Well over 100 people, most of them physically disabled in some way, many in wheelchairs, were crammed into a large dining hall, overflowing into two annexes, one of which was reserved for most of the 'babies', so called because they were deemed to be severely 'confused', and most of whom were fed by staff. Meals were served from a large hatch by staff who queued up with trays; ready plated meals were plonked on to the trays and in turn plonked in front of residents. It was the duty of every care assistant to serve everyone. As with nearly all other regular tasks in the place, there were officially no individual relationships or connections between staff and residents – hence the aptness of the phrase 'Block Treatment'. In fact often residents got left out when the food came round.

There were other problems too: insufficient cutlery and crockery, people trying to eat a boiled egg with a tablespoon, care assistants having to rush backwards and forwards taking cups or spoons from those who had finished at one end of the hall to those who were waiting to start at the other. Some people never got to the dining room in the first place. Although part of the pre-meal preparation for staff was to collect residents from all the big lounges downstairs, quickly checking round the toilets and passages, inevitably people got missed.

The process was a headlong but disorganised rush. While there were many other routine tasks to perform, breaks and staff meal-times were integral parts of a rigid pattern of 'early' and 'late' shifts; so, as soon as the serving of a meal had finished at one end of the dining hall, the clearing of tables and moving of residents started at the other. Many residents were then 'toileted', another task which was performed in a hurried, mechanical, production-line fashion which meant that some residents did not wear under-clothes and doors were not locked, or even shut, as frail old people were hauled on and off lavatories.

The eradication of this deeply rooted institutional abuse required fundamental changes in structure and social relations.

I began by remarking on the importance and significance of meal times in any residential living situation. We were faced with the problem of creating a context for social relations, the association of people with each other, for the existence and fostering of groups and groupings which would allow mealtimes to become convivial, therapeutic, and nourishing in every sense. Where to begin? We couldn't isolate mealtimes from the myriad of other problems which beset this institution, but it was as good a place as any to start.

We had already established that different opinions were not only tolerable but essential in working towards agreed plans of action. So in our shift meetings and the newly developing staff meetings, mealtimes were high on the agenda. No one was happy with them as they were, but, by feeling so unhappy with them and by previously being unable to find a way to substantially improve matters, the staff initially tended to be as defensive about the mealtime practices as they were about many of the other seemingly unchangeable rules and routines.

However, we did find some ways through. We discovered four different sets of expensive crockery which had been bought a year before but hidden away in a store 'because it would get broken' (the existing 'crockery' was plastic) and we divided the dining room up into four sections. There were four floors at Inglewood and the plans were to create at least that number of 'group living units', so this division of the dining room was quite a significant first step in several ways. We were at least just beginning to think *groups*.

Because we had not yet got anywhere near to dividing the staff up into teams, we went through a discussion at every shift meeting of who was going to serve which section, but after a couple of weeks workers began to prefer particular sections and to learn residents' food preferences, to know who on their section was going to be out at hospital that morning, and to take special care and thought when taking particular people to the lavatory. Some began to be taken before the meal or to be changed into clean clothes before eating. If there was a resident in bed it became a matter of concern and pride that she would be properly looked after and get the sort of meal she wanted or needed. There began to be the scope and opportunity at mealtimes to have, as a worker, one's own sphere of influence and decision making, a defined area and limited group of people with whom one could improve the service and have some assurance of being able to build on day to day achievements.

One of the other constant concerns in our meetings was the divisions which existed between all the people in the place, 'officers' and care assistants, care assistants and domestic workers, staff and residents. These divisions were perhaps most obvious at mealtimes. We not only ate separately, we ate different food, off different plates, at different times.

As discussion proceeded, staff were already beginning to experiment with not being so separated. With encouragement and example, staff at all levels were sitting with their group of residents after a meal, having a cup of tea, a smoke, talking rather than rushing to get the plates cleared away and get into the staff room to sit down and do the same things away from the residents. 'Work', the mundane tasks of simple physical labour, began to merge with a sort of relaxation which was also quite legitimate work. People found that they could move in and out of each form freely and often do both at the same time, so that conversations did not stop with the group when tea was being poured out or someone was being fed.

The more the idea and practice of convivial meals began to take hold, the more absurd seemed the institutional practice of taking set lunch and tea breaks. Why did staff have to go away into a slum of a staff room at the moment when some of their best, most satisfying and pleasurable work could be done? Why should they leave at the moment when some residents were physically relaxed and pleased to sit and talk?

After long discussions at the staff meetings we took the bold step of doing away with formal breaks, although it always remained an option for any worker to decide to take a break as long as she arranged it with her colleagues on the shift.

In residential child care it had long been accepted that workers not only ate with residents, but that doing so would be seen as a normal part of work, and staff would not of course have to pay for the meals. Predictably we had quite a lot of trouble getting our employers and unions to accept that the same conditions would be good for us as workers and improve the service we offered. This opposition and uncertainty constantly washed back into the staff group undermining the gradual build-up of new practice. However, the change was eventually accepted, mainly because of the determination of most of the workforce, and it proved to be one of the crucial structural changes we made in support of group development.

Now, mealtimes are very different on different units. On the respite care unit, breakfast TV will be on and the small group of short-stay residents there will get into long discussions about the news, politics, home, relations, the past. Like any undirected, informal group of people, they range widely in their conversations, much depending on their interests and backgrounds.

On another, long-stay, unit mealtimes may be quieter and less animated, but staff take care to sit with residents and will often engage them in conversation, whether it's about something in the daily paper, or what events or activities are on that day, about families, children, or friends.

The arrangements around mealtimes are also shared by tenants and all grades of staff. This tradition began in the big dining hall before the small group living units started up. Laying tables, preparing some food, clearing, and washing-up get done by a mixture of people and are again a chance for ordinary group interaction.

Included in such interaction are the easy, sociable experiences of doing things together and making a communal contribution, but also prominent are the sort of rows that go on in most households about such chores. People do too much and give up. 'Let's make a rota'. 'John doesn't dry the plates properly'. 'Margaret uses too much washing-up liquid'. There are objections that, 'This is what staff get paid for'. Someone decides she's had enough and calls in the union or refers to her job description which can provide little guidance on questions of the demarcation of personal household chores. At whatever point one is in such disagreement, it is difficult. There really are no external rules that can sort out these problems. Without institutional rulings, a group is thrown back on its own resources and finds a way through. No solution is permanent; the situation will recur as the group and context change.

It is this sort of group work which is inherent in residential community living. While it is ordinary and natural, its survival and growth are essential if residential life is to be a positive and fulfilling experience for people. Such a reality is far from simple or straightforward to achieve in institutions embedded in moribund routines and regimes.

CHANGE – WHERE DO YOU START?

So what was going on with the staff group while some of the early changes to do with mealtimes were taking place?

It would be useful at this stage just to give more details of the staffing and organisation of Inglewood before we began to develop group living. While the staffing numbers and grades were disgracefully inadequate for such a large establishment (up to 119 residents), there was a very big staff group by any standards. Well over fifty people, nearly all full-timers, worked at Inglewood in 1982 and although staffing ratios improved because the overall maximum number of residents was reduced by thirty two, approximately the same establishment five years later left us, unable to fully utilise the resident accommodation because we were still considerably understaffed.

As is traditional in old people's homes, the staff fell into three broad groups, officers, care staff, and domestic workers, and were divided in many ways by the organisation of the home, by employment conditions and by nationality and race. The officers worked, ate, congregated socially and had any informal meetings in the office; the 'rest' the weekly paid workers, used a dirty, overcrowded staff room which was as far away as possible from the residential part of the building. It was unusual and somewhat daunting for an officer to enter this room because it was the location of staff relaxation, gossip, grumbles – a whole virulent counter culture where bad work and bad feelings grew and found support, and were ineffectually directed at everything outside – the officers, the residents, colleagues who weren't there at the time, and the employer and the department's management. There was even a lock on the inside of the door.

The office had all the same characteristics. Weekly-paid workers ventured inside only when summoned on official business. It was the place for dressing people down, for receiving visitors or new residents, although often newcomers were just deposited in the hall with no proper welcome or introduction. It was the location of all that was 'official' – time sheets, money, pensions, the staff absence and sickness book, the lines of communication with the outside world, letters and 'phones, residents' files, all the petty paraphernalia of officialdom and status. But open a drawer and you would find cutlery and sauce bottles for the officers who had their meals brought in here on trays; or investigate the filing cabinets and find a dirty assortment of electric razors, spectacles, false teeth, and hearing aids. Essentially the same social interaction went on between officers as between manual staff – gossip, recrimination, moaning, ineffectual allegations of bad practice against almost everyone outside the office, domestics, care workers, and management.

These sketches of the rooms or work bases of two staff groups in a residential home are quite typical. Any deep change in such a setting must begin with a change in staff relationships.

As a new manager at Inglewood in 1982, I had the advantage of being able to start work without the constrictions of the powerful existing traditions of group solidarity and antagonism which provided such fertile ground for the prevailing bad practice. I was able to ignore the surprise and hostility with which my early intrusion into the staff room or my spurning of the office were met. But I was also able to directly and openly pick up the many positive signs from colleagues and use all attempts to raise important issues, to float ideas, to work at problems as the starting points for changes. A culture of open debate began to take root and everyone, in whatever job or context, could and should start contributing.

I would be quite as likely to be talking to a domestic worker about care, the problems of privacy, the management of continence or even the staffing situation, as I would be to an assistant officer in charge. My first twelve weeks at Inglewood were spent working shifts with care assistants. In a short space of time I became familiar with all staff and all residents and they with me. I was purposely disregarding group boundaries, not normally the recommended path when entering a strongly delineated social setting.

When I discovered that, predictably, there were no regular staff meetings, we started them within a week. I chaired the first two meetings but made clear that, from the third, chairing and minuting would rotate between a group of any staff willing to take on those roles . . . 'any volunteers?' Luckily there were some, and ever since there has been a weekly staff meeting. Since the group living units started with their own separate staff teams, the meetings alternate between unit team meetings one week and the full staff meeting the next.

MEETING TOGETHER

Readers may question what's so special about having regular staff meetings and what have they got to do with groups in residential work?

First there are features of these meetings which are unusual and, although they may seem only to be common sense, there are in fact very few residential centres (or social services settings of any kind) which genuinely follow the same principles. *All* staff are rostered to be on duty and to attend the staff meeting (and remember at Inglewood that means fifty or more people including the handiperson, kitchen staff, laundry workers) and the meeting is open to residents who sometimes attend. The full staff meetings have a simple but regular form. The chairing and minuting rotate between a changing group of volunteers – again *all* grades of staff are involved. The minutes of the previous meeting are read, agreed, and commented on. There are then reports from each of the units, made again by a range of staff and sometimes tenants from the units. These reports will include news of all sorts, successful new bits of work, new equipment, plans for the next two weeks, staff on training, events, sickness, holidays, births and deaths, congratulations and condolences; the possibilities are endless. The meeting acknowledges each report by clapping, a response which started quite spontaneously when we began having unit reports.

After the reports comes the main agenda, pinned up a few days before the meeting for any individual or group to put down an agenda item. Anyone who wishes to speak must put up her or his hand and wait to be called by the chair. The meetings last up to $1^{1}/_{2}$ hours and usually end within time.

This fortnightly general staff meeting is a major event in the life of the place and has a strong influence both in form and content on the many other meetings which occur regularly or occasionally. All workers are used to simple meeting procedure which is adapted according to the size, setting, and purpose of whatever group is meeting. Most workers have developed experience and some expertise in chairing and minuting meetings. There is much common ground established on such areas as timekeeping, listening, and tolerating, indeed valuing, disagreement which means that group meetings have become one of the central work methods and supports in the establishment.

A tradition of group discussion, decision making, and action help workers naturally to think from a groupwork base. If someone has an idea, if there is an event to be organised, funds to be raised, the word will go round, or an announcement be made at the staff meeting; a notice will go up on the crowded notice board in the information and poster area in reception to say that something's being organised, 'There will be a meeting on . . . .'

As officer in charge of Inglewood, I sometimes found that groups were operating or getting on with work in the place before I knew anything about it. There grew a discipline within this co-operative and self-managing style which meant that usually all the learned experience of workers (mostly women, many of whom were used to the complex organisation of households) was used in a creative, and mainly non-conflictual way and had its own progressive momentum.

GROUPS – FORMAL AND INFORMAL, PERMANENT AND PASSING

For at least six months of the year, when the sun shines, two oldish men, John and Charlie, take chairs to a sunny spot outside and sunbathe. They are often joined by others and the venue has changed about three times in three years. They are the same two men who every morning at about 10.15 make tea for some of the small group of people they live with, a couple of people from other units who come to join them at that time, for Joyce and a friend, another John, who run the shop together. (This John lived temporarily at Inglewood for a few weeks when his flat was flooded and now helps with the shop and comes for his meal at the luncheon club.)

At about 11 a.m. most mornings, Steve comes down in his wheelchair from the first floor unit to go to the shop. He buys a can of lager which he drinks while he's talking at the shop counter, and usually he buys one or two things for his wife, Gladys, who stays upstairs. A little bunch of people gather round the shop; some of them are there to buy, some to talk, some to do both.

People wander up to get their tickets for the luncheon club – outsiders, residents from the ground floor units (short stay or semi-independent), people coming in for a social group or adult education class, and staff who don't work on one of the long-stay units and so will have their lunch in the luncheon club – all need to get tickets at the shop.

Rene is waiting in the reception area for her friend to give her a lift to do her weekly shopping at a supermarket. In spite of being severely disabled and using a wheelchair, she cooks all her own meals, does her own washing, and has a private telephone in her room. (The scene in her unit's kitchen is sometimes hectic, for there are several people trying to do different jobs at the same time – not unusual in a kitchen anywhere.)

In the reception area people come and go all the time – talking, meeting, and parting. The automatic front doors open and close constantly as visitors, friends, residents, and staff come in and out.

In the licensed social club, a public lounge during the day, the Music Morning is just beginning and about twenty residents from all units gather to sing, dance a bit, have coffee and enjoy themselves. Pam, who is retired but used to work at Inglewood, plays the piano; Margaret, who is 82 and seems to know all the songs ever sung, leads the singing in a strong, clear voice. Ellen and Viola, a domestic worker and a care assistant, are running the event this morning, and dance enthusiastically with the older people.

Prominent in the reception area is a board showing 'What's On Today?' on which are listed such things as meetings, groups, visitors, events, outings. It is quite common for the board to be full, but of course it shows only pre-planned and more formal occasions.

Increasingly other organisations and groups are using the good public facilities of Inglewood. A carers' support group meets; local organisations working with older people in the neighbourhood hold their monthly meetings; a group for isolated elderly people use one of the large public lounges. Most groups have some strong connections with the users, staff, or the work of the place and often people from Inglewood will be members of or in some way contributing to these groups. As yet no resident has joined the philatelic society which meets monthly in the big hall, but there is free membership for anyone who does!

Staff training events, internal and borough wide, and similar meetings of staff groups, including workers from other homes and day centres, are well provided for. For a long time staff involved with tenants' groups at Inglewood had their own training and development meetings, supported by one of the borough's groupworkers as consultant.

On individual units there are many small groups and groupings – cards, games, handicrafts, the groups of people who find they watch the same TV programmes, the people who habitually sit together in a small lounge, who go to events together, who eat together, the tenants' committees which keep starting up, flourish for a while and fade.

Most groups come and go; the only permanent ones are the large staff meetings, unit meetings, shift meetings, and management team meetings. The forms and contents of these may change but they always happen.

BEING PRIVATE AND PUBLIC

Inglewood is a place where many things happen. A lot of the time it is lively and bustling, and a good place to be. Between 120 and 150 people live or work there and many more use it, visit it regularly, or come there as part of their work. The liveliness and sociableness are a result of people coming together in groups – an ordinary part of social life except in highly institutionalised settings.

Inglewood's size was both a liability and an asset. Our aim in planning changes was to enhance the advantages of size and minimise the disadvantages.

Since the overwhelming problems for residents were a lack of privacy, personal care, and personal relationships, it was essential to establish ways in which people could be individual and private. We worked on a theory of the importance of both *private* and *public* areas of life, relationships, and physical space. The idea was that you could not exist publicly without having the opportunity to be on your own, to have some secure part of the building which you controlled and you could call your own, and to pursue your own private relationships – spiritual, intellectual, emotional, sexual – with others. It would be this sense and experience of privacy which would enable you to live a full community life. The converse was also true and demonstrated the advantages of a large establishment: a rich diversity of communal life with a wide variety of changing opportunities to associate and enjoy living with other people, and to do things together would enhance one's private life in an institution. Obviously we would have to cater for the whole range of public and private people: those who hardly moved from their rooms and would set them up in such a way to reduce to an absolute minimum their need to associate with any groups, and those who lived for the public area of their lives and disliked being on their own at all.

With this *public* and *private* notion, we set about making it possible for people to *be* private. Locks and bath taps were altered so that it was possible to have a bath without staff supervision. Residents were encouraged to create their own rooms; friends and relatives helped to redecorate and refurnish; new curtains were hung, kettles and televisions bought and carpets laid, none of this at any extra expense to the local authority. Inevitably, all of it took a long time.

As usual, the main obstruction to such internal changes were staff, residents', and relatives' attitudes. For years there were people who would not lock their rooms because they were 'not allowed to' in spite of repeated assurances that they were, and staff who could not bear the anxiety of a resident's telling them they could *not* come in when they knocked on a room door, or relatives who refused to accept that older people can decide to take risks in pursuit of independence and privacy.

We also concentrated on establishing a degree of privacy and sense of territory for each of the group living units. Only those who live or work in the unit have free access; everyone else must ring the front door bell, and 'everyone' means the officer in charge, outside visitors, and workers and residents from other units. The units are private to the group of residents and their staff team. However, there are no private staff facilities, no staff rooms or staff lavatories, which helps to ensure that the facilities are shared and kept to a high standard. This identification and territorial exclusiveness initially contributed to an unhelpful rivalry between units, which still surfaces at times of stress and loss of confidence, but increasingly growing differences between units are valued. Communal rooms are furnished differently; meals are at different times; decoration and tradition are varied and reflect the wishes, tastes and interests of groups of people who respect and value their own and each other's diversity.

The public areas became really public. Automatic front doors, plants and new lighting in the reception area, the shop, the public notice boards, and changed attitudes to 'outsiders' all spelled out a message: '*This is the public part of a public building. Can we help you? Welcome!*' The influx of outsiders was seen as an achievement, not a threat.

A variety of posters and announcements in the reception area demonstrated that what was going on in the outside world was relevant to this social services centre and that it, in turn, had a relevance, use, and identity in the environment in which it existed. A programme for the local cinema in Brixton; political, church, social information, local authority and benefits leaflets, newspaper cuttings, news of local events and organisations; a collection of pictures of women and men of many nationalities who made their mark in their seventies, eighties and nineties, underneath which was written the slogan 'Old Age is not a Problem; it is an Achievement.'

THE PAINFUL AND PERSONAL PROCESS OF CHANGE

The contradictions and dilemmas of *group living* are widespread and perpetual. What becomes of those people who had managed to make the institution, as it was, work for them? Was their achievement of a reasonably happy and satisfying way of life to be sacrificed to the promised, but doubtful, attainment of a better life for all? In the early days of reorganising the dining room, there were times when the results seemed to be even worse than what we were trying to replace. Over and over again staff were put in the position of apologising for and attempting to explain a new pattern of work which, at times, only a minority believed had a chance of succeeding.

Residents and staff were exposed to risks and anxiety which they had never before experienced in the work: knowing that someone who was very frail and forgetful was going to take a bath by herself, having to stand by while people took their own risks. In such situations the 'failures' are immediate and frightening, but the 'successes' are long-term and not so readily connected with a change in regime.

When, about two years after major change had begun, a man died while taking a bath very early in the morning, my competence, concern, and even fitness to manage Inglewood were questioned, not for the first time, at the highest levels in the department. He had died, apparently peacefully, of causes completely unrelated to his being in the bath. He liked taking a bath at that time, and wouldn't dream of allowing other people into the room with him. My concern was to reassure the night staff and the officer who was 'on call'. We were all very fond of this rather eccentric man and were upset by his unexpected death, yet it seemed probable that, for him, dying while relaxing in a hot bath was a good way to go. The concerns of senior managers appeared very different: dying in the bath looks bad if it becomes public; it could imply mismanagement and negligence. They were angered by my refusal to agree that the event should have been differently handled; they seemed to be stuck at a stage we had long since left. I was shaken by their lack of confidence in me and their failure to hold fast to the principles which underpinned the changes we were implementing.

Staff and residents who expected a 'good' head of home who would look after people, tell them what to do, minimise risks, and who, by her or his detachment and status, would be in a position to take the major decisions in the home, were initially disappointed and angered by my general approach.

Admittedly, in several ways, I was ideal to fill the patriarchal role prepared for me, and inevitably I must have slipped into it on occasions. As an English, white, middle class male in my mid-thirties at the time of my appointment, I did not have many elements in my identity and background which would ally me to either my colleagues or the residents.

How could I understand the point of view and experience of my colleagues? Nearly all of them were women, many black, many Irish, many older than me, many in this weekly-paid, low-status work for years, most having wanted to do a good job but prevented by a host of major structural forces – sexism, racism, low pay, and the hierarchical and demeaning nature of their employment. How was I to know what life was like for 80- and 90-year-old working class women? I knew little about their life experience and current position in residential care. And, while by class, race and sex, fitting accurately the mould of the 'new manager', I had the gall to constantly ask them to take on the very responsibilities and decisions for which I was being comparatively highly paid.

My acceptance and winning of trust would take more than words. First, I had to admit and accept my own ignorance. No, I didn't know what it was like to work at Inglewood or to be the object of the sort of discrimination and injustice which oppressed both most of my colleagues and most of the residents; neither was I likely ever to experience such oppression. Nor would I be able to claim to be free from the prejudice and privilege which was the other side of that oppression. While not denying either my position or my own useful knowledge and experience, I had to learn fast about myself in this new situation and about the realities of the job, about my colleagues and the tenants.

By working *with* care staff and domestic workers for my first three months in the post, I was able to gain at first hand some of the experience I needed. With my eyes wide open I saw the conditions of life and work in the place. I felt disgusted and degraded; I felt an anger that was physically and emotionally driven, no longer intellectually conceptualised. My responses were in my stomach and heart, and I did not have to rely solely on other people's feelings refined in my head. I understood at least some of the reality of this 'women's work', what it was like to work hard against all the odds with no satisfaction, no appreciation, and no power to effect change, but always facing the possibility of blame and even of losing one's job if the reality leaked out. This was the essence of 'women's work', paid and unpaid.

Here was the most crude embodiment of *unequal opportunities*, and I was part of it. It would be reasonable to assume that I would accept my part and play it. But changing Inglewood must mean changing parts, taking on new roles, learning, developing, surprising ourselves and other people. My chosen method of doing a crash course in care work was a dramatic first step in my own process of change and to changing relationships within Inglewood.

As I have already written, I was not always welcome in the staff room, and I was often pushing changes which were not initially supported by the majority of staff or even tenants. I was certainly not universally trusted – would other people be left to pick up the pieces? In spite of my efforts, for some, the doubt and resentment remained. Why couldn't I act more in keeping with my role? My own doubts were strong – was I being authentic? Was I trying to run with the hare and hunt with the hounds?

But colleagues, themselves wrestling with change, helped me along. For instance, the laundry person, under the critical eye of all, had the courage regularly to chair the large staff meeting, and, with others, led the way by daring to voice criticism of bad practice and support for change. Other staff risked writing reports and attending outside meetings, standing exposed on the very ground where they felt themselves to be weakest, or going on training courses where they would be vulnerable in the company of trained and more 'educated' social services staff. There were colleagues who admitted and spoke about their feelings, their grief, love, anger, disgust, and who were still able to cry or to say they cared. Some workers campaigned on issues such as racism and heterosexism within the place, resolving to uncover undercurrents which affected everyone but which most wanted to stay safely covered up. Another group of people who were prepared to stand up and be counted in the pursuit of improved services whether in a union meeting, a management group, a council committee or with their colleagues in a unit staff meeting. Major personal changes were going on around me as I struggled with my own position in a situation which I would have wished to be otherwise, but of which I was part. As we struggled, we suffered severe emotional pressure and confusion.

The exhilaration of new work and taking on new roles is often matched by the anxiety, tension, and sense of loss involved in letting go of or discarding old attitudes and work patterns, especially in the context of a wider organisation which is full of jumbled messages, policies and practices. While much effort was made within Inglewood to set up supporting systems for staff involved in change, the extent of support in the Social Services Directorate was far from certain. There were individuals outside who gave practical and moral encouragement, and constructive criticism, but they were few. The general attitude to the changes at Inglewood was hostile. Why?

THE INEVITABLE CONFLICT GENERATED BY GROUP ACTION IN A HIERARCHICAL ORGANISATION

Such grand proclamations as an Equal Opportunities Policy and a Residents' Rights Charter are fine in any organisation until workers at a lower level or users of services get hold of the idea that, as the people most affected by the wrongs these policies seek to put right, *they* will do something about them.

Groupwork in residential settings is, as I have implied earlier in the chapter, about finding, creating, and exercising the collective power to change things. The steady growth of self-managing and self-sufficient collective work in institutions is inimical to the organisations which run them. Traditionally all policy initiatives are 'top down' processes. In the case of very major policies such as an Equal Opportunities Policy, the senior staff appointed to implement the strategy quickly become swamped with work as all the responsibilities for a universal policy get landed on them. Instead of being able to operate as leaders and developers, they get stuck with a policing role and instead of the policy becoming indigenous and deeply rooted in the organisation, it sits heavily but superficially imposed on the workforce and users. A few 'show trials' emphasise its punitive and controlling, rather than creative and positive, nature.

Attempts by groups in the workforce to bring such policies into everyday work practice are frequently blocked or diverted at higher levels in the organisation.

If there is one clear implication for action in the two policies I have mentioned, it is that people who have hitherto been discriminated against in employment and denied access to and use of services, will start to take their fair shares: that users who have had their rights taken away will take them back and exercise them.

It is inescapable that the process of establishing equal opportunities and rights, of people taking their own power back, involves a loss of power for currently powerful groups and individuals. Power holders will always be reluctant to let go and will close ranks very quickly at the first signs of change. A display of vigour and enthusiasm for progressive policies, particularly unexpected and unwelcome in the area of residential care for older people, is just such a dangerous sign.

The sort of life and work which I have described in this chapter is challenging to a wider organisation which is run very much from the top down. A large social services centre which has a strong but minimal core of formal structure, providing a basis for a multitude of self-managing groups and free-wheeling groupings, does not fit easily with a predominantly patriarchal, bureaucratic local authority department. Each is a serious threat to the other.

The weekly-paid women workers and the elderly women users of residential care, oppressed by sexism, racism, and ageism, many having spent their lives doing two jobs, one paid and one unpaid, unable to afford for their own dependants the care they give to others, make a stark and telling contrast with most of the organisation's managers – well paid, highly educated, and trained white men who need never get their hands dirty at home or at work. Organisational harmony is achieved at the expense of the independence and self-determination of the users and workers. This cost is levied particularly on residential centres for older people. A centre which develops differently and in which people gather, work, live, and take action together in self-directed groups, using the organising abilities and experience of the residents and staff, will always be at odds with a centralised hierarchy.

For *group living* to become a dynamic reality in residential centres, (and not simply a hollow description of dividing people into more manageable and convenient, smaller groups, and providing them with kitchens and dining rooms), social services departments have to change. They will have to start by learning from a different and more successful form of management, a looser and less bureaucratic form of organisation, and from the ordinary group activities of workers and users in institutions where convivial social life is able to take root and flourish.

This chapter is based on events between 1982 and 1987 at Inglewood in the London Borough of Lambeth. Places and groups change constantly; some of the circumstances are now different and some of the people referred to have died or, like the author, have moved to other jobs. In many centres, such as Inglewood, workers and users continue to struggle to create good work and a good life in the most adverse conditions. This chapter recognises that such states are achievable in local authorities, even though, as yet, they are fleeting and rare.

Chapter Five

GROUPS AND GROUPINGS IN A FAMILY CENTRE

CHRISTINE STONES

CONTEXT AND BACKGROUND

Family Centre is a title covering a multiplicity of establishments which vary in terms of users, aims, methods, and styles. It is therefore necessary to provide some context and background before exploring groups and groupings in a specific family centre.

Fulford Family Centre is a non-residential, neighbourhood-based project established by Barnardo's, on a large housing estate on the southern outskirts of Bristol, to work with families with pre-school children. The DHSS Under Fives Initiative provided a proportion of funding which was subsequently replaced by local authority grant aid (County of Avon Social Services Department). Further developments in the project have obtained additional funding from the Health Authority and the Inner Area Programme.

The project was allocated accommodation by the local housing authority and is housed, at the end of a rank of shops, in a small three-storey building which was previously three 'hard to let' flats. It primarily serves the community of Hartcliffe but is also used by some families from the adjacent estate of Withywood. There are no clear boundaries between the two estates which have a joint population of 35,000, the size of a small town, but include very few of the facilities which residents in a town would expect and enjoy. The estates, built in the 1950s, comprise, a mixture of high- and low-rise flats and houses; the population includes a high proportion of children under 5.

The family centre was established in response to local health and social services agencies identifying an urgent need for additional provision for families with children under 5 years. In the three months prior to the centre opening to families in October 1984, the staff undertook a detailed assessment of need in order to develop appropriate services. One hundred families living in the neighbourhood were interviewed to obtain their views as to the needs of young families in the area and the services they would consider most relevant. The survey provided some vivid illustrations of the impact on families of living on an estate with some of the highest levels of social stress in the city and county. In response to the question, 'What are the best things about living in the area?' the most frequent response was 'nothing'. Asked, 'What do you not like about living in Hartcliffe?' the majority of parents responded with several items, the most common answers included a lack of safe play areas and other facilities for children, isolation and absence of community feeling, burglaries, vandalism, and glue sniffers. Isolation from wider families was found to be an issue for 43 per cent of the families interviewed.

The findings of the survey together with the views of representatives of local agencies refined the aim of the project and informed the design of the centre's programme.

AIMS AND PHILOSOPHY

The stated aim of Fulford Family Centre is, through partnership with parents to facilitate opportunities for growth and development for parents and under fives, and, where appropriate, to prevent the reception into care of young children. The ways in which this aim is pursued are influenced by the philosophy, values, and theoretical framework held by Barnardo's and by the particular project team.

The growth and development of pre-school children (and of their parents) involves physical, cognitive, emotional, and social components. The centre's philosophy includes an interactional and multifactoral view of the problems and possibilities facing families with young children. Such a perspective refuses to locate issues of child development, neglect, or abuse solely within the individual family nor simply within the community or social structure. It rather recognises the multiple, interconnected factors which can encourage or impede the development of children and the fulfilment of all family members.

CATEGORISATION OF THE CENTRE'S GROUPS AND GROUPINGS

A varied programme and a range of facilities have been developed to achieve the aim of the centre in accord with its philosophy. A combination of theories and approaches are used in work with individual parents, children, and whole families. But for the purpose of this chapter the description of the project's work will concentrate on the constellation of groups and groupings arising within or associated with the centre. Some groups interlock, some overlap, others are quite separate; the majority can be outlined using the typology in Chapter 2 as a guideline.

The whole community of the centre

Occasional meetings are organised to which all recent users are invited (e.g. to set up a *parents council*) but obviously, with over 200 users in a year, 100 per cent attendance is unlikely. Thus, because of the size and nature of the project, the whole community never meets. It has a large, changing, unclear membership and permeable boundaries and is made up of a number of smaller groups, plus individual users who may not belong to any group but receive welfare rights advice or individual/family counselling.

The definition of the whole community is also blurred by the project's involvement in promoting and supporting community provision for young families on other local sites. Thus a development worker and a high rise resource worker are involved with a number of groups of parents and children, some of whom may never enter the centre building.

Informal friendship/affinity groups

These exist throughout the centre's programme but are particularly apparent in larger groups. A core activity of the centre is a twice weekly open session to which any local family with a pre-school child is welcome. This has become known as the *drop-in* and on a typical morning there will be fifteen to twenty parents and more than twenty young children. The large grouping is a changing population with a nucleus of regular attenders and comprises a number of informal friendship groups. Some of these sub-groups have arisen within the centre and strengthen their attachments by outside meetings; others may already exist in the neighbourhood and subsequently participate together in centre activities.

Groups organised to discuss group living issues

The preface to the aim of the centre is 'through partnership with parents' and this is a primary influence in the design, style, and content of the programme. Since its inception the project has striven to develop processes and structures which involve users in decision-making. A *parents council* comprising representatives of the different centre activities has been established to participate in decisions relating to resources, priorities, and programme. The *parents council* meets regularly with the staff team. Problems arising within or between groups may be channelled through the *parents council* and its sub-committees for resolution. For example, disagreement amongst users about how conflicts between children should be handled led to the issue being referred to the *parents council*.

Structured organised groups for specific purposes

A range of different groups belong to this category and can be clustered into three areas:

Adult education/leisure activities. These include cookery, sewing, mural painting, literacy, photography. Whilst each of these groups meet, a crèche is provided for the children so that the adults can pursue the particular activity. A small group of parents have participated in a welfare rights course as they wished to be equipped with the knowledge and skills necessary for basic advice work.

Parenting groups. A *parents course* is run as a closed group over ten weeks and its objectives include recognising children's developmental needs and understanding and facilitating play.

One day a week is used mainly as a *family group day* when intensive work is undertaken with a small group of families. For some of the families there is a risk of the children being removed by the local authority or courts due to neglect or abuse. This closed group of three or four families meets for twelve weeks and most families attend for at least two series of twelve weeks. The *family group day* includes movement and play sessions which both involve parents and children working together. Later in the morning parents have a discussion group including the use of role play and video while the children have a play session.

Mutual self-help groups. Three self-help groups have been initiated in the centre and each of these had staff involvement in the early stages. A group for prisoners' wives has now become completely autonomous and has moved to a different venue. A single parents group and a group for parents of hyperactive children provide their members with mutual aid and support.

Groups organised by consumers to manage particular events

These may sometimes be a sub-group of the parents' council or an ad hoc group to organise a specific event. A number of events occur during a year which lead to the evolution of such groups and they might include a bonfire night party, a trip to the pantomime, and the provision of a stall at the local fayre.

Staff group/s

The staff group comprises five full-time and three part-time professional workers, one project secretary, a part-time cook/cleaner, and a part-time handyperson. The staff team meets weekly except for the cook/cleaner and handyperson although they are invited to occasional gatherings. 'Away days' are held with a major aim being team building. Various pairs and sub-groups exist within the team and these mainly relate to areas of joint work or common interest. Two of the part-time staff are partners who share a project worker post whilst sharing the care of their children. For most of the year the centre enjoys the presence of a professional social work student on placement and each is seen as a member of the team.

Groupings for particular events

Occasional 'special' meetings, events, and outings are opportunities for various groups or some of their members to come together in a new grouping. Outings are held regularly and the different groups are encouraged to participate. The constituent groups may not interact much and may retain their identities sitting together on the coach, and remaining together throughout the day.

Groups which embrace both insiders and outsiders

As suggested earlier, it can be difficult to identify who is an insider and who an outsider, due to the permeability of the boundary of the whole community. However, tenants' groups may meet at the centre where a core are parents who use the centre, but others may not have children under 5 so cannot be termed insiders. Also under this category, one would place regular meetings which are held with groups of other professionals. Some of these meetings will involve both centre staff and users and others may only involve staff.

THE APPLICATION OF A GROUP PERSPECTIVE

In order to work effectively in a family centre it is helpful to use a group perspective. This perspective needs to apply insights from small groups, large groups, and intergroup theory, whilst also recognising that those too rarely take into account an environment made up of complex inter-related groups.

Planning activities and programme to meet the aim

In making choices between different methods of work the particular strengths and weaknesses of the varied options are considered. There are several potential advantages of using groups as the context, medium or focus of work. Brown (1986) identifies these advantages and they can be considered in relation to the three ways in which groups are used.

The group as the context for work in a family centre. The centre's aims of individual growth and development for young children and their parents involves gaining knowledge and learning skills. In many instances this may require a teacher or tutor, for example in literacy or cookery. There are obvious economic considerations in using a group context, in these circumstances. However, a group will also have other benefits, such as the context for individual learning which includes mutual encouragement and support.

The group as the medium for work in a family centre. It is under this heading that much of the work undertaken at the centre can be considered. Awareness that groups of people with similar needs or common problems can be a source of both support and problem-solving resulted in the encouragement and establishment of self-help groups. Many people experiencing difficulties feel isolated and unique, so to meet others in similar circumstances (e.g. other women whose men are in prison) can provide reassurance and friendship.

The use of a social service, whether statutory or voluntary, can be experienced as undermining; thus a great advantage of a group is that each member can give as well as receive help. This may be sharing information about cheap sources of clothing or contributing ideas about managing temper tantrums. Taking a 'helping role' in a group increases self-esteem and thus encourages personal growth in a parent. Recognition that attitudes and behaviour may be altered in a group through modelling, reinforcement, and multiple ideas is a reason for working on parenting issues in a group.

Some vital developmental needs of children can be met best in a group. Both co-operative play and social learning require the presence of others. The group of children at drop-in, at family group day, and the crèches held whilst parents attend adult groups, provide an opportunity for the children to develop social skills.

The tenet of partnership with parents involves sharing power with parents. Parents are more powerful in a group than individually. Thus, when planning a joint parent/staff meeting to discuss aims and priorities, staff suggested that the *parents council* met together first with an 'external' facilitator to do some initial work on their views. This led to the parents attending the joint meeting with a clear set of proposals and confidence in presenting them.

The group as a focus for work in a family centre. In using the group as a focus for work, one is immediately aware of common bonds between groupwork and family therapy and between groupwork and community work; all these methods are utilised within the project. In working with *an individual family as a unit, one is using the natural group of the family as the focus for work.*

Families attending the centre are often isolated or alienated from their wider family and from others in their neighbourhood. It sometimes is clear that an important way in which an individual family needs help is to extend or strengthen their social network. The existing social network will then become the focus of work.

Factors in group planning

Once the choice has been made of using a group as the context, medium, or focus of work then a number of factors need to be considered in order to aid the effectiveness of a group approach.

For instance, thought needs to be given to how the group fits into the centre as a whole. How will users and staff not involved in the group view it? Resources for a group need to be available and increasingly with the establishment of a busy programme there can be problems in ensuring that both staff and appropriate accommodation are available at the same time. It is vital for communication and negotiation to take place with other groups and groupings.

The recruitment and selection of members of a new group can often be a difficult issue. Criteria for the group composition will relate to the aim of the group and many groups at the centre are self-selecting. Studies in group composition identify the degree of homogeneity/heterogeneity amongst members as a key concept. Bertcher and Maple (1977) suggest that stability in a group is facilitated by members sharing certain 'descriptive' attributes and vitality is engendered by group members differing in 'behaviourial' characteristics (see Chapter 2 of this book). Similarity in 'descriptive' attributes requires agreed definitions and can provoke disagreement. One user of the centre thought she should be eligible to join the single-parents group as she was divorced from her children's father. However, the existing members of the group did not recognise her as a single parent because she was known to be living with someone else, while another parent whose husband was in prison was accepted as a single parent.

In planning a group, clarity of aim and openness in expressing the aim are important. On occasions other agencies may have a covert aim in referring a family which they do not share with the family, as when they suggest to a family that they attend the centre in order to make friends but tell the centre staff they are concerned about the standard of parenting. A preparatory stage for the group which attends on *family group day* includes the negotiation of a contract with both the family and the referrer so that hidden agendas are avoided.

In planning a group, timescales need to be considered and one factor will be whether membership will be open or closed. In the early stages of its development, *family group day* involved an open group with new members being added at any time providing there was room in the group. This approach was soon found to be very disruptive, new members were often resented, and it could be difficult to integrate them into the group. The group is now closed for twelve weeks. As indicated earlier, many families will attend more than one twelve-week series but new members are not added until the start of a new series.

WORKING WITH FORMAL AND INFORMAL GROUPS TO ACHIEVE THE AIM

Once a group has been set up or an existing group has been selected as an appropriate target of intervention, then a group perspective provides numerous insights to aid effective work (or at least understanding ineffectiveness!) Three major areas will be explored in this section, first, stages of development, then leadership, and third, inter-group relations.

Stages of development

As group theory indicates, a group goes through a number of different stages of development. Most models of group stages appear to portray a linear development but their proponents always include a warning word about oscillation between stages. Recognition of the different phases of development has often helped to make sense of group behaviour or difficulties experienced by members.

In a neighbourhood family centre users attending groups may have prior knowledge of one another. Thus in starting any new group, attention needs to be paid in the early stages to existing friendships and alliances which will be brought to the group and the integration of 'new' centre users or 'strangers' in the group. During the first sessions of the group, it can be useful to undertake exercises in two's or three's which mix new and 'existing' centre users.

The beginning of every session often involves re-forming for a group. It can be useful to introduce a structure to aid re-forming such as a *good news/bad news* exercise which enables members of the group and workers to be aware of important events that have occurred during the intervening week.

A stage in the life of a group which can pose difficulties for members and group workers involves struggles concerning power and control. When a group is in such a *storming* phase it is important that workers remain consistent and the conflict is handled constructively. In the earliest days of *family group day* workers were tempted to keep adjusting the programme as members objected strongly to various components and sometimes refused to participate. However, it was soon recognised that this was a feature of the storming phase of the group and it was important to maintain the structure of the programme whilst tolerating members' rebellion.

Establishing ways in which all members can find a role in the group and their contribution valued is important. A danger apparent in the *storming* stage can be that the most forcefully assertive members have greatest influence. In the *parents council* two members may form a powerful alliance and consistently seek to influence the group; inadvertently workers may reinforce positions by asking for volunteers for various tasks, such as working parties when frequently confident and articulate users will be the first to respond. When first the *parents council and committees* were being set up, it was rapidly apparent that several parents were interested in participating and thus wished to hold some influence in the centre but were unwilling to stand in an election. As a result committee/council places are allocated by selection not election. The method of selection is by a draw and this reduces the feelings of competition between members.

It is often in the *storming* phase that sub-groups form and re-form; such sub-groups may be fluid throughout the life of a group but more commonly they will become fairly fixed. The larger the group or grouping, the more likely it is that sub-groups will form. Sub-groups may strengthen the total group but they will hamper the overall group if they develop into cliques and thus become exclusive. The large drop-in inevitably has a number of sub-groups some of which appear cliquish, such as when people make frequent references to a shared history which is not explained to a newcomer.

Most groups over time develop their own culture and establish group norms, the *norming stage*. In any situation where groups and groupings have common or overlapping membership, it is likely that the culture and norms of one group will influence another. The culture and norms experienced in one group may be ascribed by members to the centre as a whole. This can pose difficulties since groups and groupings with different tasks and format may need different kinds of culture. An obvious example of this is that the *drop-in* is often the first grouping that users experience at the centre. As its title suggests, it is a session when any user can call in between certain times. They are encouraged to sit and chat, and *drop-ins* can be attended as frequently or rarely as an individual desires. When activity or educational groups are set up, potential members may be recruited at *drop-in*. These groups frequently have patterns of irregular attendance and quite a high drop-out rate. This may, in part, reflect a much wider picture found in adult education where there is a considerable discrepancy between numbers registering for classes and those attending. However, this problem is compounded at the centre by expecting users to move easily from *drop-in* norms to those of another centre group where membership is closed, the group starts at a specific time and attendance is expected for every session.

Leadership

Two ways of viewing leadership aid effective work with groups. The first is to see leadership as the performance of acts that help the group achieve its tasks and maintain effective working relationships among its members. Such leadership functions may be distributed between group members. This approach means, for example, that when a self-help group is being established its effectiveness will relate to the distribution of task and maintenance behaviour among group members.

The distribution of task and maintenance functions within the staff team makes a major contribution to the team's productivity and to the satisfaction individuals express about belonging to the team. Thus at staff meetings, the activity of some members ensures that the agenda is pursued whilst the contribution of others particularly encourages harmonious relationships.

Leadership can also be understood in terms of a position held and from this perspective the leader is the person fulfilling an ascribed role. However much group workers may view their aim as facilitating members to undertake leadership functions, group members may expect workers to be more active and directive as they occupy a 'position' of leadership.

In addition, the stage of development a group has reached needs to be taken into account when considering appropriate leadership behaviour. When the *parents council* was first established workers suggested that it should be chaired by a parent and the parents also supported this. They decided that they would rotate the responsibility for chairing. After the first few chaotic meetings, the parents requested that the member of staff attending the meeting should be the chairperson. On reflection, it was unrealistic to expect the members of the group who had little, if any, experience of formal meetings and were in the early stages of working together as a group to undertake positional leadership.

When acting as leader, workers may use different styles. It is appropriate that workers vary their style of leadership both between groups and within groups in correlation with various factors. Both the aim of the group and its composition are elements which affect leadership style. However, users may find it difficult to understand and adjust to changes in behaviour of staff. *Family group day* and *drop-in* provide one of the biggest contrasts. In the programme comprising *family group day*, staff are actively focusing on parent/child interactions and suggesting alternative ways of relating. At *drop-ins*, staff are much less directive and more informal in style.

Individual staff vary in their natural or preferred style of leadership and a range exists within the staff team. a great advantage of this new project was that all staff were recruited specifically for it and a factor given attention in recruitment was the provision of a range of skills and experience. This led to a variety in approach from family therapy to community work and differences in stance from psychodynamic to behaviourist. The team shares an enthusiastic commitment to the aims and philosophy of the centre and this, together with respect for each other's ways of working, has led to the development of a cohesive group. Compared to most fieldwork settings, work in a centre as a team provides numerous opportunities for developing knowledge and skill through observing other team members and by giving and receiving feedback. Team-building days have explored differences in approach and style and have included sharing observations of each other's practice.

To work effectively as a team requires openness and trust between members and a willingness to explore disagreement. The inevitable diversity in workers' style has enormous advantages for users and for team members but can also lead to difficulties. An example of this is difference in the degree of self disclosure practised by staff. A member of the team high on self disclosure may inadvertently disclose information about another team member when asked by users.

If the other team member is low on self disclosure they may not wish the material to be shared. A number of incidents resulting from this led to a frank and productive exploration of individual attitudes and use of self disclosure and concluded with the establishment of team ground rules for disclosure.

Intergroup relations

In any day or residential unit workers are managing a range of different groups and are thus working with processes both within and between groups. Most studies and theory of inter-group relations focus on the interaction between discrete groups with separate membership. Like most, if not all, residential and day care activity, the family centre's work is also affected by the processes arising between numerous groups with differing and varying degrees of common membership. The complexity of this can be expressed diagrammatically.

Important processes to consider in working with any small group comprise the internal dynamics and the context of the group (Figure 5.1).

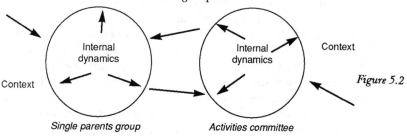

Figure 5.1

Context

Internal dynamics

Single parents group

In intergroup relations some of the environmental influences are other small groups.

Context

Internal dynamics

Single parents group

Internal dynamics

Context

Figure 5.2

Activities committee

But at the centre many groups overlap and interlock.

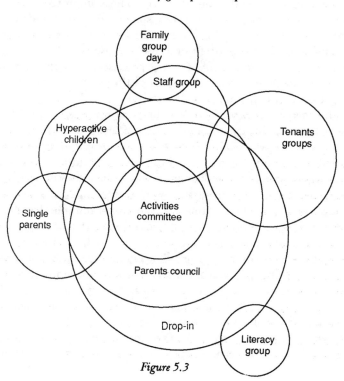

Family group day

Staff group

Hyperactive children

Tenants groups

Single parents

Activities committee

Parents council

Drop-in

Literacy group

Figure 5.3

Thus part of a group's environment may be other discrete small groups and part is other groups with which there is a degree of common membership. This provides a situation in which the interaction is complex.

In looking at the norming stage of group development reference was made to the relationship and influence between groups. Another aspect of inter-group relations which influences their effectiveness and the efficacy of the centre as a whole is that of conflict between groups. Conflict between groups occurs when activities of different groups are incompatible. As Zander (1982) outlines, this may relate to 'competition for scarce resources, barriers to self determination for a group, differences in basic beliefs or fears that actions by those in one group will create discomfort for those in the other group'.

Examples of conflict at the centre can be fairly readily provided. The activities committee, whose members did not include anyone from the single parents' group, objected to a request for finance for an outing from this other group. The committee organise outings for the whole centre and suggested that if individual groups wished to arrange expeditions restricted to their membership they should fund these themselves. This conflict involved both competition for scarce resources (the outings budget) and differences in belief as to the centre's relationship with constituent groups.

The *parents council* and the staff group may experience disagreement, the cause of which is different beliefs. A clear example is the two groups' incongruent views about appropriate controls and sanctions to use with young children. The staff discourage parents from using physical punishment whereas, when the issue was discussed with the *parents council*, most members supported smacking children and recommended that a child who bit another child should be bitten by their parent.

Concerns of both gender and race can be explored and understood from an inter-group viewpoint. The family centre has found difficulty in involving men in group activities. In work focused on individual families, such as family therapy and the *family group day*, workers have been more 'successful' in engaging the whole family. In spite of some changes in sex roles, society still sees child care as primarily the concern of women. Such stereotyping does appear stronger in working class culture and

94

although there are high levels of unemployment on the estate, and thus greater opportunities for contact between fathers and children, the degree of shared child care seems low. One or two men attended drop-in but usually appeared uncomfortable. Staff were concerned that, as a family centre, some activities should be provided which attracted fathers and felt that greater involvement of men should be a priority.

Several of the mothers attending the centre were ambivalent about the proposal that male staff members would allocate some time to seeking ideas from fathers about possible activities. Some mothers were opposed to the proposal and argued that none of the existing activities excluded men. It would seem that for many women experiences in the centre contrasted with most other experiences, i.e. all the parents on the *council* are women and thus it is a relatively rare place in which women hold power and influence. Thus the proposal to seek greater participation by men raised the possibility of both competing for limited resources and threat to the existing status of the women using the centre.

The centre's location is on an estate whose population is largely white with a small minority of black families. The centre has had contact with a few black parents and there have been incidents of both overt and covert racism. The small number of black parents using the centre have been recipients of a colour-blind attitude – 'I don't think of you as black you're just like one of us'. A school-age child of one family suffered considerable racial harassment at school and most of the other *drop-in* users were unsympathetic and suggested that the child and his mother were at fault. During *drop-in* and other groups, often there are racist conversations. The staff group are committed to establishing an anti-racist policy but receive little support for this from users. Families accurately view their local community as under-resourced and thus there are feelings of being disadvantaged and frustrated. Media coverage of the inner city (as opposed to outer city estates), with emphasis on the multi-racial population and on any new resources being allocated to such an area, encourages and reinforces existing prejudice which scapegoats the black population for the economic hardship of white families.

ISSUES AND IMPLICATIONS

A major implication of the mosaic of groups and groupings is that both staff and users are concurrently members of different groups. There can be advantages to users of having an opportunity to take different roles in different groups but this may be confusing and stressful.

An added dimension to the movement between roles in groups is that some users may see staff in a context of individual counselling and family therapy which further extends the number and type of roles and styles experienced. As indicated earlier, the existence of varying cultures, norms, and leadership styles are likely to cause uncertainty and anxiety for some users. All these factors point to the importance of staff and users finding ways of managing movement between groups and suggests that the different boundaries should be marked.

The greatest contrast is often between *drop-in* and other activities. When users are recruited from *drop-in* for more highly structured groups it is helpful to emphasise the structure of the new group: regular attendance, starting and finishing times, limitations on membership. In some instances, difficulties may be compounded by holding groups with contrasting cultures consecutively on the same day. The *parents council* is usually held in the afternoon following a *drop-in* and it is often hard to create an atmosphere in which only one member talks at a time and where contributions are listened to and responded to seriously. This is perhaps not surprising when one reflects that most of the members will have spent the morning together in a noisy *drop-in*, and over a communal lunch will have maintained the lively informality. Careful timetabling may help to emphasise boundaries and assist movement between groups.

An issue which arises in most open-ended groups is how to enable them to be both cohesive units with strong bonds between members but also welcoming to new members. In most groups, it is often the staff who take the role of welcoming newcomers. Although existing users were aware of the problem of *drop-in* being daunting to first-time users, the majority of parents seemed to lack the social skills which would aid integration of newcomers. Sometimes existing users are also ambivalent about visitors as there is always a risk that their presence will mean fewer resources for established parents. The problem of integrating parents new to the centre is being tackled by a scheme to use existing parents as volunteers. In this process a new parent is linked with a current user to assist integration.

Group composition in some instances can raise difficult issues. As outlined above, an important advantage of groups is the provision of different role models for members. When the focus of the group is on parenting it can be difficult to identify which are critical attributes to produce the optimum composition. This may be because the descriptive attributes which need to be homogeneous are likely to be correlated with similar instead of varied behavioural attributes. In *family group day*, families are more able to identify with each other if they all think there is risk of their children being removed or at least acknowledge that they face serious problems in caring for their children. However, this descriptive characteristic of 'parents whose children may be removed' is certain to mean that all the group members experience difficulty in parenting behaviour and are unlikely to provide each other with suitable alternative role models. Composing effective parenting groups is therefore a difficult task.

Staff have identified various difficulties in work which aims to make groups self-supporting. The development worker has found that where she is successful in encouraging leadership within a group the effects are often short-lived. The parent who has taken on some responsibility for leadership will, frequently and understandably, use their increased confidence and skill to move out of the group and into some other activity. Thus the aim of growth and development for parents may militate against a goal of self-supporting groups. This problem is further exacerbated by the quite high degree of transience within the estate. A tenants' group which was supported by a centre worker experienced a complete turnover of 'officers' within a year of the group's existence. Many individual tenants also have a personal goal of obtaining rehousing and such an objective leads to a lack of interest in, or energy for, co-operative action to improve their present housing situation.

One of the issues identified earlier in the chapter is the conflict that may arise between the staff group and users' groups in terms of values. A current and crucial example relates to the development of an anti-racist policy. Staff would place this as a

97

high priority but the *parents council* view it as a low priority and some members question its relevance altogether. The conflicting views of users and staff in this produces a further conceptual conflict for staff. Pursuing a policy of partnership with parents involves giving weight to parents' views and priorities, but if in some instances these reflect racist attitudes staff then wish to oppose the views strongly.

Some conflicts arise from lack of clarity about who holds responsibility and power as the centre is subject to different sources of influence. In addition to the power which staff hold and aim to share with parents, there is the power held by Barnardo's and by three other funding sources. Emphasis on partnership with parents without clarifying the limits of partnership and without adequate attention to other partnerships may lead to disillusionment for users who are suddenly faced by an external constraint to their use of power.

An issue which arises recurrently is the integration of individual groups within the overall grouping of the project. Groups vary in the degree to which they identify with the Family Centre and this only becomes problematic when relationships between groups are strained. On occasions there are feelings of rivalry between groups and there can be a danger of the stigmatisation of one group by another. To some degree this relates to the project's efforts to provide both a community resource for any young family and a service for families under particular stress. In the main, one of the results of providing a community resource has been that the centre is not stigmatised within the local neighbourhood. It does not appear to be viewed by most local people as a 'place for problem families' nor as 'somewhere you are sent if you batter your child' which are labels some family centres have to contend with.

However, publicity has sometimes caused concern for users; for example, a local newspaper, when reporting on a visit of the President of Barnardo's, the Princess of Wales, to the centre, described it as helping people with social and emotional problems. A number of users were understandably angered by this limited account and there was a tendency for *drop-in* users to see such stigmatisation as caused by other groups such as *family group day* or *prisoners' wives group*. Thus some groups may wish to emphasise their distinction from other groups at the centre.

The family centre is still developing and changing and, if it is to be effective, it must continue to be responsive to the needs of young families in its particular neighbourhood. This requires the establishment of a culture in which particular groups are not seen as 'permanent' fixtures. Thus there will probably always be a slowly shifting constellation of groups and groupings in which new groups come into being and existing groups change or end.

Chapter Six

DEVELOPMENT OF THE SOCIAL CLIMATE IN A MENTAL HEALTH CENTRE

BEN BANO

Mental health day services have been seen, rightly, as an essential component in the overall provision of mental health service provision. *Better Services for the Mentally Ill* (DHSS 1975) discussed the need for a network of day centres and day hospitals for people with mental health problems. A minimum level of provision was proposed – for example, there would be 120 day centre places and 60 day hospital places for a population of 200,000.

But vital questions were left unanswered and lack of clarity has affected the planning of even the most recent services. One example is the question of organisation. What should be the difference between day hospitals and day centres ? The White Paper envisaged day centres being concerned with the client's needs for 'shelter, occupation and social activities'; centres were to relieve the strain on families, help individuals to readjust to the demands of work, and 'encourage the realisation of the individual's potential'. Day hospitals, on the other hand, would provide a treatment setting. There was also an expectation that day centres would be run by Social Services Departments and voluntary organisations, while day hospitals would be run by the National Health Service.

Five years later, in a national study, Carter (1981) found that frequently day hospitals and day centres were pursuing similar activities, particularly in areas where there was a deficit of one or the other type of provision. There was also a very uneven spread of provision across the country, with very few areas achieving the DHSS guidelines of service.

However, there were philosophical as well as organisational

questions. The centres and hospitals suggested in the DHSS guidelines did not reflect the trend in the 1980s towards smaller facilities nearer to the local community of the users. The 'care' component of 'day care' became an increasingly unclear term as mental health services moved away from a medical model. Increasingly day services were expected to satisfy a variety of demands, from rehabilitation of those already in the community to the ongoing care of those with long term illnesses discharged from hospital. Employment rehabilitation became difficult as opportunities for employment of people with mental health problems declined during the 1980s.

The delivery of mental health day services has also been influenced by newer service philosophies. Normalisation theory, having had a considerable influence on services for people with a mental handicap, has begun to influence mental health services, bringing an emphasis on equality between clients and service providers, and on the need to provide a climate and activities which are appropriate to everyday adult roles.

Consumerism, similarly, has had an impact on services. For example, there has been an increased emphasis on users' involvement in the day-to-day running and planning of services. At the same time gender and race issues in service delivery in mental health have had to be adequately faced.

These services, therefore, have been characterised by confusion of organisation and a constantly evolving service philosophy. Staff and planners have also had to address the issue of the *type* of service appropriate to the needs and wants of each user. A psychotherapeutic approach may not be appropriate for people with little insight, just as an approach based purely on practical activities may not be relevant for people who require greater understanding of themselves. Some users may respond only to a drop-in style, while others will welcome a structured programme. Some people may need a day service as a form of continuing support while other people may need it only for a brief period.

Other people may profit from a day service in which the emotional climate is deliberately lowered. The research on expressed emotion in the families of people with schizophrenia (Leff *et al.* 1985) shows that by reducing high expressed emotion in some families, some people with schizophrenia were able to stay out of hospital for longer periods. It would be counterproductive for the same people to leave their families during the day to attend a day service in which high degrees of emotional expression were experienced.

In fact several styles of day service are appropriate. Blake and Millard (1981) suggest that *planned variety* is important. Because the ethos of a service is particularly important, a centre should not attempt to provide too many different styles of work since the result could be confusion for both staff and users of the service. Blake and Millard's models of service provision could be described as follows.

Supportive services aim to give individuals (and sometimes their families) ongoing social support which will help to meet their social needs and to prevent social isolation. Drop-in clubs and psychiatric social clubs are examples of this type of service, as are centres which aim to assist in one or more of three ways: maintaining the quality of life for their users; preventing readmission to hospital; and in providing relief for carers.

Re-educative services help the user to relearn lost skills, learn new ones, and develop a sense of purpose through providing a time structure which can in turn be linked to 'work' type roles. Re-educative services offer their users a sense of purpose and achievement, and an opportunity to develop social confidence and social skills. This type of service may be particularly helpful in restoring self esteem to people who may have lost a job through redundancy and suffered a reactive depression as a result.

Reconstructive services are based on approaches which seek to develop growth through expression of feelings, self understanding, and learning through interaction with other users. This approach requires a higher level of intellectual functioning so that the exploration and understanding of thoughts and feelings can gradually 'reconstruct' the individuals' views of themselves and the world around them.

This chapter describes the experience of a re-educative approach in a large, purpose built mental health day centre in which I was manager from 1981 to 1987. It is concerned with the development of a social climate which had to assist people to develop the social confidence, self responsibility, and other skills which they would need in remaining as independent as possible of mental health services. This climate had to enable users to feel a sense of purpose and achievement following what may have been a debilitating mental illness. It also had to allow for the delicate balance between the patterns of group life, and individual needs and wants within the group.

Bedford House is a day centre situated near the city centre in Southampton. It opened in 1978 and was one of the few purpose built centres which were planned by a local authority as a response to the 1975 White Paper. The centre contains excellent facilities for practical activities as well as meeting rooms for groups. It was designed to accommodate up to 100 clients per day but early experience showed that this was too large a number for individuals to feel part of a community. In practice the numbers of people attending rarely exceeded fifty per day and the extra space was used by various self-help and community groups.

Over the nine years since its opening Bedford House has developed as a resource centre for mental health. In addition to providing a structured rehabilitative and support programme it became a base for clubs run by MIND. There is a drop-in centre on one afternoon a week, a mental health social club, and meetings held by various community organisations. Self-help groups, such as Alcoholics Anonymous, also meet in the centre. Two satellite centres developed, one in the eastern side and the other in the western side of the city. These are clubs which run independently of the centre and which people attend either separately or in conjunction with attendance at Bedford House.

This extensive use of the building brought its difficulties in the first few years following the opening of the centre. As Blake and Millard point out, a centre cannot meet too many needs at the same time. Even so it was important to show that such a large centre could provide a service to meet a variety of needs. Boundary management issues became important when, for example, users expecting to meet for a discussion group found that their room had been booked for a training course, or when users attending for the structured programme had to cope with 'their' space being invaded by the drop-in centre.

For users of the structured programme of a centre such as Bedford House, the main part of their experience will be the variety of *formed groups* and *informal groupings*. Formed groups include art and crafts, pottery, wood and metalwork, cookery, and clerical activities. There are verbal groups such as social skills and discussion groups, as well as sports and recreation groups. There are community meetings at which staff and users are expected to be present.

But interspersed with these formed groups are many forms of informal groupings. Users will generally arrive earlier than the start of the programme to have a cup of tea or coffee. Some people will have lunch between groups. At the end of the day many people will want to 'wind down' over a chat. At these times some people may want to talk to their friends. Others may want to sit on their own, even though they run the risk of being seen as 'anti-social' or 'socially isolated'.

Why this reliance on groups and groupings in Bedford House? First, in most day settings the staffing ratio means that one-to-one contact between staff and users is necessarily limited. Second, mental health day settings have perhaps inherited from the therapeutic community tradition a belief that it is within the group context that users will be able to explore themselves in relation to others and that the total group experience is both powerful and curative. In Bedford House this belief has often extended to referrers. How often do workers in mental health centres come across the sincerely held beliefs of social workers or doctors that it would be 'good' for someone socially withdrawn to mix with others?

Indeed the group experience in a centre such as Bedford House can be helpful to people who use the service. Carter (1981) found that a large number of users valued their attendance not on account of the formed groups but because of the opportunities to gain support in an informal way. In fact other users were valued more than staff as sources of support. At the same time users discovered an affinity with other people of similar background and experiences.

But the group experience can also be negative. We know from researchers such as Wing and Brown (1970) about the depersonalising effects of group process in long stay hospitals on people with schizophrenia. In these hospitals the needs of the organisation became more important than the needs of the individual. Goffman (1968) showed how the institution could stifle the individuality of staff and patients alike. As a 'second generation' mental health setting we had to be careful at Bedford House to avoid the same experience.

The informal 'affinity' groups which users found so helpful bring other problems. What about the anxious, withdrawn individual? Levinson and Astrachan (1976) describe the course of several experiments in large group and inter-group process undertaken by the Tavistock Institute in which participants had to find their own way to groups and take part in them from a large informal gathering. They found that the choice of 'affinity' group for some people was based on an immediate desire to avoid anxiety. Once they were members of a group they wanted to be accepted and did not challenge the fantasies of the group since this involved the risk of unpopularity.

Similar problems were encountered in Bedford House. How would the anxious or withdrawn individual, or a newcomer, cope with the tendency for groups to 'close ranks'? People needed to make friends and be accepted. But in doing so they needed to retain their individuality in stating their own opinions and in not colluding with 'groupthink'.

Formed groups also had their problems as well as their benefits. It was important to ensure that participation in groups was based on the wants and needs of users. To accomplish this we had to provide a range of groups which made differing demands on the user. For example, a problem-solving group may be useful for some people but inappropriate for others. But some formed groups were compulsory for everyone. Community meetings, which are common in centres such as Bedford House, were a good example. They were opportunities for communication, decision making, consultation, as well as for the setting of boundaries. They were also opportunities for testing reality. What should be done with the money left in the amenity fund? Did the drop-in members really cause a disturbance? What should be the centre's policy on smoking? These are some issues out of many that the community meeting had to tackle. As Peter Hawkins points out in another chapter, the community meeting is an opprtunity to attend to the health of all the community rather than just the individuals within it.

Nevertheless, the process can be painful for many participants. Anxiety can be raised and people can feel depersonalised. Main (1975), describing early community meetings at the Cassel Hospital, sees some of these meetings as a powerful and mysterious force within which individuals do not communicate with each other but to the 'group'. Personal thoughts such as 'I think' give way to thoughts such as 'People here think that...'

In the community meetings at Bedford House the need to attend to the community's health had to be balanced against the possible damage to some people by too much emotional expression. The format of meetings needed to change as the composition of the group changed: some people had great difficulty in coping with an open-ended agenda for one hour but were able to handle a fixed, preplanned agenda for a half-hour meeting.

Community meetings and other formed groups are inevitably linked with what happens in informal groupings. A difficult meeting would have its effect on staff and users for the rest of the day and the issues would be discussed around the centre. Someone might have had a satisfying experience in the pottery studio or in a creative writing group and then may have felt rejected or despondent through a discussion at lunchtime. As a staff group we needed to help users to understand and reflect on the variety of their experience in the centre, whether this be over a cup of tea in the morning or in a problem-solving group.

The climate also needed to help users to develop the progress they may have made in formed groups. Social skills groups help in developing social confidence and assertiveness. But could users practise the skills they had learned in the controlled setting of the group elsewhere in the centre as well as in their daily living situation ?

We realised that the first step in developing a helpful social climate was to identify and state the core value system of the service, as Brown and Clough suggest in Chapter 1. Questions arose which were not always comfortable to address. Were people treated as adults, with potential to develop skills and use adult roles? Did the climate encourage behaviour which was based on health rather than illness? Were users seen as equal to the providers of the service? Were users seen as consumers, entitled to be consulted about the way the service is run and developed? Was sexual and racial harassment seen as wrong and challenged when it occurred?

These were some of the issues which had to be faced every day in different situations. The way in which people collected their travel money, or the way they were served at lunch were all examples of the numerous situations in the daily life of the centre which were influenced by the value system of the whole place.

The first stage in the development of a value system was to develop a service philosophy which was the baseline for the operational policy of the centre. Perhaps the most important principle which needed to be stated in this philosophy was that the client should be seen as an adult, and that roles appropriate to adult behaviour should be reinforced in the centre. What would this actually mean in practice?

Argyris (1968), writing in the context of work performance, suggests a number of criteria within which adult roles can be measured. Using his criteria, the centre's ethos should stress roles based on maturity rather than childhood, activity rather than passivity, autonomy and independence rather than dependence, a focus on a deeper perspective rather than on shallow interests, and equality rather than a subordinate position.

The transfer of these ideas to the centre's daily life was often difficult. As adults we need fun and laughter, particularly in a mental health setting where there is sometimes a depressive group atmosphere. Centres such as Bedford House often have their rituals which can fulfill a positive function in reinforcing group identity. But what type of fun is appropriate for adults? What is the place of a disco in the afternoon, or an Easter Bonnet parade? For some years the Christmas dinner at Bedford House was followed by party games and a disco. But how many adults in our society follow their Christmas dinners with games and dancing in the afternoon? After some reflection and discussion with users it was decided last Christmas that the dinner should be followed by time to relax and, possibly, a video.

What should be the balance between activity and passivity? This was an issue in the daily life of the centre which was not easy to resolve. Time was needed for more spaces in the day for talk and relaxation. While activity is useful, too much close organisation of the day could remind users and staff of sometimes unhappy days at school. But activity and a structure within a day can fulfill another aspect of adult behaviour, that of a work role.

Shepherd (1981), writing in relation to the needs of clients with chronic illness, suggests that it is important to model everyday adult experiences by providing work type experiences. While some clients, such as mothers recovering from post-natal depression, will not welcome or need a structured day, others who find boredom and lack of routine a major problem often find that a work role forms part of developing a fuller and more independent life.

As Freud suggested, work is perhaps our strongest link with reality. Jahoda *et al.* (1972) stresses the psychological value of work beyond merely earning a living, if indeed this was a reality for people with mental health problems in the present employment environment. She suggests that adults need an imposed time structure, a regular shared experience outside the family, a change from goals that are personal to purposes other than one's own, and a reinforcement to oneself of personal worth and identity.

Equality between the providers and users of the service was another key issue which had to be addressed as it influenced so much of the daily life of the centre. In spite of good intentions there could be subtle differences in equality. *Access to space* in the building was an indicator of degrees of equality. Staff may carry keys which give access to an office where they can 'get away from it all'. They could lock their valuables in an office while users had to use a locker. Staff could use their own cups and mugs for tea and coffee while users had those provided by the centre.

The principles of *normalisation* were central to the development of the service philosophy. Wolfensberger (1980) stated that the normalisation principle means 'making available . . . patterns of life and conditions of everyday living which are as close as possible to the regular circumstances and ways of life of society'.

For Bedford House this meant that we had to evaluate many aspects of the centre's daily life. Different perceptions of what were the 'regular circumstances and ways of life of society' were debated with much feeling. Should tea and coffee be served in cups and saucers or mugs? Should the minibus no longer convey groups of twelve people for sporting activities in favour of smaller groups of perhaps three or four people? What about the loss of cameraderie and group identity which many people enjoyed? Could outings in the minibus be justified, or should people use public transport if this was available?

In spite of the difficult issues which were involved, normalisation brought its benefits. It was realised that *choice* was all important. People should have a choice of having a drink in a cup or a mug. The minibus continued to be used to convey groups for sporting activities but these sessions were interspersed with sessions when the minibus was not used and people went out in smaller groups.

Perhaps the greatest benefit from normalisation was the realisation that appropriate community facilities should be used wherever possible. Many users, having spent some time at Bedford House, needed to find ways of using their spare time other than attending a day centre. A large amount of time was spent by staff in helping users to use adult education facilities, to take courses at the local technical college and to link with facilities such as the Volunteer Bureau in offering their skills as volunteers. The centre's 'satellite' groups assumed added importance as they provided a base to help users to link with networks in their local communities.

The climate also had to encourage individual expression rather than 'groupthink', the process whereby groups refuse to face difficult issues and experience the 'fight/flight' tendencies described by Bion (1968) in his commentary on group process. The climate had to encourage individuals, particularly those who were more shy, to assert their opinions in the face of more dominant people. Those who contributed the least at meetings were often those with the most sensible ideas!

Users of mental health services are also *consumers*. People who attended Bedford House were entitled to influence the service offered for many reasons. If we were to encourage a climate of autonomy rather than dependence, and of health rather than illness, people had to feel that they *could* influence the service. This influence could be over both the details of daily life and over wider issues such as the future development of services.

The path towards genuine implementation of consumerism was not easy in Bedford House. It was necessary to clarify the responsibilities and powers of the whole community, the staff (as a group and as individuals), and the users themselves. Those involved in a particular forum needed to know whether they were being asked to make a decision or were being consulted.

A members' council, similar to a patients' council, was proposed for Bedford House. Patients' councils, which started in Holland, and are now spreading through experience in Nottingham to many other parts of the country, are examples of groups in which ex-users of services are representing the interests of individual users. People who had had devaluing experiences themselves were reluctant to put themselves forward for membership of a steering group. They were concerned about being seen as 'elitist' by other users. They were worried about the effect on their own mental health and felt it was not worth the trouble.

In Bedford House the steering group involved the participation of people who were in a city-wide support group. They were ex-users of services. The members of the support group were put under considerable pressure by users of Bedford House who saw them as meddling in the internal affairs of the centre. It was fortunate that some users risked unpopularity in speaking out and were able to break the impasse in these discussions.

We found that feedback by consumers affected nearly every situation in the daily life of the centre. When should a group take its tea break? What should the policy be towards smoking both in formed groups and in informal groupings? David Brandon (1987) suggests that in developing genuine participation, consumers need skilled support in decision making since both they and junior staff are socialised into not 'rocking the boat'. Consumers also needed help in ensuring that quieter, less assertive individuals were able to contribute to a decision.

Reference has already been made to the service philosophy of the centre. What impact did this have on people from ethnic minorities? Few black people came to the centre. On reflection, if the place were to be more attractive to black people, we would have had to take account of the experience gained in the developing field of transcultural psychiatry to see whether we could make the place more relevant to their interests. Similarly, if users from ethnic minorities were to gain confidence to attend, and, along with other users, to gain self-esteem within it, then they had to feel valued. The climate had to reflect cultural pluralism rather than just the values of the white community; and racism, both institutional and personal, had to be tackled in the centre as a whole and when it arose in small groups and groupings.

If the centre was to seem relevant to ethnic minority users, cultural and religious factors had to be taken into account. For example, different social skills would seem important to different groups of people – young white males could value the contact with the opposite sex but Asian women users may well have felt uncomfortable at the presence of other men, both users and staff. The feelings of their husbands and families about a mixed environment needed to be acknowledged. Facilities for religious practice as well as for different food had to be arranged.

Gender issues also needed to be addressed. Societal expect-ations could be reflected in the daily life of the centre when 'service' roles such as washing up or making tea were directed towards women. There was a tendency for 'work'-oriented activities to be geared more towards men. Progress was made when some women organised a clerical skills group which came to give many people, both women and men, opportunities to gain relevant skills for eventual employment.

Sexual harassment of women, both users and staff, was a recurrent problem. Services such as the drop-in centre tend to predominantly attract men, often with a poor history of making relationships. The establishment of a separate women's group as part of the drop-in centre provided some space for women, but men had to be confronted with the unacceptability of their behaviour.

The development of the service philosophy was a useful strategy since daily events could be measured against clear guidelines. But there were other factors which had to be considered if the climate was to mirror in more than a token way the key points of the service philosophy. Users needed a warm and cohesive experience but they also had to feel safe to talk about emotions. They had to be able to express conflict as well as consensus if the centre was to help them to grow in self confidence.

The ideas of I.D. Yalom (1975) were useful in helping staff and users to bring out these features of the climate. Yalom suggests that *all* groups have a number of 'curative factors' in addition to their stated purpose. Mounsey (1983), writing about his experience in a centre in Worcester, suggests that these factors are equally applicable to the climate of a mental health centre. Some of the most relevant factors are listed below.

Installation of hope. The climate should reflect optimism and a belief that unsatisfactory parts of life can be changed. Empowerment, the theme of much of the service philosophy, is impossible to bring about in a climate in which people believe that nothing will ever change. For example, if gender issues were to be properly tackled, women had to feel that they *could* challenge the status quo.

Imparting of information. Many users had fears which could be alleviated by the right information. We found that often people attending the centre had not been told about the true nature of their illness or the effect of their medication; for example, the side effects of phenothiazines, or the possible addictive effects of minor tranquillisers. There was a need to talk about mental illness in a factual way and to encourage people to ask relevant questions. They would not tackle the wider issues of the empowerment of themselves and others while they were worried and uncertain about their treatment.

Altruism – or helping oneself through helping others – is another factor which spanned much of the service philosophy. Consumers of mental health services were used to receiving services rather than giving to others. Users found that they were able to support other people in a crisis. They could share skills within groups or take part in a members' committee and so develop the self esteem which was often the first step towards their empowerment. But there was sometimes a thin line between altruism and exploitation – for example, when the person making the drinks also had to do the washing up, or when the same person was preparing a room for several weeks. The responsibilities of others had to be stressed alongside the desirability of helping others.

Existential factors. People were faced with a variety of situations for which there were no ready solutions in their lives. Bereavement, unemployment, separation and divorce, were all experiences of loss which had to be confronted and which weighed heavily with people as they sat together at the start of a week in the centre.

It was tempting to ignore these issues, to lighten the conversation, and to adopt Bion's fight/flight behaviour discussed earlier. However, in confronting issues, and in recognising what cannot as well as what can be changed, people were encouraged to move towards a deeper understanding of the meaning of life for themselves. As Argyris (1968) suggests, adult behaviour consists of a deeper perspective rather than shallow interests. It was important for the climate to encourage this discussion as people sought to identify the wider causes of their situations.

The implementation of these 'curative factors' in the daily

climate of the centre was not easy. As Mounsey suggests, staff had to be open enough with each other and receive both training and support to be able to model these curative factors in their day-to-day behaviour. It was clearly demanding, and often felt intrusive, for staff to intervene in the multiplicity of situations in which the curative factors could be used. After all, at 10 a.m. on a Monday morning, staff are struggling to reorientate themselves from their weekend as well as cope with the subtle nuances of the social climate!

The final area to be considered is the link between the climate and the needs and wants of *individuals*. Harrison and Lubin (1965) suggested that much groupwork consists of the building of 'castles' and 'battlefields'. All those who used the centre needed a sense of security and a feeling of warmth and cohesion. Yet they then had to take risks at different paces and in different ways. One person might feel a sense of achievement having chaired a community meeting, while another would be satisfied with the ability to go into a room with just a few people. Time keeping was another issue since lateness of arrival could be due to many causes: family pressures, side effects of drugs, or perhaps just laziness!

The *management of transition* had to encompass perceptions of fairness but also of individual need. As Brown and Clough point out (in Chapter 2), staff and users have to cope with many changes during the day as formed groups merge into informal groupings and vice versa. Sometimes a person was too distressed to attend a group immediately and wanted to talk with a key worker. Should the person running the second-hand shop be able to count the takings and so be late for her afternoon group? Should a deep and satisfying conversation between two people come to an end because an activity was about to start? These were questions which had to be tackled each day. As staff we had to create a climate in which there was a balance between routines and individual needs.

The difficulties for new members of joining the centre have already been mentioned. At a time when they were feeling most vulnerable they had to face strangers who may feel more concerned about themselves than about new people. The routines of the centre had to be assimilated, and the layout of the building had to be learnt. Moos (1974), describing helpful treatment environments, suggests that preparation is all important in facilitating the entry of new users.

We found that it was helpful to give as much information as possible in advance to all concerned. Existing users were more welcoming if they knew who was expected. Prospective users were sent an information sheet about the centre. They were also invited to a meeting during which they could ask questions about the centre, make a more detailed tour of the building, and then make a decision as to whether they would like to come.

Both new and existing users had specific needs and wants. Thus it might be agreed that one person should come for only half a day per week while someone else attended three days per week. People who had difficulty in getting up found that it was easier to come just for the afternoons. Users had many differing social needs. One person had to learn how to become more assertive just as another person needed to control aggression when with other people. How could the climate incorporate these various needs and wants?

After new users had settled in we found that it was important, both for themselves and for staff, to be aware of the reasons for attendance at the centre. The key worker system enabled users to work out with a member of staff (and other interested people) what they expected to gain from the centre. For some this could mean the development of helpful routines; others might want to increase their social confidence. From these general needs and wants a specific objective could be identified, such as the ability to concentrate on a task for a certain time.

Once a particular objective was agreed with the user, progress towards it could be developed in the course of the daily experience of informal groupings as well as formed groups. Someone might practise using their concentration in a woodwork class, but they may achieve the same result through an informal game of 'Trivial Pursuit'. A discussion at the end of the day among friends could lead to benefits which an organised problem-solving group might not be able to give.

At the end of a typical day there was a temptation to settle into small talk. But the climate needed to encourage staff and users to *reflect* on their experience if the day had had a particular significance. As Yalom (1975) points out, experience has to be followed by reflection if genuine learning is to follow.

In summary, the development of the social climate in Bedford House had several stages. As a staff group we had to be aware of the unhelpful as well as the helpful aspects of group process. A service

114

philosophy had to be developed and then tested out in the daily life of the centre. The 'curative factors' had to be promoted in many different situations. Individuality had to be encouraged within the groups and groupings of the centre.

We had to guard against false security. A comfortable climate may have given staff a feeling of being in control and of being wanted but it did not always provide the challenge which could lead to the development of self confidence for our users. Consequently we had to come to terms with our own attitudes about the values which we wanted for the social climate. Were we really seeing the users as adults with their right to self determination and self responsibility? 'Empowerment' as a term often felt positive until, as staff, we experienced loss of power, when, for example, the annual Christmas fair was organised entirely by the users of the centre.

Honesty and exploration of our feelings of resentment as well as optimism needed to be followed by training and exploration of these issues with the users of the service. In our discussions of the application of normalisation principles users were often as angry as some of the staff group about the implications of normalisation on the daily life of the centre. They shared the hostility of many of the staff at the idea that we might decide to give up the minibus because it represented an institutional method of transport.

The rapidly changing field of mental health meant that there was always a contentious subject for debate related to our service philosophy. In a safe, secure but challenging climate, there was room for controversy. People could move from being passive recipients of services to being active contributors to change, both in their own lives and in the services which they experienced. When the daily life of the centre contained a blend of both 'castles' and 'battlefields' for each individual, we could be reasonably confident that a constructive climate had been brought about.

Chapter Seven

GROUPS AND GROUPINGS IN A PROBATION HOSTEL

CAROL SAPSED

INTRODUCTION

Probation and bail hostels were introduced by the Home Office and voluntary agencies approximately 45 years ago, but the majority stem from the 1960s and 1970s. There are national guidelines regarding their governance but considerable local variations in style and composition. This chapter is concerned with living and working in a probation and bail hostel in Bristol.

My underlying belief is that offending behaviour is produced by inappropriate responses to circumstances, often beyond the clients' developed sphere of influence and understanding. Many offenders nurture the expectation that they can, and would, cease to offend if the circumstances were propitious. I think my task as a probation officer is to enable clients to develop resources either personal or political to have greater control over their circumstances and themselves, and to reduce the risk of further offences. Before describing the various groups and groupings of the hostel, I want to describe the hostel, its environment, the hostel residents and its programme, to create the backcloth against which staff and residents work, live and interact.

THE HOSTEL AND ITS SETTING

The hostel was inaugurated 10 years ago to provide a south-west resource for adult offenders on bail or probation. The aims of the hostel are to offer the courts and offenders a viable alternative to a custodial sentence and to offer the courts a residential facility for people on bail. The objectives are to assist and to prepare them to leave the hostel at the end of their period of residence in a planned and purposeful manner.

Initially the hostel consisted of two terraced houses with residential accommodation for staff and residents. The similarity between the renowned Topsy and the hostel is obvious. The hostel now occupies five houses. It has a staff group of seven social work staff, one clerical officer, one cook/housekeeper, one assistant cook and two part-time cleaners – and twenty nine residents. The house is divided into nineteen beds for male probationers aged twenty one and over, two bail beds for women, and eight beds for male bailees aged seventeen and over. The problems of the building and its development are obvious to visitors; the buildings were incorporated as the opportunity arose, there are odd cupboards, narrow corridors and an excessive number of front doors (five). The bail and probation beds are at opposite ends of the terrace with a secure office and staff accommodation wedged between. Thus physical communication between various sections of the hostel is restricted, indeed the easiest route between the main office and the bail wing may be by going through one front door and down the road to another. The physical separation of the two groups can reinforce the feelings of 'them' and 'us' between probationers and bailees. This affects inter-group behaviour, and on occasion disparaging remarks are made by individuals to each other. House meetings, held on separate evenings for the two groups, may include a discussion on the various iniquities of the other group. The staff have to be aware of this tension and to utilise their understanding of how to overcome it when working with the total group – for example, on a hostel expedition.

The hostel is situated on the edge of a deprived inner city area. Formal contact between the community and the hostel is mainly limited to links with local agencies. Informally, there are some links with the local residents, on a basis of mutual acceptance. The location of the hostel in that particular situation does result in the residents' excesses of behaviour passing unchallenged by local residents as the area is busy with a plethora of inner-city activity. This is in contrast to some other hostels which frequently face active public criticism from their neighbours.

Within the work of the probation section of the hostel there has always been a commitment to a programme whereby residents can engage in the complex issue of reducing the risk of further

117

offending. Initially the programme focussed upon improving residents' prospects for employment, use of the well-equipped workshop being an integral component. It was based upon the theory and available evidence that the risk of further offences was reduced if a man was in work. Much of the programme was undertaken corporately by the whole hostel group. Today, however, where the prospect for full employment for all is extremely remote, and where the evidence is that before a man can consider work other issues need to be examined, residents and staff create individual packages comprising some corporate hostel activities, using outside specialist resources, for example, drug and alcohol centres, and employment specialists. Individual residents still believe that work will reduce their offending and frequently the problem for staff is to encourage men to examine the issues around their offending behaviour before trying to obtain work. These issues can include personal areas such as addiction, sexual abuse, and physical or verbal aggression.

Referrals for the probation section come from probation officers. The criteria for referral are that the man should be at risk of a custodial sentence and should be prepared to agree to the conditions and rules of the hostel. Prospective probationers are placed at the hostel for one month's assessment period following conviction. This allows time for both staff and resident to assess what needs to be done to reduce the risk of further offending. A court report is prepared by the individual 'key worker' detailing the work to be undertaken and the methods used, for example, referral to employment resources, counselling techniques. Whilst it may be argued that many residents do not have a choice regarding the probation order – or prison – it is important that all parties concerned think that the probation order is viable. The order can be made for a period of up to three years, the most usual being a two-year probation order with a six month condition of residence.

Daily life

How does a person pass his day at the hostel? Breakfast is available on a 'help yourself' basis from 7.30–8.15 am; staff officially ask residents to be up and about by 9.30 am when the hostel is cleared so that cleaning, repairs (endless), and individual work can be completed. A resident may be seeing his key worker, or visiting the DHSS, a frequent event given the vagaries of both the postal system and the social security. He may be joining in an activity such as hostel football or outdoor pursuits organised by Fairbridge Drake. He may stay in the hostel to help paint a room, dig the garden, or repair something. From 12.30 pm onwards he prepares his own lunch - bacon saved from breakfast being the usual dish. In the afternoon, the procedure may be the same, returning to the hostel for a cooked tea at 5.45 pm. TV, snooker, darts, seeing the key worker or visiting the local hostelry may be the evening format. At 10.45 pm for bailees, 11.00 pm for probationers – the timing spaced to allow staff to cover the five houses – the building is locked up. Many residents watch TV, cook more bacon – or, hopefully retire to bed.

On certain days groups are run in the hostel by staff: a group for bailees to discuss their feelings about being on bail, for residents to explore issues of self-help, or to hear speakers from outside agencies (e.g. on health matters). The subject of hostel programmes is a wide one and I can only hope to touch upon how one hostel tries both to meet individual needs and to manage a total group.

Staff have to complete formal tasks, such as mealtimes, handing out post, seeing individuals, taking bail referrals, inducting new bailees, and packing up departed residents' belongings. Then there are the tasks defined in job descriptions as 'any other duties' such as showing a workman how to find Room 4, House 12 in order that he may mend a broken basin, unpacking vast amounts of frozen food, helping a resident dig the vegetable patch, and answering the front door to unexpected callers ranging from the police for a cup of tea, to a person looking for accommodation.

Bail referrals are taken on a daily basis by telephone, on average ten people arrive each month. The criteria for acceptance are extremely wide, the most usual reason for refusal being lack of a spare bed. Bailees arrive at the hostel any-time following their release from the court or prison. They are frequently anxious, uncertain as to why they are at the hostel and unsure of themselves. Staff may have to counsel people with very little knowledge of their history or the circumstances of the charges. Once the initial settling in process has occurred, bailees will pursue a similar routine to those on probation.

Hostel rules

Hostels are empowered to devise their own rules; there are significant variations between hostels, although the majority impose a night curfew. The reasons for abiding by them can be accepted as a commitment by the resident to the hostel as an alternative to custody, and they do afford some security for those whose lives are not circumscribed by internal controls. In addition to a curfew, the rules include no alcohol or unprescibed drugs on the premises, payment of weekly rent, and no violence against residents/staff. Interestingly, one exercise used in the formal group requires group members to plan a hostel programme and rules. The devised rules are usually extremely stringent.

Infringements of the hostel rules by bailees can result in staff taking breach action, the offender can be asked to leave the hostel immediately, returned to court via police custody, and either rebailed to another address or remanded in custody. Thus departures can be precipitate and unplanned. Probationers are subject to the same hostel rules but for them the outcome may be more protracted; breach hearings currently taking up to three weeks to be heard by the court. During this period staff and residents may, or may not, be able to construct a further working agreement to put before the court. The subject of rule making and breaking is an enormous one; the hostel tries to apply them in a flexibly consistent manner.

To summarise, it can be seen that the hostel is a complex organism/system; it has a boundary which is penetrated both by individuals and organisations. It is a self-determining body within a constellation of external systems mutually dependent, sometimes in conflict, sometimes in agreement. It is fuelled by external sources such as the courts and resourced financially entirely by the Home Office. It has to comply with conflicting demands and maintain an uneasy balance between various bodies. Within its physical boundary there are further groups between which there are tensions, alliances, and fusions. Viewed objectively from outside, a total of forty one people form the hostel. This large grouping is separated formally into a staff group and a residents' group.

RESIDENTS' AND STAFF GROUPS

The residents group

The residential group can be subdivided into long-term (which can include bailees) and short-term; some people place themselves within these groups, others are defined as members by those around them. Further, an unofficial sub-division of the residents' group could be an openly delinquent group and a conforming group; the former displaying to the world around it manifestations of its delinquency, e.g. people driving cars to the hostel whilst disqualified, abusing themselves by either drinking, taking drugs, or gambling to the edge of disaster. The latter group appears to be (and the hostel staff devoutly hope it is) conforming to the hostel's expectations; it is relatively pliable, and acquiescent. Again the group's membership may be self-defined or externally attributed. Residents may define themselves as members of a particular group; this can be in order to gain advantages for themselves, for example, peer group status.

Often, to the staff cost, membership of the conforming group may abruptly change to the delinquent, leaving staff perplexed as to the cause. However, this type of change from the conforming to the delinquent group can in part be attributed to pressure from the delinquent group. In addition, it may appear that the delinquent group is achieving more in terms of subcultural goals, for example, power, attention, or prestige.

Many of the residents will have considerable experience of institutions and have strategies for coping with their pressure. However, institutions are powerful organisms which do not easily accommodate individuals needs. Nowhere is this more evident than when black residents, who form a small percentage of referrals, are placed at the hostel. It is imperative that the hostel continues to develop, monitor, and evaluate positive action against institutional racism.

Further analysis of the hostel residents group is necessary before we can discuss the various groups as a medium for work. There are the two statutorily defined groups of bailees and probationers. The former is a small group of ten, eight men and two women, rather isolated from the main hostel by physical segregation. The latter is a larger group of twelve men which may contain some overspill bailees, and one or more parolees; and it has easy physical access to staff via one main office door. A further sub-group comprises seven self-catering probationers and parolees, housed in three self-contained units. Their physical movements are discreet and they can avoid contact with the staff and other residents for long periods.

Across the sub-groups further groupings will occur, those of friendship, various but loyal, perhaps having been forged in the context of a shared prison cell or wing, or made by arriving at the hostel from the same court, or through sharing one of the six shared bedrooms (still surprisingly popular amongst residents). There are groups formed by staff for specific purposes; an offending (induction) group, parole group, activities (usually sporting), repair and maintenance groups. There may be groups set up for a 'one-off' particular purpose, such as video filming, visiting the cinema, or coping with a difficult resident. These groupings can include a mix of bailees, probationers, and parolees in varying numbers.

The staff group

The staff group is organised into a formally designated social work group and a support group, the latter being sub-divided into catering and clerical, full and part-time. There are other 'divisions' according to age, race and gender, work role and hierarchical position. Other sub-groups of staff are formed by the staff group itself for specific tasks such as planning an event, reviewing procedures and training sessions. Notwithstanding these various differences, all staff are engaged to a greater or lesser degree in the social work task of negotiating with, supporting, and confronting hostel clients. Shared experience of crisis events can create sub-groupings across formal boundaries as, for example, when three colleagues on duty one morning, a part-time cleaner, relief worker, and social worker, had the shared experience of coping with a serious suicide attempt by a resident.

Within the staff group there may be discreet sub-groups sharing a commonality which can delay or enhance the overall group process. Decisions to be taken regarding residents are often debated by staff using different theoretical and value bases. For example, men who continually abuse alcohol form a large section of the residents. How we work with them and if, or when, we return them to court for failure to abide by the rules is a constant topic of debate. Within the hostel, staff have to work closely together, trust and understand each other; the process of achieving this takes place partially within the context of the staff meetings and can prove both painful and enlightening. Evidence of racism and sexism is not unknown and the team's development is not always even or uneventful. The staff may wish, because of issues of control, to present a united front to the hostel residents regarding decisions, hostel activities, etc.

The practice of upholding other staff may be indicative of the extremely powerful maxim 'united we stand, divided we fall'; the fear of being overwhelmed by the resident group taking precedence over other responses. The danger of this maxim is that the implementation of rules and the decision-making process can become excessively rigid. It is necessary for staff to monitor this and try to maintain a 'flexible consistent' attitude towards the application of rules.

A GROUP PERSPECTIVE – RELATING THEORY TO PRACTICE

I have a special interest in groupwork and, whilst I understand and occasionally apply a number of different groupwork theories, I consistently apply the Group Focal Conflict Theory (Whitaker and Lieberman 1964) which states that groups have two processes continually at work within them. One process is the sharing of collective experience; whilst the other is a fear of the consequences of that sharing. Thus, within the hostel a collection of individuals may be united in their stated aim to achieve intimacy, but individuals voice their fear of ridicule if they do so.

The other theory I find particularly helpful is Tuckman's linear model of stages of group development (Tuckman 1965) which is outlined in another chapter. By applying both theoretical models I can consider the total hostel group or certain sections of it, and try to understand what is happening in terms of group process. To claim that my understanding and perspective of the process is objective is to ignore the fact that I am a component of the total group , have membership of a number of sub-groups or groupings, and have the most powerful formal position. I can, by commenting upon what I perceive, try to increase my personal skills and raise other people's consciousness; however, to claim that I have an objective overview is an assumption that should be, and frequently is, challenged by others. Furthermore, my view of the hostel will enable others to articulate their own view so that together we may compose a picture, jigsaw or mosaic of the whole. Any one of us would like to claim a uniqueness of perspective, uncontaminated by our personal beliefs and values. This, I believe, is not possible – my chosen area of residential work says as much about me as any other facet of myself, and recognition of this gives my work a peculiarity of its own.

It may be that my enjoyment of working and 'quasi living' with a group of people, within the confines of hostel life, affords me experiences of both security and risks. I doubt that any social work can be 'value free'. I cannot claim that working with offenders is purely altruistic, enabling others to change; theory and experience tells me that I will be influenced by those whom I seek to influence and this will deepen and inform my work. One theory suggests that we empathise most closely with our chosen client group. We may choose to work with offenders because we acknowledge those parts of ourselves which could be offenders and, by working with others on their offences, clarify our own offending behaviour. In the formal groups the staff participate in many of the exercises; thus diminishing the boundary of 'us' and 'them'. This may assist considerably in the process of group development, for example the 'forming' and 'norming' stages as defined by Tuckman. However, boundary crossing will undoubtedly reduce the leaders' objective views of the group process, and possibly diminish their ability to influence it. An awareness of these factors can assist us all in our work.

Formal groups

In the total mosaic of the hostel life some groups emerge as having an apparently greater importance than others; these would appear to be those that have the label of 'groupwork': in particular the induction or offending group. The hostel tends to attribute to it qualities that it does not possess; the leaders may be seen as omnipotent, highly skilled, and its contents can be wrapped in mystery. It is a relatively high status group, possibly because it forms the major initial intervention for a probation client, because its programme is predefined and because membership also includes residents from a neighbouring probation hostel.

'Induction groups' have been used in the probation service for approximately ten years. Initially they were closed groups for probationers at the commencement of their orders. They were designed to overcome the potentially collusive nature of 'one-to-one' supervision and reduce the power base of the probation officer by using group dynamics and peer processes to focus upon ways of reducing the possibility of further offences. Their use remains highly popular, particulary in fieldwork.

The fieldwork induction group model used at the hostel has undergone a number of evolutionary changes since the introduction a few years ago by the then Warden and Deputy. This model, which was a closed one, used two leaders and was designed to include all new probationers. The task of the group was to consider and discuss four questions:

Why do people commit offences?
Why do I (the client) commit offences?
What can I personally do to stop committing offences?
Do I want to stop committing offences?

Clients would complete the group having defined a number of areas that they wished to continue to examine with their individual key workers, specialised agencies etc.

It was realised that application of the model in its closed form was not possible, there rarely being sufficient residents on bail assessment to form a core group, and that therefore an open group model would have to be used. In practice this meant that clients joined the group when they arrived on bail assessment and left it after six weeks. Obviously this required that the original four questions needed to be adapted.

The present format which consists of six topics such as relationships, addiction, self-and-others, uses a variety of exercises, games, and discussion.

The advantages of running a formal open group includes sharing group leadership between the two hostels. This is both exciting and challenging; at present all staff have the opportunity to lead an induction group; the set six-session programme reduces the anxieties of inexperienced leaders to a manageable level; and it is sufficiently flexible to allow individuals a chance, within the programme, to 'try out' different skills, games, etc. Second, residents join the group on arrival at the hostel. The impetus achieved by beginning soon after the court's decision for a four-week assessment period gives the man a forum for focussed work. Third, a formal group allows leaders to practise different skills and develop expertise.

Inevitably, there are difficulties. No rota system known to the residential world allows for two workers from different hostels always to be available at the same time every week, shifts have to be changed and, on occasions, continuity of leadership has to be abandoned with staff coming in to replace one or other of the leaders. The current practice is for each worker to undertake a total of twelve sessions of the programme to assist continuity.

Initially one leader does only six weeks, then leaves, being replaced by a worker from the same hostel. The remaining leader completes a further six weeks, then is replaced, and so on. This allows for the development of skills and is intended to increase feelings of competence among staff. It is noticeable that by the end of the twelve weeks staff demonstrate considerable confidence in their group skills. However, given the physical and rota constraints, leaders do have difficulty in having time to discuss and review the group. All groupwork writers emphasise the need for time to prepare and review the group, and rightly so; but this may have to be reduced to telephone discussions and mean loss of time off-duty. It is frequently observed that a leader will have accrued considerable 'lieu' hours when she/he completes a series of groups.

In addition to the prepared material, group leaders have to learn to manage a number of confusing issues. Gender issues are an important dynamic; a female leader may find that she is marginalised by a male-dominated group discussing relationships. For example, one session focussing upon a 'What I need to go straight' brainstorm exercise, produced 'a woman to look after me', a statement which I felt had to be confronted when we were examining the contents of the brainstorm. Unwisely perhaps, I questioned the assumption that a woman's role was to act as a mother and I was roundly dismissed as being bound to say that – as a woman. When a similar example occurred in a later group, my male co-leader confronted the group to better effect in that individuals acknowledged that their lack of confidence led them to believe a woman would be both a prize and support for their own uncertainties. Furthermore the group, to manage their own inadequacies, may project upon the female leader qualities she may or may not possess; strengths and more commonly weaknesses are perceived and commented upon; 'just like a woman' is a phrase frequently used as I have struggled with recalcitrant Blutack – 'cannot put up a sheet of paper without us to help you'. Preparation for such issues is essential, and both leaders need to acknowledge their position on gender issues.

Leaders need to be aware also of their own attitudes to racism. The hostel group is predominantly white, and black residents can find themselves severely disadvantaged if leaders do not confront white residents regarding their racist remarks. It is important for leaders to challenge racist remarks in context; there is no doubt that this can be demanding particularly if a leader is struggling to articulate anti-racist views. The group member who stated that black people received positive discrimination by housing associations because black people made a fuss was confronted, first in his use of language and second on the evidence and reasons behind his remarks. On reflection I consider that I should have ignored the language and tackled the statement, but anxiety and 'gut reaction' had encouraged me to intervene upon the emotive words first.

Many groupwork writers advocate encouraging a group to define its own values and this can prove a minefield regarding the relative merits or otherwise of various offences. Leaders have to struggle with a desire to get a 'correct' answer, for example, assaulting someone is more reprehensible than stealing dog food, and avoid imposing their own values.

I would like now to explore issues of group dynamics, particularly those of a group composed entirely of male members aged between 21 and 60. At this point an understanding of group focal conflict theory which states that individuals will fear a loss of personal identity in a group is particularly useful. Our residents, being predominantly in the older age group, do experience difficulties in working in a group composed partly, as they see it, of 'youngsters'. To enable themselves to maintain their individuality they may adopt the 'older statesman' role, issuing portentous

127

utterances which can be extremely useful; an insider's view of a maximum-security prison when those around him have yet to enter the custodial system by the lowly portals of a detention centre, gives a member prestige and status. However, this may be of mixed benefit to leaders trying to focus the group's attention upon personal strengths and weaknesses.

In contrast to the fieldwork model which is usually held at a probation office, the residential group takes place at a hostel with the influence of the members' own territory affecting its process. Individuals will know quite a lot about each others idiosyncracies, and the group is potentially an extremely powerful agent for confrontation and catharsis.

However, one of the benefits of residential formal group work is that the process of forming may have occurred within each hostel sub-group; residents and staff will have met in groupings; joint hostel activities will have facilitated the process. The three probation hostels in Bristol are developing a practice of joint activities, for example, competitive 'sports days' which are usually very arduous for our residents (30-year-old plus bodies abused by alcohol/nicotine being no match for 20-year-olds). All this aids the group settling into work; but difficulties can arise when the group moves to 'norming'. Here, 'hostel relationships' between leaders and group members can lead to a situation where ideas are not explored and collusions between members allow possibilities for important discussions to pass by.

However, this permeable boundary between the 'formal' group and groupings can be useful. A hostel event can be used directly by group leaders to assist the group in its task. Group members are able to confront each other based upon directly observed incidents; two men who shared a room were able to examine their perceptions of personal hygiene based upon reality.

Endings of individual sessions or formal groups can be less painful than those of fieldwork groups, although difficult to utilise fully. Members know that thay will be in contact with each other on a daily basis. Sadly, sometimes the context may be different; a confrontation between staff and residents regarding behaviour being one example.

The interaction between the two groups, clients/residents and staff is a fascinating arena. It is obviously the hope and expectation that the staff group will positively effect change (and covertly establish compliance and conformity) within the resident group. Evaluation of change in behaviour is still speculative and residents may have learned that verbal protestations of reformation satisfy staff, who equally accept such protestations as evidence of a change. We need to retain the client's stated aims of how he wishes to conduct his life and measure it against observed behaviour recorded by both the man and others. Only then can we conclude that the group experience may have been in part responsible for progress.

The practice of review meetings is used in the hostel so that keyworker, group leader, and client can evaluate the group and agree subjects for future work.

The exploration of group process and dynamics by the leaders is assisted if consultancy is available. A full discussion of the use of consultancy lies outside the scope of this chapter. However, in the hostel where leaders and members frequently meet informally as well as formally the opportunity to discuss the group either in a staff meeting or with an individual in order to disentangle the various elements is found to be of considerable benefit to the leaders.

To conclude this section, formal groups have a place and a function within the total hostel programme but they need to be adaptable to fit the circumstances and to be congruous with the hostel ethos, not enshrined on tablets of stone.

INFORMAL GROUPS/GROUPINGS

There are a number of opportunities, some natural, others developed, for informal groupwork in the hostel. The most obvious natural ones are shared mealtimes which can offer a useful context. I do not wish to conjure up a picture of cosy domesticity, an enlarged, distorted image of an extended nuclear family with blue-ringed china, honey and a striking church clock, but they do present staff and residents with an opportunity, which can be grasped to discuss issues informally. The dining rooms at the hostel are furnished with small tables and the policy is for one staff member to sit in each of the two rooms. An unfortunate factor, not easily overcome, is for food to be eaten as if in readiness for the starter's gun; meals – three-course ones including washing up – can be completed in under twenty minutes. So staff and residents have to utilise time available effectively. However, time spent after a meal can be expanded into informal discussion. Staff can use the time to discuss hostel life, individual issues, sharing of the good as well as the bad events. The need for individuals to feel nurtured and supported is evident when one knows that hostel life with its impersonal physical features and rules and regulations frequently denies individuality. Residents are often prepared to support each other when staff model a caring approach. The physical restrictions of communal living can produce individual or group anger and overt violence, and staff have to be aware of the potential for this; and to be prepared to intervene, support or challenge the group whilst retaining an understanding of their own role. Food, so symbolic of caring and needs, is a constant focus of hostel life and there is a tendency to become resistant to the complaints of residents.

The evening shift, ending as it does with the hostel being locked up and residents signing in, is notable for residents seeking staff for discussion, advice, or company. It is unfortunate that on occasion they are somewhat intoxicated and staff have to be sensitive in their approach. Abrupt termination of contact may actually prolong the end of their shift; whilst a short discussion regarding the meaning of life may be quicker in the long run. A resident announced at 11.15 pm that he intended leaving the hostel 'right now and you're not to stop me'. 'Of course not, I wouldn't want to try – would you like a cup of tea before you go?' Half an hour later all retired to bed, including the resident who had threatened departure.

As mentioned earlier, groups/groupings can form following particular events; a commonality of experience following a night of internal or external disturbances is not uncommon. Staff can utilise this unity actively to facilitate change, using the experience to illustrate for residents the shared desire of hoped for change.

There are house meetings held every week allowing residents a forum to discuss house affairs. Viewed negatively they are an opportunity for residents to complain about those minor and major irritations of institutional life – food, bath water, noise, lack of adequate corporate cleaning, etc. I have observed a tendency for the hostel group to focus upon one issue – e.g. the allocation of food – for several weeks, with staff attempting in vain to deal with the problem when suddenly, one week, as unexpectedly as it arose, it subsides into the sea again. The management of the house groups which are not compulsory, rests upon staff on duty, and minutes are taken and distributed. It is difficult for the leaders not to adopt a defensive posture when complaints are voiced, and it requires diplomacy of high order to ensure that the group has aired an issue which may not have a practical solution. One 'textbook' approach is to attempt to unveil the pressures and irritations that lie behind the issues in a manner that is not challenging and derogatory. Bearing in mind group theories, I am aware that the group may remain in a 'forming' stage for considerable periods of time due in part to the group being an open one particularly the bail section of the hostel where arrivals and departures of individuals are unplanned. Commitment by both staff and residents also affects the group process; it is not easy even with a well-developed understanding of group process to facilitate a group when staff have been confronting individuals concerning their behaviour in another context. The sense of the house meetings being stuck can be overwhelming to all members including staff, and the need to reflect upon this in both the group and staff meetings is essential. The blurring of the boundary between staff and resident is easy to envisage when everyone has suffered from the ravages of institutional food. The mood of the resident group be it sad, energetic, angry or impatient will affect staff. Staff can use the feelings aroused in them by the resident group to enable discussion of the pleasures – and irritations – of hostel life. For example the demands on staff by residents following the new social security act and rent increases resulted in staff feeling defensive and becoming increasingly authoritarian in their manner. Initial discussion at the house meeting produced a defensive response 'who – us' from the residents, and a very quick change of subject. It was only weeks later that all parties could discuss their behaviour and responses in a more productive manner.

GENDER AND RACE

The hostel is predominantly male, and white; its rules and regulations reflect the assumed norms of society and make it a testing environment for those people defined otherwise by gender or race. Nowhere are these differences more explicit than regarding the preparation and production of food. Whether this is unique to offenders or a common human trait is open to question, but the exploration of alternative food is certainly seen by residents as a risky business. Equally staff, unless encouraged to consider the implications of white British food for black residents, will remain complacent and regard those who wish for a selection of food including Italian and Caribbean to be 'difficult'. It requires group vigilance if we are not to perpetuate stereotypes of imperialism.

Readers will have noted that there are only two female bail beds. Unfortunately, despite apparent evidence to the contrary, demand remains sparse and erratic and there is no acceptable argument in the current climate of high occupancy demands to increase the number to a more viable female group. Women offenders in the hostel have to cope with an overt sexism which defines them as 'available and willing'. The very fact that they have appeared before the courts renders them in male offenders' eyes as suitable for further exploitation. Equally problematic for staff is the evidence that many female bailees have developed a number of strategies for coping based upon their life experience, which can have included physical and mental abuse. It is not easy to retain a positive anti-sexist strategy when those one seeks to allow privacy and security apparently do not consider them to be worthwhile. Gender issues are not the prerogative of the residents; female staff members do experience them also, and are subjected to sexism both overt and covert. Within a group context this will manifest itself, often subtly, in a range of issues regarding attributed qualities of the sexes. Socialisation about domesticity is still largely based upon gender, and behind the hotly contested issue of washing up will lie the implication that 'it' is women's work. Female staff find that residents have expectations of them – from being a mother, to girlfriend – which will test their skills to the limit. Infatuation and excessive dependency by residents is not uncommon and the staff group has been the forum for explorations of how best to manage these issues professionally. This is not always easy when male staff may deny their reality and indeed may collude with residents in their attitudes. The watching of 'soft porn' video films by residents was the subject of much debate, the women staff feeling that it was condoning and colluding with residents' attitudes, the opposing argument being that it was entirely natural and indeed preferable to being away from the hostel in possibly nefarious pursuits.

Despite an open-door policy for all referrals, and the development of anti-racist publicity, the fact remains that black clients form a barely perceptible percentage of the hostel residents. With increasing evidence that black offenders are remanded in custody unnecessarily, the residential sector and others have to work to challenge the institutionalised racism of the criminal justice system, to redress these injustices. Whilst the hostel considers its own racist practices and seeks to change them, this will be unavailing if alterations do not occur in other sections of the system; Avon Probation Service as a whole has a commitment to anti-racist strategies and this is a positive step. The current system of monitoring social enquiry reports should encourage the service to consider its practice more thoroughly. The hostel needs to be alert to its own behaviour and to ensure that a black perspective is visible. Limited changes are evident, but monitoring and evaluation show that for many black offenders the hostel remains a hostile environment. Written information by the hostel can help to dispel some of this, but it requires strenuous effort by all sections of the service if we are to offer black offenders an acceptable alternative to custody.

Within the setting of the hostel, discrimination by residents can be problematic. Not only women and black people suffer, but those whose offences are defined as abnormal. The hostel accepts men charged with, and those convicted of, sexual offences. The task of working with these men can be very stressful in its own right; in addition, staff have to challenge attitudes expressed by other residents in regard to sexual offenders. Perhaps challenge has connotations of confrontation which is not always the best approach.

Staff have to question the triple assumption of white, male, heterosexual superiority. When a resident requested that women friends should be allowed to stay overnight the answer, that this made an assumption of universal heterosexuality and that some men would feel pressure because of this, produced a discussion at the house meeting. The group tentatively explored sexual attitudes and concluded that the rule of no guests overnight was a useful one.

Residential living provides opportunities for staff and residents to explore the strengths of groupwork, and the pleasures of groupings, as well as their disadvantages. Because of the nature of their period at the hostels, the element of compulsion and the boundaries imposed, many residents feel unable to separate the process from the content of their experience. We can enable this reflection by allowing time to discuss, to evaluate, to consider and to prompt by 'do you remember when we were all talking about . . . ?'

Chapter Eight

GROUPWORK IN INTERMEDIATE TREATMENT

LUCY BALL AND THEO SOWA

This chapter is written predominantly from our experiences at the Junction Project, a community-based intermediate treatment (IT) project operating as an alternative to custody in the London Borough of Lambeth. The project worked with groups of serious or persistent young offenders aged 14–17 who would otherwise have been given custodial sentences at their court appearances, on the basis of a joint contract and a court order. However, this chapter is not a description of the work of the Junction Project. We attempt to describe and analyse a framework for groupwork with young ex-offenders which is also informed by our work as groupwork trainers and consultants and is based on our belief that groupwork is a method of empowering people.

The criminal justice system has long operated to control certain parts of the population. This can be illustrated by studying the nature of the majority of criminal charges and those against whom these charges are brought, predominantly the working class. The juvenile justice system has also been shown to discriminate regularly against young black people who are processed through it (National IT 1985, Landau and Nathan 1983, Taylor 1981). Black young people are more likely to be stopped and searched by the police than their white peers and are less likely than white young offenders to be cautioned and offered a way out of the justice system. This discrimination continues throughout the operation of the justice system with black young people being more likely to be the recipients of racist or negative Social Inquiry Reports, school reports, and psychiatric reports. Possibly the most damaging element of this discrimination is that young black people are more liable to receive custodial sentences than their white counterparts.

This trend has been demonstrated in a number of local court studies and also by the Home Office's statistics on the ethnic origin of prisoners (Home Office 1986, 1987). Another group who are treated in a distinct way in the justice system are young women who are processed quite differently to young men (Casburn 1979, Genders and Player 1986). There are far fewer young women brought into the system, although their numbers appear to be growing and the percentage of young female offenders being given custodial sentences is rising far more rapidly than that for young males.

Therefore, as a result of the Junction Project's chosen target group and the operation of the justice system, particularly in an inner city area, almost all of the young people we worked with were from working class backgrounds, approximately 50 per cent were black, and there were few young women.

Although we have worked in an IT project which operated as an alternative to custody, when we write of intermediate treatment we broaden our definition of IT to include all projects or schemes which work with adjudicated juvenile offenders. However, it is important to realise that even within this definition of IT there are various types of IT provision: projects which offer daycare or evening facilities, projects which operate for differing lengths of time, and projects which offer various and sometimes very different types of programmes, e.g. motor projects, offence oriented, educational or activity-based projects, or combinations of these. Although young people in IT are sometimes taken away for short 'residentials' as part of their programmes, there is little full time, residential IT provision. Young offenders seen as being in need of full time care are likely to be placed in Community Homes with Education rather than in IT which is seen as community-based provision.

Various people in numerous IT projects state that they are 'doing groupwork'. This can vary from entire programmes based around groupwork, to one-off groupwork sessions; sometimes groupwork is seen as anything that involves more than three young people doing the same activity at the same time. We see groupwork as more. A groupwork programme in our definition would have clear aims and objectives, targeted participants, identified methods, planned content and structure, with the whole process being regularly evaluated. Less structured situations we would define as working with groupings of young people.

Originally, one group of eleven young people attended the project on a fulltime daycare basis with occasional evening sessions. This later changed to two groups of eight young people who attended the project together, with the first group starting about six weeks before the second. Each young person was expected to attend the project for three months full-time, which meant attending Monday to Friday from 9.30 am to 4.00 pm (1.30 pm on Wednesdays) and from 10 am to 1.00 pm every other Saturday morning. They were then expected to attend for three months part-time, which involved attending a group one evening a week for three hours and meeting with a member of staff individually as arranged. The full-time programme was organised around a formal groupwork programme, individual work for all young people with specified workers and some work in groupings. This meant that all young people who attended the project would take part in the formal groupwork sessions which focused on the topics: law and offending, employment and unemployment, civil rights and rules, and life skills. Additionally each young person attending the project was allocated a special worker with whom they met regularly on an individual basis in order to work on issues based around the family, any individual project matters and future plans for the young person.

Much of the work in groupings focused around the links in the day's activities for young people. Once a week there was a community meeting for everyone at the project. At these meetings issues affecting everyone at the project, young people and staff, would be discussed. These included topics such as food, media attention on the project, and developing overall rules or sanctions.

On the other mornings of the week there were group meetings for each of the two groups of young people attending the project at any one time. These meetings brought the group together first thing in the morning and were used to clarify the day's plans, including explanations for absences (staff and young people) for court appearances, ill health etc. We found these meetings a useful method of refocusing group attention on project matters each day and of encouraging a cohesive and positive atmosphere. The meetings were also useful as a means for young people to negotiate with each other and staff members about various issues including programme content and style; for example they could complain about the over use of a particular method in groupwork sessions (such as questionnaires) or suggest group outings. Once the group meetings had been established, young people would take turns to chair them. This was in line with the project's aim of attempting to empower.

Lunch breaks, breaks between sessions, and the beginning and end of each day were times when young people from both groups spent time informally together. While this could be positive in allowing young people to share experiences and enjoy each other's company, these were also times which could be volatile, depending on the experiences being brought into the grouping. For example, if one group had had a very constructive, enjoyable session they could affect the mood of the other group positively, or negatively if the session had been difficult. The midday meal was seen as an important time when everyone who was at the project would spend time together. Young people took turns cooking the meal for the whole project with a member of staff. Menus were the cook's choice, but were often discussed at group and community meetings so that everyone could make menu suggestions.

We found that the work in groupings often affected the group dynamics during formal groupwork sessions, and vice versa. Residential outings were a good example of this. Though they were usually very hard work, residentials were a way of speeding up group cohesion, which in turn meant that more could be achieved through the formal groupwork sessions more quickly. The planning of the residential was as important as the residential itself in this respect, with the group and staff members jointly deciding on activities, menus and ground rules.

In the IT field the fashion for groupwork as a method of working with young offenders has come and gone several times. There has been a very unhelpful tendency either to run a programme totally this way or to reject a groupwork approach altogether. We found that groupwork was a very useful method to use with young people but that it wasn't the only method needed. With certain young people or when tackling some situations, other methods served more usefully. For example, at times it may be more appropriate to deal with a specific young person's problem, for example drug abuse, individually. Workers need to look at the strengths of groupwork and then use this method when appropriate.

We think that groupwork is a good way to increase the power of young people and it can be a forum in which they can find their voice. It is important to remember that this society operates through the concentration of power in groups. Groupwork can empower young people in the midst of a justice system which disenfranchises and strips them of the little power they may have gained elsewhere. Workers need to recognise that just as they need and want peer support, so do young people. Often the individual worker/young person relationship will be unable to provide this, as most workers, with the best of intentions will be unable to understand what it is like to be a young ex-offender or to provide all the support that a young person might need at different times.

Although it is important to remember that different workers will feel more or less comfortable working in different situations and with different methods, and that this can affect the success or failures of those situations and methods, our experience indicates that many workers are afraid of the power that groupwork can afford young people.

VALUES

Values affect all levels of work. For example, they influence the reason why groupwork is chosen as a method, why certain topics are focused on in the programme, and the way these topics are approached. We believe that it is not possible or even necessarily desirable to become value free. However, it is important that workers are clear about their personal values so that they can minimise the negative effects these might have on their work. Some of the values held by workers will enhance the delivery of the programme, but others may be at odds with the aims and objectives and thus disrupt their achievement. For example, if one aim of the programme is to reduce the numbers of young people in custody, then strong prejudices against people who commit certain crimes such as sexual offences or violence against older people may undermine the enactment of that aim.

Groupwork programmes, especially those which involve young ex-offenders, constantly raise issues of what is right and what is wrong, acceptable or unacceptable, good or bad, both in moral and legal terms and implicitly or explicitly, and these must be dealt with. Workers and young people are liable to hold strong views, for instance about the role of the police, crimes such as street robbery, burglary, and car theft. These views are often influenced by values which have been internalised without much thought. This can be problematic when values clash.

Young people are rarely asked to explore or challenge their beliefs or values and can therefore find this very difficult. There are imaginative methods that can be used to help young people in this process. We regularly used popular films as a stimulus to discussion on specific issues such as violence.

As a staff team our values were often very different. This was often beneficial, allowing us to question our assumptions and enabling us to look at situations from different angles. However, there were times when it became problematic and this tended to be when personal values contradicted the project or programme aims or when differences in values between staff made it hard for them to work together. An example of this was a disagreement about whether staff could occasionally take young people to the pub. As with other issues we had to spend time as a team deciding which ground rules needed to operate in order to enhance the aims of the project and enable staff to work with rather than against each other. For this process to succeed, staff had to follow agreed ground rules even if those rules conflicted with their personal values. In the above case it was decided that project staff would not take young people to pubs as this was illegal and we were working with young ex-offenders. However, staff could buy alchohol to be served at celebratory meals at the project, for example at Christmas.

When the Junction Project first started, one of the few ground rules that staff or young people could be excluded for breaking was 'no violence'. It was only after many sessions of values clarification that the staff as a team acknowledged that black young people and workers experienced racist behaviour by other workers or young people as a form of violence. The same process occurred at different stages in relation to sexist or homophobic behaviour. As a result, our interpretation of the 'no violence' ground rule was adapted so that all young people and workers would find the project a safe environment to operate within.

In the same way that young people can be excluded from a

project if their behaviour consistently transgresses agreed project boundaries, it is important for the staff team to recognise that if the behaviour of a worker consistently transgresses agreed project boundaries, there may be no place for them in that project.

Structures need to be created and time allowed for staff to work on values. At the Junction Project one of the ways we ensured that this time was created was by making sure that we met every week for an hour and a half to look at 'non business' issues which affected the project. It was mandatory that all staff attended these sessions. The topics discussed varied greatly, but included long-term future plans, examination of specific incidents at the project, the confrontation of racism in the project, problems with the programme, and personal differences between staff which were affecting project practice. We found it helpful to use various groupwork techniques to help us tackle and explore issues in an effective and imaginative way. Role play, values continuums, and group sculpts (Brandes and Phillips 1978, Dearling and Armstrong 1980, Ball and Sowa 1985) were particularly useful in values clarification.

Personal values are an integral part of people's personalities and their psychological make-up. Questioning such values can therefore make people feel threatened and defensive and differences in values held can make people angry and attacking. We found that for the more difficult or emotive topics that we tackled we needed an outside facilitator both to set and maintain boundaries and to ensure that all staff members participated constructively and effectively. We also found that it was essential to find a good facilitator who could move the team forward and who was clear about the issues we wished to tackle.

However, discussion on values can only be a beginning. Insights gained and action agreed in discussions must be followed through and practice improved. We found it helpful to set dates when we would review changes in our practice following values clarification work. On many issues we had to acknowledge that this monitoring was a never-ending process.

AIMS

The starting point for any groupwork programme is the identification of clear aims. Central aims are needed for the programme as a whole, while short-term objectives are needed for daily operation. Staff need to make sure that programme aims are consistent with project aims, and in themselves. It is essential for aims to be realistic, clear, and jargon free. A few short-term objectives can give both group members and workers a sense of achievement.

The aims of a groupwork programme are clearly influenced by values. These may be those of the staff team, but they could also reflect the values of others such as funders of the project, the management committee, the local authority. The following examples of IT programme aims show the influence of different values.

> To stop young people from offending
> To contain young people
> To provide an alternative to custody
> To develop self awareness about offending
> To change offending patterns

Workers need to be clear about the extent to which young people participate in the setting of aims at different levels of the programme and need to be honest about this. It is destructive to state that young people can set the aims for their group if for example you are unable to guarantee this, or if you later change your mind because you do not agree with the aims set.

Aims should be shared with young people as they are less likely to be achieved if group members are unaware of them. We sometimes did this by writing aims on large sheets of paper which were then pinned to the walls of the room. It is important that workers share *all* their aims with group members – hidden agendas can be very counter-productive. Young people may well feel manipulated by the confusion that hidden agendas can cause. For example, if you do not tell group members that you aim to increase their self awareness regarding offending they may well resent and not co-operate with exercises which could be seen as intrusive.

The aims of a groupwork programme should affect its content and both the aims and the content should affect the way in which the group then operates and develops. For example, a group which is intended to focus on familial relationships is likely to have a very different content to one that is focused on specified young people pursuing group sports together. The type of group interaction which workers might encourage is likely to differ considerably as are the group dynamics.

Aims need to be monitored and evaluated in themselves and to be used to monitor and evaluate the programme. In this way if the programme is not working, it is possible to judge if that is because aims need to be changed or for other reasons. Factors external to the group can also lead to the changing of aims. At the Junction Project we rethought some of our aims after the introduction of the Criminal Justice Act 1982.

PLANNING AND EVALUATION

Planning and evaluation hinge on the groupwork programme aims and are essential to the smooth running of the programme. When work becomes pressured these can become marginalised. We had to make sure that we both set time aside and adhered to those times.

When the overall structure of the programme is planned, a decision needs to be made about how much of the detailed programme will be planned before the start of the group and how much will be planned with the group. It helps to timetable regular evaluation sessions for the time during which the programme is operating, before the group starts. With regular evaluation, problems that arise can be ironed out quickly.

We found it useful to have an evaluation and planning session timetabled for two weeks after the start of each group. At these sessions we could begin to modify the programme and methods on the basis of the knowledge we had gained about group members, such as levels of literacy, individual interests, techniques preferred by group members, group dynamics.

In addition to intensive evaluation sessions at the beginning, middle and end of the programme, there was on-going planning and evaluation of each groupwork session. Being imaginative about both planning and evaluation, for example, using video for your evaluation exercises or group sculpts for looking at group interaction, can improve the quality of the whole exercise.

The groups for whom you evaluate will affect the types of questions asked, so it is important to be clear for whom you are evaluating the programme – group members, colleagues, parents, funders, the general public, yourselves? Any evaluation needs to refer to the aims initially set for the group.

GROUP PROCESS

All groups are different, and although it is possible to draw out trends and common elements, workers must not expect any patterns for group operation to be hard and fast. Regular evaluation can help workers keep abreast of changes in group dynamics. Workers can use the knowledge gained through evaluation to keep the programme relevant.

It is essential for successful group process that worker and participant expectations are aired and agreed early in the life of the group. This should include more than work on the aims of the group, for example, work on the expectations regarding commitment, different ways that individuals operate, physical and emotional boundaries, content and methods likely to be used. At the Junction Project we included this process as part of a more general and quite far reaching induction programme which we found invaluable in the establishment of a good basis for group process.

Groupwork methods and the content of programmes need to be interesting and relevant to the young people involved. For example, it is not appropriate constantly to plan written work for young people who are not good at reading and writing. We found that many of the groups we worked with enjoyed video as a method though this was not the case with all groups, and over use of this method, or any other, could lead to boredom. Workers may need to find techniques or exercises which ensure that all group members participate.

The ending of a group can be as difficult for workers as for young people and often affects group dynamics. It is important to plan the ending in a way that eases this process. One method we used was gradually to lessen the amount of time spent in the group and at the project as the group progressed. It was also essential that the project maintained and strengthened the links that young people had in their communities and resisted the temptation to make the project the central experience in the group members' lives.

Groupwork texts often describe the development of group

process in terms of forming, storming, norming and performing (Tuckman 1965). These terms are used to describe the stages that different groups can go through: forming – the early stages during which the group members begin to learn about each other and the boundaries set for the group; storming – the stage during which the group starts to test the boundaries which have been set and also to test the group leaders, both workers and peers; norming – the stage during which group relations and rules are solidified; and performing – the stage during which the group has settled and members have begun to work well in the group. Although we have sometimes found these descriptions of group processes useful in identifying behaviour, we have also found that group processes are not so easily categorised and that these descriptions of group processes do not necessarily appear in the given order, if they appear at all. In their attempts to find easy formulas, workers sometimes cling to such categorisations rather than use their own analyses of group process; for example, workers can attribute group misbehaviour to their being in their 'storming' phase rather than recognising other factors such as bad leadership, sloppy planning, external pressures on group members, boredom, etc. and taking appropriate action.

Problems in the running of a group are inevitable, and regular evaluation not only enables the early identification of such problems, it aids in pinpointing exactly where the problems are based such as in the programme content, in incompatible aims, in bad preparation, in difficult group dynamics. Problems with group dynamics can occur as a result of personality clashes within the group, but our experience has been that it is far more often a result of some of the above listed problems not being dealt with effectively.

Sometimes when everything is feeling too much like hard work we have found it useful to organise a fun session. More can be gained if workers and young people enjoy the group process.

LEADERSHIP

Group leaders need to create an environment in which the aims of the groupwork programme can be achieved. Individual staff members may have different styles and these may vary at different stages of the programme but whatever style is adopted must relate to the aims. For example, if an aim of the group is to allow young people to reflect upon their behaviour and make choices about their lives, an authoritarian style of leadership will not facilitate the achievement of that aim.

Group leaders have a responsibility to help the group achieve its aims but are also in powerful positions which may be abused. In their attempts to facilitate the success of the group, group leaders need to ensure that their power is used creatively and meets the needs of the individuals in the group rather than their own. Although project workers are usually the formal group leaders, other group leaders will inevitably arise in the group. These leaders play an important role in the group and can be crucial in the group process and its dynamics. Often, the more powerful these 'informal' group leaders are, the more threatened the 'formal' group leaders can feel. We have found that it is in this situation that workers can find themselves, sometimes knowingly, sometimes not, using their power to undermine the roles of individuals in the group. A different danger can occur when the formal group leaders try to 'buy into' a powerful group dynamic and collude with some members of the group in undermining others in the group.

LEADERSHIP AND BOUNDARIES

It is essential that both staff and young people are clear about the boundaries for the group regarding rules, expectations, leadership styles, etc., and why those boundaries exist. Boundaries are more likely to be kept if they both have and are seen to have logical reasons, so it is helpful to have clarity from the beginning of the group programme.

One boundary to define early on is confidentiality. The group needs to know what sorts of information will be kept confidential and what will be shared with either parents, social workers, probation officers, the courts, or the police. In particular young people in IT should know how freely they can talk about past or present crimes. Staff need to be honest with themselves and group members about what information cannot be kept confidential.

Staff and young people should know what will happen if set boundaries are crossed. Some sanctions may be decided on before the group begins, others may be negotiated with the group. We

146

have found that some of the most effective sanctions can be those established by group members themselves. However, it must be very clear which sanctions are open to negotiation and which are not.

The transgression of boundaries can be approached in different ways. It may be appropriate, for instance, to deal with the matter by using an existing group meeting, by calling an emergency group meeting, preparing a workshop to deal directly or indirectly with the issue, or seeing people individually. Having 'time out' when a situation gets heated can be very useful for staff as well as young people. It allows situations to be dealt with less emotionally and increases the likelihood of finding an appropriate way forward.

It is vital that all staff take responsibility for ensuring that boundaries are kept. Once a boundary is agreed all staff need to be equally strong in ensuring it is held to. Staff need also to be sensitive as to how they can support each other. Too often one staff member is left alone to enforce agreed boundaries. Frequently, for example, it is left to black staff to challenge racism and women to challenge sexism. Sometimes workers prefer to ignore the crossing of a boundary. Although this may make life easier initially, in the long term it is a disaster. The next time the boundary is crossed it will be much more difficult to deal with. Many people in IT fear violence. However, in a well-run project where young people are clear about the boundaries and immediate appropriate action is taken when they are crossed, conflict rarely leads to aggression.

The discussion of boundaries should be part of evaluation. It is useful, when examining how difficult situations were handled, to look at the way staff supported each other or not in keeping boundaries. We have found that role play is one method that can be helpful in this process.

LEADERSHIP AND CO-WORKING

At the Junction Project all our groupwork was led in pairs. We found it productive to have one worker concentrating on the group task and the other on the group process. For instance, in a group with a few very vocal members, one worker can ensure the workshop is covering the agreed material while the other encourages quiet members or regulates the noisy ones! It is also a good way for inexperienced staff to gain confidence.

When co-working, workers need to guard against being allocated fixed roles by themselves or the group, for example, one worker being the 'hard' one and the other 'soft'. Differences between co-workers can be manipulated by young people and workers can find themselves undermining each other. It is therefore important to clarify with each other the differences in values you may have such as views of the police or the amount of personal information you wish to disclose. Before the workshop, tasks need to be allocated carefully, for instance, who is going to introduce the workshop, present material, watch group dynamics. When evaluating it is important that workers are honest about the way they worked together and their personal dynamics within the group. By reviewing an awkward situation and planning how it might be dealt with, workers will be better prepared for similar situations in the future.

CONCLUSION

We think a successful groupwork programme must include clear and coherent aims and boundaries, good values clarification and leadership, consistent planning and evaluation, and active participation by all group members. With these elements a programme is more likely to achieve our basic aim, that is, to empower young people and to help them take more control of their lives.

Chapter Nine

GROUP HOMES FOR PEOPLE WITH MENTAL HANDICAP: KEY ISSUES FOR EVERYDAY LIVING

DOROTHY ATKINSON

INTRODUCTION: RESIDENTIAL CENTRE OR GROUP HOME?

This chapter is about the lives, and lifestyles, of people with mental handicap. They do not live in 'residential centres'. They live in ordinary houses. Their lives are not entirely 'ordinary' though, because they live in small groups. These people are members of 'living together groups' (Brown and Clough, Chapter 2) or 'situationally determined groups' (Brown 1979).

Small group living has its rewards but also has its pitfalls. The groups in this study were set up with the best of intentions and were meant to be rewarding experiences. Trust, co-operation, and support were anticipated between people living together at such close quarters. These positive outcomes have been achieved in practice, but not universally and not without a high cost to some people. Dissent and conflict were not anticipated at the design stage, but have surfaced in practice as significant features of small group life.

The focus here on group homes is justified on two counts; for historical reasons and on the basis of available literature. The recent history of residential care for people with mental handicap has seen some major changes. Until the 1960s, people mostly lived either at home with their families or in long-stay hospitals. The twenty-four or twenty-five-bed purpose-built hostel began to appear in the 1960s and 1970s as an alternative to the family home and hospital. Now the hostel itself is being replaced by ordinary domestic houses. 'Residential centres' are already, at least for some people, simply houses, flats, bungalows, and bedsits. As this trend is part of the widely accepted principle of 'normalisation' (Wolfensberger 1972, 1983) it is likely to continue. It seems fitting therefore, in the light of current and future trends, to focus attention here on the small group home.

The short history of the typical purpose-built hostel is reflected in the sparse literature on residential care for people with mental handicap. There are some accounts of hostel life along a series of dimensions which include size and scale; physical appearance; internal arrangements; care practices; aims and objectives; client progress; community acceptance; and opportunities for integration. (Atkinson 1988a). Groups and groupings feature little except as negative influences on people's lives. Individual wishes and needs are lost sight of in the 'block treatment' of people in traditional residential settings (King *et al.*, 1971). Social integration is precluded when people live together in large numbers, and move around their local community in groups (Mittler and Serpell 1985, Tyne 1977, Parker and Alcoe, 1984).

Group homes have an even shorter history. There is, however, a small but growing amount of literature on aspects of group home living, with some attention paid to the dynamics, and tensions, of group life. Race and Race (1979), for example, charted the fortunes of 'The Cherries' group home in the 1970s. This setting was 'home' to twelve people. The authors describe the difficulty of getting twelve people to live together 'in harmony', in a situation where sub-groups formed and there were leadership clashes. Group homes have reduced in size over the years, with four people usually regarded as the maximum number. The tensions and conflicts of small group living have been highlighted in accounts by Tyne (1978), Atkinson (1982), and Malin (1983).

The short history of group homes already contains lessons for the practitioner. These lessons are embedded in descriptive accounts of people's everyday lives and experiences. They need to be unearthed, identified and explored. This chapter aims to begin this process.

THE RESEARCH PROJECT: ILLUSTRATIVE MATERIAL

The case material which informs this analysis is drawn from the findings of a research project. This was a follow-up study of fifty five people who left long-stay hospitals in Somerset to live in flats, houses, and bedsits in the community. The information obtained from research interviews with consumers, and their social workers, and from casefiles, is supplemented by descriptive material drawn from two linked projects. Two students from the University of Bath independently undertook these related projects. One student conducted a participation observation study of three of the eight group homes featured in the main follow-up project (Atkinson 1985). A second student ran a series of meetings in a group home which was experiencing particular inter-personal difficulties.

The two linked projects provide rich descriptive accounts of life in three group homes. These three 'minimum support groups' were also part of the main research project. This 'followed up' an initial fifty five people who were discharged from hospital to the community in the decade 1971–1981. Forty five people had moved into minimum support groups, and ten into one- or two-person flats and bedsits.

In 1983, the follow-up study revealed some changes. The number of people living in minimum support groups had dropped from forty five to twenty six. One person had left the county, and three people had died. Sixteen people had actually moved out, eight of these into more structured environments, including hostels and other residential homes. A further eight people had swapped group home life for married life (three people), sharing with a friend (two people), or living alone (three people). This rate of turnover was unexpected. Was the group model not functioning? What were the features of everyday life which had led to this exodus from group homes?

This chapter is an exploration of two factors highlighted by Brown and Clough. It seeks an understanding of the group processes at work in these small groups, and it looks at the skills required by the staff engaged in supportive roles, whose task it is to intervene helpfully in these processes. The illustrative material is drawn both from the main follow-up study, and from the two linked studies of individual group homes.

KEY FEATURES OF THE GROUP HOME

The 'minimum support group' in this study was the Social

Services Department's preferred model of independent living for people with mental handicap. It was described in the departmental handbook as a 'mutually supportive group', usually of four people and often, though not always, consisting of two men and two women. People were selected on the basis of complementary skills and compatible personalities. The aim was to create a self-supporting small group of people who could run the household and, with help, their own lives.

The minimum support group was conceived as a co-operative venture; its members would be interdependent, and would offer each other support, company, and companionship. Selection of members was followed by a period of residential training and subsequent move into an allocated three-bedroomed house. Official 'minimum' support was provided through regular visits by home helps and social workers.

The minimum support group was a 'living together group' (Brown and Clough, Chapter 2). Was it a 'natural group', like a family, or a 'created group', designed and structured for a purpose? (Douglas 1983). It was a hybrid. It had aspects of a family, or natural group; it was long term and aimed to meet people's basic human needs for contact and support. It was also a specially created group, designed as a mutually supportive living unit. It was designed, however, with accommodation needs in mind rather than with an eye to the internal dynamics of small living together groups.

The two requirements of complementarity of skills and compatability of personalities were design features of an accommodation scheme. When the scheme worked well it promoted peer group support and a co-operative atmosphere. When it did not work, confined group living led instead to dissent, conflict, and even violence. Was this through a design fault at the planning stage? Or was it because the home help and social worker were unable to understand the processes at work in their group homes and were unable, therefore, to intervene helpfully?

Design faults were recognised only retrospectively. Some attention has been paid to factors which promote 'group harmony', (Malin 1983). These have been identified as group membership built around existing friendships; compatability between residents; personal motivation to succeed; joint commitment to the project; a willingness to share; and an atmosphere of trust (Atkinson 1988b). Apart from basing group membership around people's existing friendships, these factors are intangible and difficult to identify at the design stage. People's level of motivation, commitment, and willingness to share are not known at the outset, and an atmosphere of trust can only develop over time. The following example shows how group harmony can be fostered by attending to existing friendships at the design stage:

> In Edgar's group . . . the three householders are good friends. Edgar and Robert were friends for years in hospital, and now Norma has become a friend too. They go together when Edgar visits his family in another town: 'All three of us go. We go together. I always take them with me, I don't like leaving them behind. They go and see Charles and them while I see Mum and Dad. I don't like going on my own, it's not nice leaving Norma and Robert back here.' The principle of sharing is well-established in this group home. They share the decisions ('we talk it out between ourselves'), they share the budgie ('he belongs to all of us') and they share the chores ('we all help'). This companionship serves them well, and each member of this threesome seems to enjoy a full and active life both at home and out and about in the community.
>
> (Atkinson and Ward 1987)

The long-term outcome in this group was good for its three remaining members. Like the other groups in this study, it was designed as a four-person mixed group. In the intervening years a disruptive fourth member, Ada Smith, had left to get married.

Existing friendships can be built into the design of group homes. Other group harmony-promoting factors can be actively considered, but a positive outcome can not be guaranteed. Group harmony has to be worked for. This applies not only to group members but also to the frontline staff who are there to offer help and support. The latter need to understand the group processes at work, and to develop helpful interventionist skills which promote group cohesion and stability.

Where group cohesion and stability remained elusive, the groups in the research study remained vulnerable to internal dissent. Typically, an everyday disagreement would occasionally escalate into a full-scale row, frightening the group members and leading to social workers engaging in crisis intervention skills. In the research study, social workers shared their experiences of group home discord and how they handled dissent when it reached crisis level:

Example 1. 'The situation was explosive, there was evidence of tears and violence. They called me in to restore order.'

Example 2. 'I'm called in to domestic disputes which get out of hand. Being there helps calm people down. There is a good deal of trust, and they *will* listen – eventually.'

Example 3. 'Emotional tensions surface in the group, and I get called in to deal with the breakdown of interpersonal relationships. I try each time to sort it out, explain it, smoothe it over.'

Example 4. 'The group has its internal crises. I have to intervene. I try to disentangle the threads of their conflicts, to help them understand what goes wrong.'

Could these crises have been avoided? Perhaps trust between people, and an understanding of their differences, could have been promoted at an earlier stage. Could groupwork skills be developed to supplement crisis intervention skills? This chapter includes detailed accounts of group home life. These are looked at in two ways; as aids to greater understanding of the dynamics of small groups, and as pointers to the kind of groupwork skills that staff require in their day-to-day work.

EVERYDAY LIFE IN THE GROUP HOME

The following extracts are taken from notes made by the student in the linked participation observation project. They are fragments of everyday life in three group homes and, as such, give a 'feel' to small group life.

194 Abbey Road

A January afternoon, at 5 pm:
Douglas and Philip arrived back, and went immediately into the kitchen to unload the shopping. Melanie turned to me: 'Would you like tea?' I said 'Yes'. Melanie, to Douglas and Philip: 'What shall we have?' Douglas: 'Cucumber'. Melanie, to me: 'Do you like cheese?' She disappeared into the kitchen.

Their sandwiches were already made, and were on the living

room table. Melanie had made them while Douglas and Philip were shopping. Philip spoke to me, but I didn't understand. Douglas translated: 'Would you like a cup of tea?' Melanie brings my sandwiches in. Douglas carries out milk and sugar. Philip is fussing with the teapot, making the tea. Douglas returns to the living room, sorts out the crockery and lays the table. Nobody speaks. They work in silence. Everybody knows what to do.

Later, 5.30 pm:

We all sat around the table. Melanie put my sandwiches down, and poured the tea. Douglas asked me: 'How do you like your tea. Black? Milk and sugar?' I replied: 'Milk please, but no sugar.' I asked: 'Do you like living here, this house?' Melanie answered: 'Yes, since Alan's gone.' This started a conversation on the faults of Alan. They told me how he used to leave rubbish around the living room, and how he never washed or shaved. 'He smelled awful!' Douglas explained to me about shaving cream and how easy it was to shave, yet Alan never did. They told me about all the noise, and how Alan had music on late at night.

Melanie said: 'I could never sleep early when Alan was here.' Yet she had often wanted to go to bed early. 'I can sleep now that he's gone.'

The TV was on throughout the whole of tea time. They didn't look at it, or even glance in its direction. They made no comment about it.'

This tranquil scene of three people living amicably together contrasts sharply with an incident described by Melanie's sister on one of her regular visits to the house. The group then had its fourth member, Alan Perkins. The incident was graphically described in a letter to the social worker: 'Alan had already punched Melanie in the face...he was in a dangerous mood...the two boys were terrified and Melanie was crying and would not come downstairs...' (letter in casefile).

5, Melbourne Terrace

A February afternoon, 4.30 pm:
Roland is making tea in the kitchen in silence. Dennis is

sitting in the dining room listening to his tapes. Roland comes in (in silence) to lay the table. He puts the cloth on.

Isabel sits down and starts to put butter on the bread. To me: 'Do you want your egg hard or soft?' To Roland, crossly: 'These are awful knives! Get the other ones out! Get the yellow ones out!' She continues to butter the bread. Roland sets the table. They work in silence.

Dennis has turned off his tapes, and has started chatting; apparently to me, because no one else takes any notice. He chats about pottery, music, Bath, his sister . . .

Roland brings the teapot in, and Isabel pours. Crossly, to Roland: 'I said "get some more knives out". Come on!' Roland turned to me instead, and enquired: 'Do you like your egg hard or soft my dear?' There is silence as Roland boils the eggs. Isabel looks up: 'Roland, draw the curtains.' Meanwhile Dennis has started chatting again, this time about dogs. Ignoring him, Isabel confides in me: 'I'm trying to lose weight.' We talked about sweets and chocolate, and eating too many sweet things. We agreed we should stop eating them. Then she offered me some cake, and cut herself a large piece. We continued to talk about losing weight. Roland is in the kitchen making a new pot of tea. Dennis is still talking, eating very slowly. Roland returns with the tea, and eats in silence. Isabel, crossly: 'Have your tea Dennis, and stop gasbagging!

This scene has some ingredients for conflict. Yet it does not happen. Isabel is self-appointed leader, and so long as Roland and Dennis accept her interpretation of this role, conflict can be avoided. Isabel was not always the leader of this group. She was herself dominated by the second woman of the original foursome, Diana Wells, who subsequently left, thus vacating the leadership role. Isabel had been in danger of being ousted completely by Diana, who described the home situation as she saw it:

I think Isabel has to come out because she isn't doing much, she's not pulling her weight, she isn't doing nothing. She wants to come out, she's been here too long. If she do go, everything will be all right I think.

Isabel still does nothing. She has power though, and orders Roland around instead. Diana, her rival, has gone leaving the field clear.

17 Victoria Walk

A Saturday lunchtime, in February:
Daniel returns with fish and chips. Elaine lays the table and brings the plates. Daniel unwraps the chips. Suddenly, Pamela shouts: 'I don't want no fish and chips!' To Daniel: 'I don't want your fish and chips!

The others sit down in silence. They begin to eat. There is silence except for Pamela: 'I don't want your chips.' She goes in the kitchen to get something else. The rest share out Pamela's rejected food.

Pamela returns. She's changed her mind. 'I want my fish and chips. Where are they?' There's an awkward silence. Pamela glares at everybody, realising her chips have already been shared out. Crossly she returns to the kitchen. She bangs around in there. Silence continues at the dining table. Pamela returns with a cheese and tomato sandwich.

Suddenly Daniel gets up and walks out, slamming the door. Tension mounts. Then he returns, smiling, and sits down. Everyone looks relieved. This time it was only a joke.

It's still a tense situation. Howard announced: 'I think I'll stay in my room this afternoon, have a quiet afternoon.' Elaine starts to clear up. Pamela is angry: 'Let me have my dinner first!' Howard sighs; 'We can't do nothing right today.' He goes upstairs to his room. Daniel and Elaine wash up.

Pamela sits alone with her sandwich. 'I'll be glad to get away from here altogether, I've had enough of it. I shan't come back here no more.' Nobody takes any notice. She continues, to no one in particular: 'I shan't be here for tea. I won't be back. I'll have tea out.'

Daniel returns from washing up and smiles: 'All right Pamela?' 'Shut up you! I don't want to hear another word from you.' Meanwhile Howard has put a record on loudly. Pamela goes upstairs to get ready to go out, with a parting shot: 'I'm leaving soon! I'm getting out of here. The noise is getting on my nerves.'

This is far from a tranquil scene. It is a group troubled by differences between people. Conflict is never far away. What did group members themselves feel was going wrong?

Pamela: 'We don't agree with one another. If we could pull ourselves together and help one another we'd be all right. That's what we've got to do.'

Howard: 'When we're all here together it goes to pot. I think arguments start when everybody is in the kitchen together.'

In the linked groupwork project, people identified some of the sources of their conflict. These included:

Daniel goes to sleep in the chair in the evenings. Why couldn't he go to bed?

Daniel is hopeless at getting up in the mornings. Other people feel responsible, and get annoyed with him.

Elaine constantly nags people. Everyone hates being nagged by her ('Who does she think she is?'), and they get angry.

Some people don't pull their weight, and don't take their turn at doing chores.

There's a general lack of politeness. People object to being told what to do by others.

Who is the leader? Is it Howard or is it June? Howard says of June: 'I think June causes arguments because she bosses people about.' June says of Howard: 'I know Howard thinks I'm bossy, but I'm not. I'm only trying to help.'

GROUP COMPOSITION

These snippets from everyday life in three group homes illustrate some design features which also occurred in other groups in the study.

Size

Most groups were designed as four-person units. Most houses used to accommodate them were three-bedroomed family style council houses. This meant that two people had to share and someone else was allocated the typically small third bedroom. The two established groups at Abbey Road and Melbourne Terrace had each shed a fourth person and had subsequently remained as threesomes. In the newer group at Victoria Walk, already people were saying Elaine would have to go.

At the design stage, four people was thought to be the optimum size. In practice, three often became the norm. This applied to five of the eight group homes surveyed in the main follow-up study.

Gender

The groups were designed to be mixed sex, comprising two men and two women. In practice, the preferred threesome turned out to be one woman living with two men. In those situations where a group shed a member, it was usually a woman. The Melbourne Terrace group was an illustration of this trend. (See also the description of Edgar's group on page 153, which had 'lost' Ada Smith).

Sexuality

Close, sexually intimate friendships between men and women in groups seemed rare. One such friendship had blossomed in the context of a group home, and the couple had married. Mostly the group home seemed to be the 'family base' where roles and relationships were based on household tasks rather than sexual attraction. Close friends, lovers, and potential marital partners were more likely to be sought outside the group home rather than within. Where a sexual relationship did develop 'at home', other group members were observed to react with hostility.

Ethnic background

The population followed up in this study was drawn from long-stay hospitals. All the respondents were white, British people. It has not proved possible, therefore, to consider issues of racial mix in groups or to highlight factors affecting people from varied ethnic backgrounds.

Characteristics

The three detailed examples illustrate some important characteristics of the small living-together groups featured in the follow-up study.

Visible differences. The small size meant that differences were very visible and could not be easily tolerated. Alan and Diana had already left their groups. Elaine and Daniel were showing the kind of visibility which could lead either or both of them to leave Victoria Walk.

Pressure towards conformity. Group norms were fixed early and deviation from these norms was not welcomed. There was meant to be a daily routine in the groups. This had usually been established and adopted at the training stage. Most people subscribed to it rigidly, but sometimes a group would produce someone who was out of step with the daily routine. Pressure towards conformity would be brought to bear on the offender – such as Daniel – and either they conformed or they left.

Friendship bonds. Douglas and Philip, at Abbey Road, had a long-standing friendship from hospital days. They had already survived the break-up of one minimum support group, and the early years under Alan Perkins' tyranny in their present group. Their friendship was an important source of strength to them, helping them survive the rigours of small group life. There were no comparable friendship bonds at Melbourne Terrace or Victoria Walk. The lack of natural bonds of affection show through in the descriptive passages, where people failed to show respect for each other or adopt a pleasant and polite manner of address.

Intensification of relationships. The tranquil scenes captured at Abbey Road and Melbourne Terrace belied the stormy histories of these small groups. In the days when Alan and Diana lived in them, these groups were prone to conflict, dissent, and violence. The group at Victoria Walk was poised on a knife-edge. The observer caught the tensions in her descriptions. That day it was Pamela who was out of step. Mostly it was Daniel or Elaine, and on those days differences led to verbal abuse and sometimes physical violence. The small size of the groups somehow intensified personal relationships and magnified differences out of all proportion.

GROUP CONFLICT

Group homes were set up with good intentions. They were to enable people with mental handicap to live in a shared household, with ready access to help and support from peers, and opportunities to maintain and develop friendships. It was assumed that tasks and chores would be shared, and that people could enjoy one another's company.

Some groups never achieved cohesion and stability. The groups which had developed a co-operative approach to life, and an atmosphere of trust, had usually done so after a turbulent history which included the departure of one member. The Abbey Road and Melbourne Terrace groups, described in detail above, had settled into stability if not cohesion, but only after they had lost Alan and Diana respectively. The Victoria Walk residents were still experiencing daily conflict and differences. Perhaps that group would need to lose one or two members before it settled into routines and practices which suited everybody else.

Interpersonal difficulties are likely to occur in any small group. People in minimum support groups often spent their days in each other's company as well as living together. Not surprisingly, this day-to-day contact led to tensions between people. Conflict is not confined to the group homes in this study. For example, Tyne (1978) observed 'the frequent upsets within the group'; the 'troubles which ruffle the calm from time to time'; and the 'periodic upheavals' caused by 'tensions'. Similarly, Malin (1983) recorded 'many instances of petty quarrelling' as well as 'more hard edged conflict' between people in the group homes he studied. And some people in Mason's study (1983) 'admitted to tensions, and talked of their "ups and downs"'.

In the present study, the most common conflicts were based around the issues of leadership and roles. Leadership was often assumed by the most dominant member of the group, and tended to be autocratic in style. Leaders tended to focus on the fulfilment of tasks; issuing orders and instructions to group members about what had to be done and when. This worked only if other group members tolerated their subservient role and adopted a 'follower response' (Malin 1983). The focus on task achievement left other needs unmet. Groups also need to give attention to people's feelings and the relationships between them; 'group maintenance leadership'. (Brown 1986).

Lack of care about, and concern for, individuals within the group led to periodic rows and hard-edged conflict. It also led to individual unhappiness. It could lead to isolation, rejection, and scapegoating. Three examples illustrate these individual outcomes:

Richard Evans: isolated within the group
Tensions remain within the group . . . with four separate individuals leading rather different lives, and personalities and temperaments somehow failing to match. Richard has no friends. His household companions are just that and no more. In interview he commented: 'We do try to make an effort to get on. I try to keep me pecker up.' He does not enjoy the group tensions, and looks forward to getting away from the difficulties when he visits his sister.

(Atkinson 1984)

Glenda Potts: rejected by the group
The home help and social worker began to suspect that Glenda was being mistreated; that Helen and Bruce were treating her badly, refusing her food and making her spend her own money on groceries. Certainly Glenda was showing signs of unhappiness; she looked 'unwell and unhappy' (casenotes) and had taken to spending her spare time in the village cafe.

(Atkinson 1984)

Elaine Court: the group scapegoat
Several people in Victoria Walk identified Elaine as the source of their difficulties. For example:
Martin Forest: 'Elaine upsets Daniel. She makes him go to the fish and chip shop. She should go herself. She's not very good, she gets on our nerves. She will keep on, gets us all worked up. She plays up, and gets at everybody.'
Howard Bell: 'Get rid of Elaine, she's too difficult to live with. She wants to be first all the time, wants all the attention. She fights with Daniel, but she starts it. She keeps on. She gets on everyone's nerves, its just that Daniel breaks first.'

The present author has identified four roles adopted by people in minimum support groups (Atkinson 1983). These are:
the group home dependant;
the group home conformist;
the group home dominant;
the group home rebel.

The model works, or at least remains stable, if most people adopt the conformist role, and only one person tries to become dominant. Some examples, taken from social workers' casefiles, illustrate these roles:

Group home dependant

Martin Forest
He is partially sighted and is to some degree dependent on the good will of his junior partners. The rest of the group are kind and helpful to Martin, cooking for him and escorting him to and from the Centre, and helping him cross main roads. In his turn, Martin makes a valuable social contribution to the household.

Group home conformist

Roland Masters
Roland is endlessly patient and long-suffering. He complains about Dennis's hygiene and appearance, but politely continues to share a bedroom with him. He runs errands to neighbours, shops and post office on behalf of both Dennis and Isabel. He never refuses their requests.

Group home dominant

Isabel Squires
Isabel is self-appointed housekeeper. She dominates her two male companions, Dennis and Roland, and runs much of the house from the comfort of her chair.

Group home rebel

Alan Perkins
Alan proved to be the most competent member of the group, his frustration towards his companions showing in outbursts of temper and occasional aggressive acts. He made no concessions to group living, he lived his own life with scant regard to the comfort or happiness of others, scattering his belongings everywhere, sleeping on the settee and tampering with electrical fittings to the extent that the 'whole house is a fire hazard'. Complaints from his household companions,

together with his evident unhappiness with his lot, led to Alan moving into his own flat at last.

(Atkinson 1986)

INTERVENTIONS IN GROUPS

Interventions in the dynamics of these small groups have tended to be of three kinds:

Groupwork.
Crisis intervention.
Removal of individuals.

Groupwork

Groupwork skills were rarely consciously employed. In the linked groupwork project, a series of focused weekly group meetings was set up with the residents of Victoria Walk. This was a conscious attempt to explore people's differences, and work towards group cohesion and stability. It proved to be a difficult route to negotiate as this extract from the report indicates:

In this meeting, members openly displayed their hostility towards each other and towards me. Throughout the session the atmosphere was tense, and despite my efforts people were unwilling to talk or even listen. For example, Elaine giggled throughout, Pamela sulked and Martin bickered with Daniel. The more I tried to help members recognise their feelings and discover the causes of their anger, the more they retreated into themselves. The meeting made me feel very despondent, and left me wondering if the fault lay in my skills, or in the members' personalities. Had the situation in the home got beyond repair?

Crisis intervention

Examples of crisis intervention were given earlier in the chapter. Social workers, when drawn into group conflict, tended to reassure people, reduce tension, smooth over the difficulties and attempt to find explanations for the dispute. These interventions usually worked in the short term, but crises recurred. A truce, handshake, or apology might help; but only until diferences surfaced the next time.

Removal of individuals

Some people, like Alan Perkins, wanted to leave their group homes. Alan's disruptive behaviour led, in time, to his acquiring a flat of his own. Others, like Glenda Potts, were rescued from unhappy situations. She was found a place in a hostel.

In the research study, sixteen people had moved out of group homes; eight had chosen to go, and eight had been rescued.

FUTURE TRENDS

Residents of group homes are members of small groups. Staff involved in creating and supporting group homes need a knowledge and understanding of group dynamics when considering group composition and continuing support. This entails a shift in attitude; from thinking of group homes as accommodation units to regarding them as dynamic, interactive entities. This entails two strategies – attention to design features (Douglas 1986) and the adoption of appropriate 'group practice skills' (Brown and Clough). These skills include informal group work, role modelling, and group counselling.

Strategy 1: Design features

The four-person (two men and two women) model needs to be reconsidered in the light of people's actual preference for a smaller size and different composition. Friendship bonds clearly matter and these need to be built into the group structure wherever possible.

Assumptions were built into the model, and these could usefully be challenged at the design stage:

tasks and chores would be shared out, and everyone would help;
the group would settle into routines and practices which worked for most people;
group members would live together and spend their days together;
this closeness of contact would lead to group cohesion, and people would enjoy each other's company;
autocratic leadership, adopted by the most dominant

member, would ensure that things got done;
anyone showing 'disruptive' behaviour would be moved out.

Some of these features could be changed. People could have the option of spending day time apart from one another. Some sort of flexibility regarding the allocation of chores could be encouraged. Some understanding of the nature and causes of 'disruptive' behaviour could be shown (Douglas 1986). Autocratic leadership could be actively discouraged.

Strategy 2: Group practice skills

Informal groupwork. Assumptions may be challenged at the design stage but small residential groups, if left to their own devices, are likely to show intensity, rigidity, conformity, conflict, and rejection. Some of these features can be ameliorated by building on existing friendship bonds between members and encouraging ties of affection.

However, there is also a place for informal groupwork. This means staff having much more day-to-day involvement and working alongside group members, particularly during the early stages of group life. It means modelling a flexibility of approach towards daily living and a tolerance for people's differences. It involves staff being there and joining in, ensuring that group norms retain some fluidity and no one attempts to become an autocratic leader. Hopefully, respect, politeness, and even affection could come to replace the silence, apathy, or actual dislike which has characterised some group homes.

Roles were not predetermined. Nobody *had* to become the dominant person. People did not have to conform, though most people did so. Rebels were exceptional people and eventually left. So too did scapegoats, but often under a cloud. Informal groupwork would involve staff within the very fabric of the group, particularly at that early settling-down stage when roles have not been adopted or assigned. A spirit of trust and co-operation could be engendered, and positive roles adopted; group members could become supportive towards each other, enabling one another to express some individuality and facilitating a range of lifestyles.

Role modelling. People who move from long-stay hospitals to live in minimum support groups may well bring with them an image of authoritarian behaviour. This may reflect not only how they were spoken to, but also how they saw their peers treated. The 'group home dominant' (Atkinson 1983) has adopted this manner towards fellow-residents. The authoritarian style leads people to become abrupt and speak sharply. They are likely to give instructions without explanation, and hand out advice which is neither sought nor welcomed. People adopting an authoritarian manner are likely to cause resentment in others, and set the scene for conflict.

Can someone with an authoritarian manner learn more socially acceptable ways of relating to people? Are dominance, resentment and conflict inevitable features of group life? If the authoritarian style was learned through imitating staff in a hospital setting, then it is likely that a pleasant and caring manner can be learned in a community environment. Staff members can act as *role models*, modelling constructive and positive ways of relating to people.

Group counselling. There are *three* stages in group counselling. First, members of staff themselves need to learn about group dynamics. It is widely accepted that the only way of learning about how groups operate is through participating in a group, and learning through personal experience. Only someone experienced in the workings of small groups can begin to help people in group homes work towards group cohesion and stability, and, where necessary, help them disentangle the threads of discord between them.

Second, residents of group homes themselves need a chance to learn about group interactions and the give-and-take of shared living. They too can benefit from gaining insight into their own role in the group, and how their behaviour has an impact on other people. This crucial area of personal learning can best be incorporated into any initial training programme. Alongside learning how to cook and shop, people can also learn about relationships. Staff members have a key part to play in this learning process. It may require imagination and innovation using, for example, pictures, games, role-play, and video recordings to facilitate the process, enabling people to learn about themselves and other people.

Third, staff have a continuing role in supporting people in group homes. A weekly group meeting may be a helpful innovation. In a regular group session, residents can be encouraged to air their grievances, and work out constructive solutions to conflicts. In addition to staged meetings, staff can implement on-the-spot discussions about specific incidents so that residents have a chance to put more generalised learning into specific use, and have new practices reinforced.

CONCLUSION: LESSONS LEARNED

People were placed in groups for reasons of companionship, social support, and economics. Initially no one realised the importance of understanding group dynamics when working with people in group homes. The research, on which this chapter is based, indicates that group home living is not just about support and company, it is also about leadership struggles, clashes, rejection, scapegoating and all the other feelings and rivalries that can exist in a small group living together. Within these groups strong forces existed and pressures were exerted on individuals. One whole group split under the strain, and sixteen people moved on.

It is imperative both for this generation of group home dwellers, and for future ones, that lessons are learned from the experiences charted here and elsewhere. Support staff – whether social workers, community nurses, home helps or care assistants – need to understand about group processes and make a positive input towards stability and cohesion.

ACKNOWLEDGEMENTS

Thanks are due to the people who took part in the main follow-up study, and gave their time so generously. This applies to those whose homes were visited, but also includes their visiting social workers who talked so long, and with such warmth, about the people they knew. Thanks are also due to other colleagues in Somerset, both in the Social Services Department and in the Health Authority, for their interest in and active support of this project. Finally, warm thanks are extended to two ex-Bath University students for sharing the rich findings of their respective projects.

Chapter Ten

THE FAMILY AS A LIVING GROUP

BRIAN CAIRNS AND KATE CAIRNS

ESTABLISHING THE GROUP

In the early 1970s we were making plans to extend our two-person family. Our work in social work and in teaching had aroused in us a concern for children in care, and particularly those children who seemed not to fit with the existing resources of residential care, fostering or adoption. Some experience of living and working in groups of various sizes had convinced us that our personal preference would be to live in a group or community of ten to twelve people, and that such a group would have the potential to promote wholesome change in all its members. Linking our concern with our preference, we decided to establish a living group in which children separated from their families of origin could find a home in our family.

We were aware of the work of David Wills (1960) in this country and elsewhere and of Bruno Bettelheim in the USA (1950, 1974), and we believed that we could establish a base for our children which would include three important elements: a carefully planned environment, the constant, consistent presence of caring adults, and a group of sufficient size to develop a potentially therapeutic network of relationships and interactions.

In 1975 we joined the Children's Family Trust, an organisation offering permanent substitute family care to separated children. Trust families usually care for about ten children including the 'home-grown' variety. They are provided with a house and garden of sufficient size to allow for shared and private space. Family running costs are met by charges made to the referring local authority and major capital costs are met by the Trust. The homes are registered with the DHSS as Voluntary Children's Homes (Cairns 1984). CFT has provided the structure and means to enable us to put our ideas into practice.

Since then four children have grown up in our family into independent adult life, still maintaining active links with us as young adults, and nine children and young people are living at home. Of these thirteen, three are 'home-grown' children born into the family; the others have been with us anything from two and half to twelve years, having joined us at ages ranging from 4 to 14.

We consider that every deliberately formed group owes its existence and much of its form to the fundamental philosophy of its leaders, and it is helpful to be as clear and explicit as possible about this underlying belief system. We hold views which lead us firstly into membership of the Society of Friends (Quakers) and secondly into a perception of human needs and potential which is based on humanistic psychology rather than on psychoanalytic or behaviourist models. Each person is to us unique, irreplaceable and infinitely valuable, with a capacity for and tendency towards wholeness and goodness which may be blocked or subverted but cannot be destroyed.

We believe that human nature at its roots includes elements of autonomy and responsibility, of having the capacity for joy and ecstasy, and of belonging in groups through which people are linked together in a complex web of interrelated systems. These are matters of faith rather than reason or observation, yet they are fundamental to the nature and style of any group we might establish, and will largely determine the practice methods we are willing to use. On this base we have built our family. Thirteen years of life together has served only to deepen our faith in the way we have chosen. Such, of course, is the fate of true believers!

THE THERAPEUTIC BASE

Thus was our family formed. Thus was our therapeutic group formed. Experience has confirmed to us our initial assumption that there need be no conflict between the two concepts (Douglas 1986: 123). If the purpose behind the establishment of a therapeutic group is to develop the potential of each individual member through interaction with other group members, then that can also be seen as the purpose of the family. But whereas therapeutic groups as traditionally viewed concentrate on one selected area of human activity or relationships, the family group has as its area of activity the whole field of living as individuals within society. There are other apparent differences, for example: traditional therapeutic groups are time-limited, short-term, whereas our family group offers (but does not demand) lifelong membership. But for a family group such as ours to succeed, we would contend that very many of the same considerations have to be borne in mind by its leaders (the parents), both at the outset and during the evolution of the group, as have to be borne in mind by the leaders of a successful traditional therapeutic group.

It seems to us that therapeutic groups come together because of something shared, but that their success is due in large measure to the ability of the group to recognise and value differences between its members.

Our family group at the moment (i.e. those who live at home for at least part of each week) numbers eleven; ourselves and nine children aged between 8 and 18. There are four female members and seven male; three 'home-grown' and six 'separated' children; seven people of white parentage, three with at least one black parent, and one whose unknown father may have been of Amerindian or Mongoloid extraction. We have not taken every child that we have been asked to take (space permitting), because we have wanted to maintain balance of sexes, of racial origins, of age, of temperament. We have carefully avoided (except in one instance) having children of the same sex close enough in age to be in the same school year, thus avoiding counter-productive constant competition or peer-group indivisibility, either of which can be damaging to the functioning of a group or to the individual development of the group members concerned.

The insistence on age spread brings many advantages. Each child has their own individual place in the family order, and is more easily seen as an individual by other family members. Each approaches 'landmarks' – school transfer, important examinations, starting work – separately, and can be helped through by those who have passed that way already. Each can assume responsibilities, accept restrictions, negotiate personal 'bonuses' (extra pocket money, joining in a school trip, riding lessons, or whatever) without a sense of competition with direct peers. Each can be assured of being not just one of a group but, at any one

171

moment 'Mum or Dad's favourite 10-year-old, or 11-year-old, or 12-year-old'. Thus group living can boost self-worth and uniqueness.

Some readers may wonder, given the present climate of opinion, about the racial mix. Our approach is not 'colour-blind'. The experience of the children in our family group mirrors their experience, present and future, in our society – membership of a white majority or a black minority. Within the family group it is safe for the issues and fears which this arouses to be shared and worked at. This might be very threatening for a single black (or white) child, but the group is large enough to avoid such a vulnerable situation. We become increasingly convinced that it is actually easier to help children to construct and inhabit a multi-cultural society in our artificially-constructed multi-racial group than in the 'natural' white suburb or black ghetto area. (Douglas 1986: 24)

The 'atmosphere' of a group is, of course, largely set by its leaders. In our case, that's ourselves – the parents. It is important that there are two of us. The same advantages which co-leaders have over single leaders in running a time-limited therapeutic group apply for us – mutual support, the opportunity for reciprocal consultation, as well as the essential external supervision which we have sought and received separately and together, the ability consciously to adopt different complementary roles at any stage, and so on. The co-leaders of such a group need to be clear about the aims and objectives of their group, to feel at ease together in the group, to have enough understanding and trust of each other to recognise what the other is doing in an unprepared situation and to avoid open conflict or pulling in opposite directions. It is essential for the functioning of a family group such as ours that the co-leaders have freely chosen to live together and enjoy a harmonious, mutually fulfilling relationship. It also seems to be essential that living in a group such as ours is something that they both want to do – a lifestyle in which both feel totally comfortable. Our relationships with the group and with each other are open to continuous scrutiny and we must be willing for that to happen. Similarly accessible and open to examination by the children are our relationships with and attitudes towards the world outside the family, just as theirs are to us.

This is perhaps the most far-reaching aspect of our application of groupwork theory to residential living. In most residential centres, staff members have 'private' lives and 'private' relationships with each other which take place on 'private territory' outside the purview of the group. The residents have no such privacy. There is an imbalance which leaves residents vulnerable. In structured therapeutic groups there has to be openness between leaders and other members within the time and space boundaries of the group, but there is a mutual awareness and acceptance of the right of all members to go away at the end of each two-hour session and lead their separate lives. In our setting we can expect no right of privacy greater than that of our children. We share their vulnerability.

We have mentioned two of the three sub-groups of people who comprise our family group – the separated children who join it, and the parents who lead it. There is a third group – our 'home-grown' children who find themselves involved in it with the least element of choice. Of our three 'home-grown' children, one was 5 months old when we started our large family group, and the other two have been born into it. Membership of the family group appears to have been of enormous value to them so far in terms of self-confidence and development as distinct individuals. The births of the younger two and infancy of all three as shared group experiences were immensely useful in cementing the group together, in allowing the older children to examine the often damaging and distressing experiences of their own early childhood, and in offering them the opportunity to exercise real responsibility for truly vulnerable human beings. The balance of numbers is such that they can, when necessary, find support from each other, whilst the other children, through sheer weight of numbers, can never feel merely appendages clinging precariously to the margins of the 'real' family, as children in foster-care may do. The catalytic influence of 'home-grown' children in the family group is considerable; their presence makes our group a 'real' family and assures its continuance.

BOUNDARIES

One of the first tasks of a group is to define its boundaries (Douglas 1986: 45). Three kinds of boundary are important – membership, time, and space. These boundaries must be clear to all group members and to outsiders. The more vague are the boundaries, the less secure and cohesive will be the group. The firmer boundaries are, the safer it becomes to drop internal defences and open up to group influences.

Our family group consists of ourselves and those of our children who live at our address, and intend to do so until moving away in the natural course of events as young adults. This membership boundary is recognised in a host of subtle ways. Family members come into the house without ringing the doorbell, have letters addressed to them without the distancing 'c/o', are assumed to have a right to answer doorbell and telephone, and to use household equipment. They have an acknowledged right to identify themselves with the group by talking about 'our house', referring to other group members as 'Mum', 'Dad', 'my brother', 'my sister', and using our surname in as many contexts as they find comfortable. We do not try to pretend that families of origin, with which there are often close ties, do not exist. But the use of family names within the group reflects the roles adopted within it, the degree of intimacy generated in a secure group, and the commitment which we offer. Similar use of names recognises the commitments made in newly-constituted living groups formed by adoption, marriage, or remarriage. Membership is not time-limited. Having once left home, they can remain welcome family visitors on the same terms as other close relations, and the opportunity to move back in at any time in the future is always open. Other 'staff' – and over the years we have employed cleaning help, gardening help, nannies while we had babies, and a valuable network of relations and friends who have stood in for us during short absences – are *not* members of the group, however easy and cordial the relationships, or however welcome their visits. These people are expected to respect the group's privacy; they do not have the automatic right of entry, and nor are more sensitive family matters aired in their presence, for they are not members of the family group.

Physical boundaries are also important. Our house is set in a large garden surrounded by hedges. Within the house there are no 'no-go' areas. We expect the children to respect each other's right of privacy in their bedrooms and infringe that right ourselves only in exceptional circumstances (Maier 1981: 42). There are no locks on internal doors or cupboards, children's files containing correspondence with social workers, medical information, statutory review notes, etc. sit openly on a shelf in the study and may be read at any time; piles of coins, wallets, purses, frequently lie for days on sills and shelves. Abuses of trust, such as stealing money, are dealt with by the group and individual discussion, but have never been allowed to alter our policy of not locking anything away. Boundaries around the family group are clearly defined and reinforced to enhance a sense of security and cohesiveness; boundaries within the group are avoided or reduced to the minimum needed for personal privacy in order to develop mutual trust and openness.

EXPECTATIONS OF MEMBERS

Group members who join groups voluntarily come with expectations of what that group is going to offer them, and how they hope to benefit from participation in it (Douglas, 1986: 137). The success of the group is not always dependent on whether or not these expectations are met; the group process may lead members to feel that their initial expectations were unrealistic or inappropriate, or they may find themselves developing in a totally unexpected, but exciting and satisfying new direction. Nevertheless there are certain expectations such as acceptance and tolerance which must always be met if membership of the group is to be of value.

Our children have come to us with very differing expectations – and apprehensions – depending largely on what they have come from. In theory, all have come voluntarily, and have visited us on a few occasions (but not too many since their status as neither-visitors-nor-group-members poses a threat to external boundaries for the existing group) before deciding to join us. In practice there may have been little alternative. All want security, a sense that they will be valued as individuals, an assurance that they will not be expected to leave bits of themselves outside. Most want to feel that they will be listened to and respected, but left to make relationships with the group at their own pace, in their own way, and at the level of intensity at which they feel comfortable. Primarily, they want honesty, but past experience has often left them suspicious and unable to trust.

A skilful group leader is aware of these issues during the first session of a group, and will manage it in such a way that every member leaves the first session relieved of some apprehensions and daring to trust that at least some of the expectations will, after all, be met.

We have a similar task to do in children's initial visits, and during the first weeks and months of their time with us. It is a task which becomes easier as time goes on and we can draw more and more on the experience of long-standing members of the family. They can vouch for the fact that our commitment to them, and theirs to each other, have continued over years. They can point to their own successes, and to those of older children who have moved away from home, whilst recalling their own uncertainties on arrival – and we, in turn, by careful handling of mealtime conversation, can, often amidst much hilarity, provoke reminiscences of family failures which have been worked through without requiring panic action or classification as major disaster. We avoid a lot of questioning of the newcomer who is the vulnerable party for whom too much self-revelation may be painful at this point, but make a point of listening attentively to anything that is offered, and of answering questions about ourselves very fully. We try to be conscious of the ways in which the newcomer's presence may enrich our lives rather than dwelling on what we, in our arrogance, may feel we have to offer.

Leaving the group is different for family members from the usual leaving of therapeutic groups in that their membership is for life if they so wish. Moving away from home is, however, a matter for some ceremony, marking the beginning of adult independence and a change in group relationships. The ceremony is not overplayed, though, as we recognise that young adults often return to the family; there is a delicate balance between offering a loving welcome when they return to the nest, and encouraging the fledgling to fly!

THE PHYSICAL ENVIRONMENT

The leaders of a therapeutic group need to structure with care the physical environment where the group meets. Size and shape of room, lighting, heating, furnishing, outlook, the pictures and objects within the room, will all influence the ease of otherwise with which the group feels comfortable with itself (Maier 1981: 40 ff.)

In establishing and maintaining the physical setting for our family group living, certain requirements have been paramount: the fact that as parents we need to feel comfortable and relaxed ourselves in our environment; the recognition that whilst we hold the purse-strings and have wider experience to draw on in decision-making, the children need to sense that they share a growing responsibility for shaping and maintaining the environment; the need for each member of the group to have a sense of personal space and for smaller groupings to be able to carry on joint activities undisturbed; the wish for the environment to strengthen the feelings of warmth, security, and calm which we try to offer children whose previous experiences have lacked these; the value of using the environment to foster cultural and spiritual awareness and to excite the imagination.

The first important consideration was the location of our house. We felt it right that the children should have basic urban facilities within walking distance, should be able to make their own way to local schools, and should be able to visit and be visited by friends without complicated transport arrangements. But we also felt that the impersonal nature of a large town could add to the alienation of children who felt at odds with society – better a small town where networks of acquaintance constantly overlap, where shopkeepers know their customers personally, where a walk down the main street will often result in a chance encounter with a friendly neighbour who will greet you by name. In such a setting the family group and its individual members can quickly find their place in the community; the community is small enough for each member to be of obvious value, and our role as 'group leaders' is to maintain and develop, both internally and externally, these community links which boost self-confidence.

Large groups of children are, however, noisy (particularly those with disrupted early experience) and active. This dictated a large garden, a house far enough away from other householders to have its own 'insulation', and easy access to open country. The house we found is a few minutes' beyond the edge of a small town, set in an acre and a half of garden, bordered by fields on three sides, and with a large area of common land beginning 100 yards away.

We wanted a house which retained something of the 'feel' of previous family occupants, which had lots of rooms to provide personal space, yet was compact enough for no one to feel isolated within it, and easy to maintain. Its architectural style needed to be cosy rather than grand, its rooms individual enough to lend themselves readily to 'personalising'. Although it needed to be a large house, it had to avoid being very obviously different from other houses around, for we wanted to establish ourselves as far as possible as an 'ordinary' family in the locality to gain maximum acceptance. Fortunately, all these factors were present, at least in potential.

Then came the equipping of the house. We improved the central heating system so that the whole house can be used, but retained open fires in the living rooms, and a solid fuel cooker in the kitchen as focal points, and live sources of warmth. The effect of the open fire on a winter's night is powerful, drawing the family group together around it, making a setting where emotions can be felt, and feelings shared. We insulated the house against noise, using the thickest carpeting that we could afford, the heaviest curtains, furnishings in soft fabric, usually 'good' second-hand, and wood rather than metal or plastic where possible. We scatter around soft cushions and pillows of various shapes and sizes, and notice how even teenagers often seem immediately more relaxed with a large cushion on their laps! (Maier 1981: 37).

A similar 'softening' of the interior of the house, mitigating the severity of vertical and horizontal lines, has been achieved by the use of indoor plants, hanging baskets, and mobiles, and by avoiding the use of central ceiling lights where possible. We have aimed for a level of tidiness, at least in shared areas of the house, which welcomes the constant presence of a certain amount of 'clutter' as evidence that living is an active business, but stops short of there never being a chair clear to sit in or a table with space on which to write a letter!

Finally: there are pictures on the walls, glassware and pottery on the shelves, musical instruments, records and tapes, and, above all, books in their hundreds, and a constant stream of newspapers and magazines, all for the using. Sooner or later every child's curiosity is aroused by something; chance remarks, throwaway questions start us all searching through shelves on an impromptu voyage of discovery that leads, as often as not, to self-discovery.

This is not a description of how our household simply happened to evolve. It has been the result of careful planning of the environment to meet the needs of the whole group. We have tried to provide 'a home that smiles, props which invite, space which allows'. (Redl and Wineman 1957, Chapter 6.)

LEADERSHIP AND MANAGEMENT

Consideration of our style of leadership and our management of interaction must be brief and selective. We shall, therefore, consider only a few aspects of our approach which relate to two of our main aims – aims which are often high priorities in groupwork. These are the bolstering of feelings of self-worth, and the building of trust in the continuing commitment of members of the family group to one another.

By comparison with time-limited, sessional groups, we have all the time in the world. We can allow change to happen slowly. Individual children, we hope, can feel that what they have to say matters, and is taken seriously, and we will strongly discourage others from closing them down. 'Not interrupting' is one of the golden rules of the household!

We are often asked how we can 'give enough attention' to so many children, and the answer may well lie in our deliberate policy of rarely being right at the centre of things. We allow individuals and smaller groupings to seek us out when they want our attention, whilst fairly unobtrusively keeping our finger on the family pulse so that we can pick up an individual child who appears to need particular attention, or take out someone who is threatening to disrupt others and meet that child's need more constructively.

The children are thus for much of the time meeting with each other's needs for attention. There are similarities with recent changes in classroom management as teachers have realised that working in small groups is more effective in increasing active participation in the learning process than a teacher-centred approach. We encourage the children to take responsibility for each other – washing a cut knee, helping a younger child with reading or polishing shoes, mending one another's punctured bicycles (Maier 1981: 54–5).

Mealtimes are important family occasions – the landmarks of the day when the whole family is usually together. Again we assume a shared responsibility for mealtimes – not rotas. We encourage the children to help in the preparation, and cleaning up afterwards is a shared task; everybody can find something to do!

We eat around one table and aim to have one general conversation rather than several disparate ones. These are the occasions on which we air matters of general interest to the family: local, national, or international interest, political issues, moral dilemmas, questions of religious belief, or domestic issues such as which room in the house might best be used for the current craze of sewing, or how we can reduce use of the telephone after today's fearsome bill. Everybody's opinion matters, everyone's suggestion is welcome. We avoid secrecy. Details of our most personal beliefs are open knowledge, as are details of the family finances.

Mealtimes are also occasions for 'building up', for publicly expressing appreciation of what someone has done, pleasure at achievement. They are occasions for drawing the attention of the whole family to positive changes in individual members. We feel, incidentally, that it is much easier for a group of our size to expect and accept change than for a smaller group where the incidence of change is rarer and the prevalence of stereotyped roles for members of the family, 'the clever one', 'the naughty one', is probably greater.

Mealtimes are not, however, appropriate occasions for challenging individual children with misdemeanours, or confronting them with failures. This is destructive at the time, and so better done in private. But having worked the matter through in private, we find it helpful to 'report back' to the whole family group, to make forgiving and being forgiven a public experience, and to appeal to the strength of the whole group to assist in the process of rebuilding.

Formal rules are few in our household in the sense of unbending precepts issued by authority. We endeavour to treat every new situation as unique, requiring decisions based on principles of reasonableness and worked out by discussion. We expect to follow the same principles ourselves. If we go out, we expect to inform the family where we are going and when we expect to return. If they feel we have omitted to take something into consideration they will tell us so! We expect the same to apply to the children. Bedtimes are a similar matter for open discussion, and will turn on the individual's apparent need for sleep or the constructiveness of the current evening activity rather than arbitrary deadlines. Once the principle of reasonableness is established, other children are often able to point out the unreasonableness of one child's apparently misguided decision and persuade them to think again without recourse to us! (Wills 1960, Chapter 6).

So much of the family's sense of self-worth arises from their perception of our interdependence. We have already mentioned older children helping younger children, and shared responsibility at mealtimes. There are other ways in which interdependence is apparent. The house and garden are large and we employ very little help. So everybody needs to wield a vacuum cleaner or a mower from time to time if we are to prevent dust or nature taking over. We generate a lot of laundry; anybody can at any time load up the washing machine, iron a few clothes, or distribute clean washing, and push the process along a little further. As our children have grown older, we have been delighted to see several develop skills – in art, in music, in home maintenance, in cookery, for example – that surpass our own, and take pleasure in putting them at the family's services.

> Experiments with residential groups constructed on the basis of an extended family have shown that people with wide disparities in age develop an ability to relate to, support, and inform each other . . . such a group is able to exploit all the different resources of experience, knowledge, energy, skill, and affection that are available to it.
>
> (Douglas 1986:32)

We also aim to build feelings of self-worth by sharing space quietly. It is important for our children to be aware that it is with them that we often choose to be, contentedly pursuing our interests in the same space as them when we could choose to be elsewhere.

HISTORY, MYTH, AND THE EXPERIENCE OF CHANGE

A common feature of group leadership is the use of summary and review to demonstrate to or remind members of progress over time – of what has been achieved over the course of an evening or a series of meetings. We can and do employ techniques which similarly make explicit the history of our family group and add to the children's security by looking confidently into the future. Reminiscence is a powerful tool; carefully-seeded conversations of the 'do you remember when . . . ?' variety can extend meal times over what seems like hours. Newer members of the family can share vicariously in experiences which preceded their arrival. Older members are confronted by the reality of change. Problems which seemed major at the time are now viewed in perspective, and we are all more able to realise that present problems will be worked through and grown through in a similar way.

Projection into the future has similarly beneficial effects. 'Just imagine', one of us can say 'in two years' time I shall be 40'. And immediately the projections come: 'I'll be 12 and able to join the drama club'; 'I'll be able to visit my mum on my own'; 'I'll have a motor-bike' – 'Only if you get a job' . . . A lot is happening here – trying on roles for size, expressing longings and so on – and fruitful discussion in private or in public can follow from the cues given. But underpinning it all is the security-building assumption that the family will still be there, that there will be no more total rejections, that we, at least, have faith in the future.

Before moving on from discussion of management of interaction, we must make mention of the importance of rituals and festivals in our family group (Maier 1981: 30). Christmas and Easter obviously have to be important times in the year for any group living together in the Christian, or nominally Christian, tradition, and, whether or not we like the symbolism, the tree, the holly, the presents, the huge meal, are elements of the traditional Christmas which we have and enjoy. But the rituals which seem to be most looked forward to every year are those which are entirely of our own making, and which grew up spontaneously over our first few Christmases: postponing the decoration of the tree until Christmas Eve, then going carol-singing to neighbours and relatives after dark and demanding mince-pies, hanging up Kate's father's largest socks in a circle in the living-room next to cartoon drawings of each of us to assist Father Christmas in identification! Somehow these make Christmas our own – a celebration of the coming together of *our* family, as well as a family in distant Bethlehem.

Worthwhile ritual is born, not made, but birth and development can be assisted, and an important group leadership task is to recognise the potential of emerging ritual and capitalise on it. So we bake hot cross buns for Good Friday and dye hard-boiled eggs for the Easter Sunday game of 'sharps and blunts' (a sort of out-of-season game of conkers, but with an edible end-product), we decorate birthday cakes, and build bonfire, masks and lanterns for Hallowe'en. Daily events can also have a ritual element which some of us need and value. Bedtime and getting up, going out and coming in, are all points of the day which have significance and which may prove reassuring and strengthening or lonely and frightening depending on the way they are carried out.

Rituals and traditions are observed by us so long as they have life and meaning. We try to remember that any family practice may become meaningless habit, and to discard it if it reaches that point. We take care, though, not to abandon long-standing traditions because some members stop observing them; this can be just part of a proper separation from us rather than a loss of value in the tradition.

In building up a sense of family history we have avoided too much use of photographs, diaries, and other records. These certainly have their place, but we think they should not be relied on as the sole or even principal source of identity building for the period after a child has joined the family group. Human memory is more subtle than a mere chronicle of events, or even a record of events and feelings. We allow the group to weave its own patterns out of the shared experiences of life, and thus to create myth as well as history. 'It is only through our imaginative construction that we shall be able to own the full heritage of the experience we have acquired through living in time' (Salmon 1985: 147). Myths are often truer than literal truth, and are nearly always far more powerful in effect. One of our children insists that Kate's sister and Brian always have an argument when they meet; this is far from true, but it expresses the impact on her of the realisation that people are able to have an argument and still remain friendly and happy together, which was completely new in her experience. Sharing our subjective memories also makes us aware of the partiality and fallibility of our perception more gently and appropriately than would recourse to 'objective' records. Someone remembers 'the day we got lost on holiday, and someone was sick, and the minibus broke down in the middle of a flock of sheep, and mum had a head-fit'; Kate's recollection of the incident was quite different!

LINKED SYSTEMS

Living groups cannot afford to be isolated from the community that surrounds them. Groups which do so become little islands which may function quite adequately within themselves, and within which individuals may also function adequately, but which lose track of the mores of society outside them, and leave their members ill-equipped for the reality of life in other systems.

We recognise that our children come to us already members of at least one system (their family of origin), and actively encourage their membership – and our own – of as many more systems 'outside' as possible. As a result, each of us is constantly refreshing our family living experience by bringing in experience from other settings, finding constant opportunity to apply in other situations social skills learned at home, and learning about ourselves by comparing the functioning of various systems and our own functioning within them.

Three outside systems which we, as parents, have brought into our family life and which have particular importance for us all are our extended family, our Quaker meeting, and our workplace. We were clear from the outset that our own extended families would have to be able to accept all our family naturally, making no distinctions, if we were to maintain more than token contact with them. We have been fortunate: both sets of 'grandparents' live nearby and have committed themselves entirely to what we are doing, throwing themselves enthusiastically into being grandparents to all the children, and other relatives have followed their lead. Happy, natural, four-generation family gatherings have become part of our regular family group experience; grand-parents' homes become a place of refuge not totally separate from home when the emotional going gets rough – retreat there carries no stigma and can be a very 'building-up' experience.

Our Quaker meeting, besides providing us with spiritual inspiration and support, offers all the family a wide and varied group of people who share our philosophy about the essential nature of human beings and are concerned for the welfare of each one of us. The children delight in mixing freely with adults of all ages who don't talk down to them, accept them as they are, and express this equality of acceptance by expecting to address and be addressed by first names. The absence of dogma and doctrine in

Quaker belief and practice is non-threatening, and personal experience and thought is validated by an approach to discussion that doesn't assume that teaching is done by adults and learning is done by children!

Throughout the twelve years of our family life, at least one of us, and currently both of us, have been employees or students in the fields of education and social work away from home. The effect of this was memorably expressed several years ago by a 7-year-old who had previously lived in conventional children's homes. 'When Dad finishes his duty', he said, 'he comes home, but when the staff at the unit finished their duties, they went away'. Our children have daily evidence that at home with them is where we choose to be, and not where we have to be. As our older children have completed their education and gone out to work themselves, the experience which they bring back is also of great value to the rest of the family.

Our children's schools are of great importance. A vital part of establishing our family involved getting to know the head teachers and staff of our local schools, explaining to them what we were about, overcoming their apprehensions, and sometimes prejudices, at dealing with the children of a family so unorthodox in construction, and with us as their parents. Once built, these relationships have to be constantly maintained. That demands involvement in school activities and attendance at parents' evenings. It means being prepared to see the school as a partner in caring for our children. For us, fostering and preserving links with school is the second most important inter-group relationship that we have to manage, second only to relationships with the children's families of origin.

As for other community links, it has been our practice to become personally involved in activities outside the family circle, and to encourage (but not pressurise) our children to join individually as many local leisure activity groups as they wish, within the limits of practicability. The diversification of experience thus gained builds individual identity and ensures that the family group is constantly bombarded with fresh stimulus from outside it.

We have tried to help our children to look and explore beyond local, and even national, boundaries. We have, on several occasions, taken family holidays abroad, off the tourist tracks, and have ensured the children's participation as far as possible in school trips to other countries. Individuals have taken part in school exchanges, and their exchange partners have been welcome guests here.

The family group is also the setting for working with the feelings aroused by painful contact with the wider community. Experiences of racism, sexism, and prejudice against children in care are brought to the family to be shared. Positive images of strong, capable people who have survived such experiences are found among friends and acquaintances, famous people in national and international life, and among older family members. Such images provide strength, comfort and inspiration. Television programmes and press articles provoke discussion which makes it clear that feelings of pain, anger, and powerlessness can be aired and accepted. Within the group we discover together possible routes to survival and the potential for positive collective action.

We mentioned the links which our children bring with them when they join us, and which continue – their membership of their families of origin; 'children do not lay aside their previous attachments and associations by a mere placement to a new care setting' (Maier 1981: 59). This is the most powerful and influential system to which they belong, however dim their memory of it, however limited by time, space, and circumstance. In some cases it has been almost the total of their past experience. In others, the involvement has been small in reality, but immense in forming self-image and fantasy. Mishandled, the relationships between our family group and the families of origin can be enormously destructive of either system or of the individual child, and to ignore them, and thus attempt to block out such a fundamental part of the child's being, would itself be a gross mishandling. To achieve an easy relationship between the two systems which allows the child to feel comfortable in either and to bring enrichment from each one into the other can take years of hard work with many setbacks and a lot of pain, but it must be attempted. Often the route is a roundabout one – via siblings, grandparents, aunts, and uncles. Often we have to take the initiative in breaking down barriers and opening up channels of communication, and often we get it wrong, so sensitive is the area. This sensitivity relates to live issues. We are writing about and in consultation with children for whom these matters involve present pain, all of whom have active, more or less regular, contact with members of the systems of which they were part before they joined our family. This is too public an arena in which to give any greater space to describing private griefs.

CONCLUSION

Grief and rage are no more abnormal than joy and delight. Within our family we aim to be as 'normal' as possible (Maier 1981: 52). We want our children to see the family life they enjoy from day to day as recognisably similar to that of their friends. We deliberately avoid anything institutional. Our planned group environment is made up of elements which could be part of the life of any other household. For us, group living is not set apart from the ordinary world, but is in itself normalising; not an alternative to the family, but an alternative family which works for us.

'The whole basis of learning about groups is not to discover some quintessential truths but to create a series of constructs about group behaviour that will enable us to make sense, of a kind, out of what occurs in our daily life' (Douglas 1986: 216). We have not attempted to form a group separate and different from the stuff of our daily lives. Instead we have considered an everyday group, the family, and realised that it has the potential to function as a therapeutic group. We have tried, by applying our ideas and knowledge about people and groups, to enable the family to become a centre of energy and healing through which all of us who are members of the group may discover strength and wholeness and the courage to be.

Chapter Eleven

A FRAMEWORK FOR PRACTICE

ALLAN BROWN AND ROGER CLOUGH

Note. References without dates are to other contributors and their chapters.

In this final chapter we draw together the main threads from the rest of the book to present a framework for thinking about practice. The framework is based on a systems perspective, which views a centre as a dynamic, interacting whole in which everything that happens is interconnected to a greater or lesser extent. Incidents that occur, say, in a staff meeting, at a mealtime, on a day-trip, in a group counselling session, or during a chat among friends, will have been influenced by, and will influence, things that are happening and being felt, elsewhere in the centre. The implications of this, for understanding the incident and for deciding about responses, are far reaching, offering choices and setting limits to the actions of both staff and users.

The centre itself is, of course, usually part of a much bigger organisation whose policies, purposes, resources, and constraints will have a profound impact on what the centre is able to achieve. (Burton shows, however, ways in which a centre did develop and change in spite of departmental constraints.) The parent organisation will, in turn, be heavily influenced by more powerful institutions and resource factors beyond its borders. Having acknowledged the significance of these wider systems, we shall concentrate here on the centre itself, not as an island, but as an open system with a permeable boundary, constantly interacting with its environment. As Hawkins says: '*Social learning* provides a language which can link the group and groupings dynamics within a home to an understanding of the total system of the home as a whole, and to the dynamics of the organisation or department which manages it.'

THE FRAMEWORK

In Chapter 2, we developed a typology of groups and groupings based primarily on their different functions. We also need a framework which views centres systemically. Centres can be thought of in terms of perspectives and levels. *Perspectives* are views of the centre which derive from what life is like for different individuals (and groups) according to their position in the centre and their relation to it. Thus perspectives combine emotional investment and location: the way in which groups and groupings matter to a person, and whether he or she feels themself to be an insider or an outsider. The idea of *levels* provides a structure for analysing how groups and groupings interact with each other and with the centre as a whole. We have identified three principal levels:

the centre as a whole, the gestalt;
the mosaic of interacting parts, the whole in relation to the parts, and the parts to the whole; and
the small groups and groupings, the discrete parts.

The centre as a whole. This refers to the totality of life in the centre. It is the level for thinking about overall purpose; establishing basic principles, values, and ground rules; and developing a climate and culture which is conducive both to achieving centre aims and making the place attractive to all those who use it.

The centre mosaic. This can be thought of as a bird's eye view of the pattern, or landscape, of interacting groups and groupings in the centre, as they are, both at any given time and over time. Atherton (1986: 93) makes the point that the worker in 'group care' needs to have a clear grasp of the whole network of relationships and groupings that make up the 'ecology' of the centre. Hawkins refers to this process as 'helicoptering'.

Small groups and groupings. These fall into three categories. The first is the special category of *single small group centres,* as in the examples given by Atkinson, and Cairns and Cairns. The second and third categories, *small groups* and *groupings* respectively, have already been defined and explained in Chapter 2. What we have not yet done is explore the implications for practice skills and the role of the worker.

A systemic framework highlights the differences for both workers and users when in a group or grouping in a centre, compared to being in a formed group in a fieldwork setting. In a centre, how people behave and feel in a grouping may be determined as much by other centre factors as by the grouping itself. This external influence factor does, of course, also apply to fieldwork groups, but there are two important distinctions. The first is that in a centre the other systems are much more immediate and pervasive; the second is that the members of a group in a centre, whether users or workers, will in all probability be encountering each other *that same day* in other contexts and guises, formal and informal. Hawkins shows the way in which what is happening in the staff team both reflects what is happening in the community as a whole, and will be mirrored by the community. The influence is two way.

This has crucial implications for staff. It means that consistency, both as an individual in different contexts, and as between different staff in similar contexts, will be of prime importance. There is nothing more undermining and confusing for users than conflicting responses from staff, and unpredictability. Staff also have more choices about how, when, and where they respond than do their fieldwork counterparts. The particular small group or grouping may, or may not, be the optimum place and time to take a particular action. In isolated groups it would be expected that problematic individual behaviours or difficulties would have to be dealt with within that system: in a centre there are many other possibilities, some of which may be more appropriate. It is, however, vital that whatever strategy is adopted, and wherever the initial intervention occurs, it is reinforced and supported elsewhere throughout the centre.

Similarly, users in centres have a potential freedom of choice, particularly if the ethos is facilitative and sensitive to their position and perspective. There is the risk that particular labels, say of scapegoat or joker, will pursue individuals whatever they are doing in a centre, but there is also the possibility that those people can take different roles in different groups and groupings; options which would be unavailable to them in an isolated fieldwork group. Benefits are more likely to accrue for users in a centre if staff are responsive and have understood that there are many different avenues available for perceiving what is going on, understanding it, and doing something about it.

It is important to remember that the part can influence the whole. Change does not only, or necessarily, happen because somebody at the top of the hierarchy decrees it. Individuals, groups and groupings, by doing things differently can create ripples which may become the waves of change. Such actions often need to be accepted and confirmed by the whole organisation; nevertheless the influence or power of the part in relation to the whole is apparent.

THE CENTRE AS A WHOLE

We focus in this section on aspects which permeate the whole establishment. If these are not given attention, much of what takes place in the smaller parts, the groups and groupings, will be ineffective.

Purpose

A centre is an 'artificial' structure, in the sense of being contrived; because of that, people should be explicit about aims and purposes, and how to achieve them. Many confusions and inconsistencies arise from muddles about what the centre is there for. In the probation setting, Sapsed emphasises that a hostel needs to be clear about its primary aim. Such aims might be to reduce the risk of offending; to enable clients to develop resources for gaining greater control over themselves; to learn social and life skills; or some combination of these and other aims.

Belief in what is going on in the place is an important component of purpose. It is only when staff believe in what they are doing, and users accept the fundamental purposes of the centre, that there is any hope of good practice. The task for the agency is to consider what is likely to enhance such belief. One factor is choice by the user: only in exceptional circumstances should anyone use the centre who has not expressed a wish to do so. Staff belief will be enhanced by an environment in which staff at all levels are encouraged to be imaginative and creative in trying to provide the best possible service.

Some basic principles

Every contributor to this book stresses particular values and working principles which are seen as fundamental to 'group living' in a centre. Although the emphasis and the language varies there is a remarkable degree of unanimity about the essentials. We now identify four of these interrelated strands, acutely aware that the test of any principle or value is whether it is manifest in the daily life and actual behaviour of staff and users. It is one thing to declare an equal opportunities policy and quite another to put it into effect in what actually happens throughout the life of the centre in all the groups and groupings.

Empowering users. By this we mean maximising people's control over their own lives and over those decisions which affect them individually and collectively. Burton, in his case-study of ways of bringing about change and of empowering of older people in a large residential home, states, 'Groupwork in residential settings is . . . about finding, creating, and exercising the collective power to change things.' In a day centre, as in Ball and Sowa's Intermediate Treatment group, the primary aim may be to use the time in the centre to try to enable people who, on account of their class, race, gender, or other factors, have little power in the community outside, to develop some conviction about their own worth and their capacity to influence their own lives and circumstances.

If empowering is to be more than a slogan and a good intention, organisational structures will be needed which build in real power for users. For example, this happened at Stones' family centre, when a parents' council made up of users met jointly with the staff to decide policy matters.

Equality of rights and opportunities. In day and residential settings this principle applies doubly: first in the familiar (but frequently not implemented) sense of ensuring that a person's sex, skin colour, age, disability, or sexual orientation does not adversely influence his or her rights and opportunities; second, in ensuring that being in a day or residential centre does not reduce in any way someone's full rights as a citizen. Underlying this is a recognition of the essential normality of people in centres, and an avoidance of labels which stigmatise, including those associated with being a user of social services.

Partnership. This is another vogue term referring to a relationship between users and staff which offers varying degrees of real power and control to users. Daines (1988) has identified a framework for thinking about partnership as consisting of support, alliance, and control. Stones explicitly refers to partnership as a basic principle underlying the approach taken in her family centre, and highlights some of the issues that arise: for example, the parents' council and the staff group held widely different views on the adoption of an anti-racist policy. Cairns and Cairns describe ways in which a considerable degree of partnership can be achieved between parents and children in their 'extended' family. However, a cautionary note needs to be repeated here: it is easy to claim to be in partnership with someone else; it is far more difficult to turn such a claim into reality. A key question is, 'Whose centre is it anyway?' There are risks attached to this style of work, and to asking this type of question, because of the ensuing uncertainty.

Another aspect of partnership is sharing critical events and struggles. Staff and users can learn from each other, and change can emerge for everyone in the centre. Hawkins discusses this in his chapter on social learning.

Seeing things from the user's perspective. Equally important is the need for a user perspective on the mosaic, tracing each person's daily pathway of experience as he or she moves through groups and groupings and protected personal space. This perspective is well presented by Bano whose approach is not about what programme can we (the staff) fit them into, but how can their total group living experience be most fruitful for them. What sort of transitions are involved and how can their movement through the mosaic be facilitated? Carter's research (1988) gives a vivid picture of the daily journey through the mosaic, not only of individual users but also of individual workers. If this journey is to be a coherent experience rather than an obstacle course, careful organisation is needed as well as specific actions and skills.

A facilitative culture and climate

A central objective is to establish a facilitative culture and climate based on a clear purpose and value-base, creating an atmosphere and way of doing things which permeates everything in the centre.

Five specific factors have been identified.

Physical environment. Several of the contributors provide evidence for what Bettelheim (1950) has said about the substantial effect which the physical environment has on people in a centre: first, there is the suitability or otherwise of the actual physical structure (Sapsed's unplanned five terraced houses, Cairns' carefully chosen house and location); next there is the quality of decorations and furnishings and whether the place looks attractive; and then there is the crucial question of how the space is used (as in Burton's attempt to distinguish 'public', private, and personal space).

Centre-meetings for the whole community. In Chapter 2 we indicated the powerful and often uncomfortable feelings that affect most of us at times in large groups, making it difficult to participate in ways that are both satisfying and productive. This means that, if large 'community' meetings are to be held with a realistic expectation of the positive outcomes indicated by Hawkins and Bano, much careful preparatory work is needed. Users, and also staff, will need assistance if they are to participate actively. They have to know how to get items on the agenda, how they can give information or make their views or requests heard, and how to respond to others.

Preparation by the convenor of the meeting, a position which may rotate between staff, or between staff and users, involves both being prepared personally, and enabling others to do things beforehand that will help them in the meeting. For example, a sub-group might meet in advance of the meeting to plan what they want to say. Everyone should know beforehand what will be on the agenda and how the meeting will be conducted. In some contexts all this will be written down, in others people will understand the system because it is explained very clearly and/or there is past experience of a consistent way of doing things. In the meeting itself much more structure will be needed than in, say, a small group of six people. Different people can have prearranged roles and opportunities to speak. Individuals can be given time to think things out personally before they are overwhelmed by the remarks of others. 'Buzz' groupings can be formed during the meeting to give people the opportunity to check out their ideas in a small group and perhaps ensure their views are fed into the main meeting via a spokesperson.

As in a small group, the person chairing the meeting has to manage both process and task. Thus it is important to take account of people's feelings, which may be displayed, for example, by angry challenges between individuals or by hostile silences; it is equally necessary to be aware of decisions which have to be reached in relation to particular items. The temptation is to pursue one of these, process or task, to the exclusion of the other. The result is that either the business has been concluded (but with many people resentful or disgruntled), or attention has been given to interaction (and vital decisions not taken because time has run out); again, people end up frustrated. Successful leaders of large groups find techniques for managing business in ways that do not 'put down' members who appear awkward: for example, 'that's a good point, but I think it is taking us away from what we're discussing at the moment; would you like to raise it later?'

Managing the 'outer boundary' of the centre. Management of the physical and psychological boundary between the centre and the outside world will vary with the type of centre and its purpose but will always be of crucial importance. There are likely to be relations with the rest of the agency, with the immediate neighbourhood, with the relatives and friends of users of the centre, and with all the other people, such as food suppliers and doctors, who have cause to cross the threshold of the centre.

In some community-based day centres the policy may be to have as open a boundary as is consistent with protecting the activities within the centre. Interestingly, Stones refers to tensions which can arise from competition for space between insiders and 'outsiders'. In other centres, such as residential therapeutic communities or intensive intermediate treatment programmes, like the one described by Ball and Sowa, the very nature of the 'closed' activities means that quite strict boundary control is needed. In an older persons' home the public/private boundary will need to balance the desirability of continuing outside contact with recognition that the centre is the personal home of the residents who have a right to be protected from uncontrolled intrusion into their private lives.

There is also the question in some centres of how to open the outer boundary deliberately to try to attract those potential users who might not otherwise enter the place. For example, men do not

195

easily enter family centres which seem to be geared to activities for women and children, and black people are unlikely to be attracted to centres which have a dominant white culture. In both these examples active steps can be taken to demonstrate to the 'under-represented' group of people that the centre offers something positive for them (assuming that it does!). Another category of 'outsiders' are the families of users, for example, the relatives of older people in a residential home. Things can be done to make them feel welcome, whilst ensuring that staff do not usurp the user's role as host or hostess.

Ground-rules for living/working together. Perhaps significantly, the two contributions on centres for offenders (Ball and Sowa; Sapsed) are the ones which discuss 'rules' explicitly. In our view, however, every centre needs to have a clear, explicit understanding, perhaps a code of practice, about the kinds of behaviour which are and are not acceptable in that place.

These ground-rules (preferably few rather than many) then provide a yardstick for all users and staff in every group and grouping in that centre. For example, a centre can make a clear statement that racist and sexist behaviour are not acceptable, neither is physical violence nor any form of harassment, and that drug and alcohol abuse will not be tolerated. Ball and Sowa make the important point that, 'it was only after many sessions of values clarification that the staff as a team acknowledged that black young people and workers experienced racist behaviour by other workers or young people as a form of violence'. Rules can provide the framework for developing a culture and climate in which power is distributed more evenly, and people treat each other with respect; the ultimate goal is that people internalise behaviours and attitudes congruent with the ethos of the centre.

If possible, users should be involved in the drawing up of rules, as happened with Sapsed's hostel regulations about overnight visitors, rather than having them imposed. Indeed, it often happens that, in resolving issues in one of the parts of the centre (in a particular group or grouping), people establish new ways of tackling issues which become accepted throughout the centre as a whole. In other words, influence permeates upwards as well as downwards, though it is often useful to get such practices confirmed by the larger system.

Role of the worker. Our contributors make it clear that the quality, style, and composition of the staff group (race and gender balance, range of skills and personal attributes) is the main determinant of centre climate and culture, and that it is a long hard struggle to establish a truly facilitative environment. Staff group dynamics and supervision are discussed in several texts (see, for example, Atherton 1986), and the implications for training are considered later in this chapter. The ways that the 'entries' and 'exits' of new and departing staff are managed is likely to be reflected in users' capacity to cope with the often frequent changes in their own membership and groupings.

The way a staff group behaves is important in any setting, but in group living settings it is doubly important because of the continuous direct influence the staff group will have on users' behaviour in all their groups and groupings. Consciously or unconsciously, users are aware of how their staff group manages issues of authority, leadership, intimacy, conflict, individual idiosyncracies, sub-groupings, alliances, roles, boundaries, and all the other basics of group relations. The mirroring of behaviour between the two groups is mentioned explicitly by Hawkins, and is implicit in other chapters. Atkinson discusses the significance for users of the role-models provided by staff, and Sapsed makes the point that the quality of caring that staff demonstrate is likely to be reflected in how users treat each other. All this is not to say that staff are not also learning a great deal from users, but most centres have paid staff whose responsibility for what happens is of a different order from that borne by the people for whom the centre has been created.

The worker in day and residential settings is much more exposed as a person than she is in fieldwork, and lives are shared to a much greater extent. Indeed, counselling or talking groups are unlikely to be successful if the behaviour of staff in activity, work or informal groupings is not in accordance with the centre's basic principles. Users will not turn up to group meetings, or will say little in them if they do, if other events in their daily lives make it clear that staff are not listening to what they say. However, as several contributors have indicated, doing things together with users in informal groupings offers rich opportunities for learning and personal development.

Lastly, but crucially, is the appointment of the person in charge.

Five of our contributors indicate how, in their different ways, they have been able to use the power and influence of their position 'in charge' to bring about significant change and development in centres where they work.

THE CENTRE MOSAIC (OF GROUPS AND GROUPINGS)

Taking account of the complexity of the mosaic, with the influence of the parts on the whole as well as of the whole on the parts, planning should include:

An overall programme which meets the aims of the centre in a way which is creative and manageable both for users and staff. This will of course vary enormously according to the type of centre and the resources available. Programme planning is an important and under-rated skill in field-based groupwork (see Ross and Thorpe 1988), but it is infinitely more complex in day and residential settings (see Stones' diagram, p.93). This makes it tempting to go for safety in terms of structures and content, and for 'tidiness', but this must not be at the expense of a 'user-led' perspective.

Spaces for people. 'Space' is a useful idea because it can refer to physical space, to space in the head, or to being with or apart from others. The balance of organised and 'free' space is a delicate one. People will benefit from an environment which is stimulating and has plenty going on, but which also leaves them free to decide what they want to do; they will want to have enough to do, but also periods for personal reflection and privacy. If staff are serious about empowering users and working with them in partnership, then the programme needs to be conducive to groupings of users being able to meet together spontaneously, or formally, to plan and develop their own ideas and aspirations.

Managing transitions and boundaries. One of the most difficult aspects of life in day and residential centres for both staff and users is coping with all the changes and adaptations involved in moving from one group or grouping to another during the course of a day or a week. Is it OK to take your pudding into the art group that meets after lunch? Can anyone join the social skills group? Can women users have their own room that men may not enter? Can staff have certain meetings from which users are excluded? What

198

are the limits to how much staff are expected to share with users about their private lives? What are the limits to staff intrusion into residents' private lives? How can a reminiscence group ensure that its members are not interrupted? Can a member of a drama group bring her friend along if she feels like it? Boundaries are difficult for all of us because one person's protection may be another person's exclusion.

Several contributors describe the problem of adapting not only to changed membership as you move into a new group or grouping, but also to differences in format and culture. For example, Stones mentions that many people first join the 'drop-in' at the family centre, with its open laissez-faire culture, and then find the transition to a more organised and demanding group difficult to make.

Procedures need to be developed for getting from one group to another, whether or not this is from a sitting room or work group to the dining room for lunch, or for children to come in from playing to join others who are watching TV or another grouping who are going to bed. Spaces and 'buffer zones' can be built in after the more demanding activities, with time and assistance for people to change gear: this may take the form of ensuring there is time for young people to unwind after a boisterous activity, or of creating an opportunity for others to discuss what has just taken place in some emotionally demanding group. It also means that the beginning of a group or grouping which follows another may need to have a transition corridor when members can be helped to make the adaptation by explicit recognition of the adjustment and help in making it. Bano mentions the idea of making sure all users have one core small group to which they belong and part of whose purpose is to help members integrate all the multifarious experiences of the day or week.

There is also the issue of personal boundaries. The more intimate the service that one person provides for another, the more it can only be carried out satisfactorily if the provider gives of her or himself. The extent to which people are prepared to share parts of their lives will vary, but successful practice, as described in many of the previous chapters, contains elements of challenging existing boundaries. For example, should officer staff have separate facilities from manual staff? Should staff of any kind have separate facilities from the users?

Facilitating intergroup relations. We know both theoretically (see Chapter 2) and from some illustrations in this book, that tension, competition, and conflict can develop all too easily between different groups. Burton describes how the establishment of separate units in his centre led initially to 'unhelpful rivalry' (other examples are found in Sapsed and Stones) but also how growing differences between units can come to be valued. With good communication between groups and some cross-membership, it is possible to establish a culture in which, as Burton says, people respect and value their own and each other's diversity. It is more difficult to develop mutual respect between groups when, as in user–staff group relations, one group has much more power than the other. Experience suggests that users relate best to staff groups which do not fudge their authority, which do not undermine users in those arenas where they can have some real power, which are consistent towards users and, perhaps most importantly, demonstrate that whilst roles are different, people are all essentially the same as human beings.

Role of the worker. It is sometimes said that to be a good residential worker you need to have eyes in the back of your head! Beedell (1984) refers to 'radar' skills, and Hawkins, in his chapter, talks about 'helicoptering'. What this means is that the skilled worker needs to be able to be deeply involved at any particular time with one individual or grouping, whilst simultaneously having an awareness both of what is going on all around her, and of the significance of any 'micro' incident in the context of the total mosaic. This requires the worker to have a sense of the whole milieu, and to draw on qualities of noticing, listening, sensitivity, and awareness.

Coping with multiple roles. Relations in the groups and groupings of the centre mosaic are characterised by multiple-role relationships, as people may encounter each other in very different contexts during the course of a day. Sapsed describes how, in the probation hostel, staff and uses have to cope with, say, switching rapidly from a shared experience in a group to an interpersonal confrontation elsewhere later on, and perhaps sharing a meal together after that! In addition to managing their own role-changes, staff have a responsibility to facilitate users' role-changes by modelling how to do it and, when appropriate, easing the changes facing users and talking about how role-transitions are experienced.

SMALL GROUPS AND GROUPINGS

Having established the significance of the context of the whole centre and the mosaic, we now consider the implications for practice in small groups and groupings within centres. This will be discussed under the three headings already identified: *small centres which comprise a single group; small formed groups (of the 'social groupwork/fieldwork' type); and small groupings.* It is very easy to forget how daunting being with others in groups can be to people who are not used to it. A core skill for workers is helping users to learn how to function in roles that are enabling: in order to do this, staff themselves need these skills, and training is the topic of our final section.

Single small group centres

Two contributors, Atkinson and Cairns and Cairns, describe centres of this special type whose characteristics are in many ways similar to those of a family. (Cairns's centre *is* a special kind of family.) Group dynamics are likely to be intense, individual roles set, and choice of companions for affinity groupings restricted, with fewer options available generally than in larger centres. On the other hand there is a good basis for stability with few changes in membership, and the opportunity to develop cohesion, close personal relationships, and group autonomy as a unit. The amount of power users have in deciding who comes into the centre is an important variable and will influence what happens after people have moved in.

The role of the worker differs from place to place. In the very unusual setting described by Cairns, the 'staff' become real parents as distinct from the quasi-parental role of staff in conventional small children's homes. By contrast, group homes for people with a mental handicap have only visiting staff, whose role is not easily defined (see Atkinson). There are difficult ethical and professional judgements to make about when and how to intervene, and how much training in group living is needed by users. Atkinson proposes that workers need to be quite deeply involved, particularly in the early stages, and she suggests 'informal groupwork' (joining in the daily life), role modelling, and group counselling as three crucial skills for the worker. In addition, she shows that in devolved, semi-autonomous group homes, users may need initial guidance from workers on how to handle boundary management.

Formed small groups

The social groupwork skills for working with this type of group are well documented elsewhere (e.g. Heap 1985, Whitaker 1985, Brown 1986) and will not be repeated here. What does need to be recognised are the special features of holding these groups in day and residential centres, where whatever happens in a group will be affected by, and will affect, other things that are going on in the centre. This has to be taken into account so that different experiences for users are positive, mutually reinforcing and not conflicting and confusing.

A few key points are only summarised here because they have been discussed elsewhere: (a) in such a group members have less freedom, than in a fieldwork group, to establish their own ground-rules because they are subject to those of the centre as a whole; (b) both workers and users have, potentially, more choice about what to do in any circumstance because people meet outside the group; (c) the management of the boundary of the group is more complex, partly again because people see others outside the group, but also because of the emotional and behavioural adjustments people have to make as they move from less formal gatherings into organised small groups, and back again; and, (d) rules have to be established about confidentiality so that there is a clear position both on what is 'imported' in the way of gossip and personal details and on how group members are expected to respect disclosures made in the group.

Small groupings

Much of the 'groupwork' in centres will be with groupings. As will now be clear, this category includes a wide range of types of gatherings, between what have been termed *aggregate* and *group*. Examples include groupings at mealtimes, in a minibus, at an educational class, round the pool table, in the TV room, in a residents' meeting, sitting in the garden, at the drop-in centre, clusters of people who gather together at the beginning of the day, (see Bano), and so on. These groupings vary greatly in the characteristics of their membership, purpose, time-scale and activities, making it difficult to generalise about appropriate actions and ways of 'working with groupings'. As with groups, the process in groupings will be profoundly influenced by the group living environment and users' cross-membership of several groups and groupings. A fundamental question is, 'What is the role of the worker in relation to the grouping, and in what ways is it different from working with formed groups?'

Before considering the role of the worker, we need to ask the question, '*Who initiated the grouping?*' Was it started by users, staff, or on some joint basis? As stated earlier, centres will vary in the extent to which there is both real encouragement to users to generate their own activities, and sufficient physical and psychological space available for informal groupings to develop. The stance of this book is that users should have the maximum opportunity to take responsibility for such decisions themselves, within the limits set by their own physical and mental capacities, and the purposes of the centre.

The role of the worker in groupings. The classical approach to the role of the worker in social groupwork is that he or she will often start the group (that they have formed) in the role of 'central person', and then as the group moves through stages of development towards maturation and a degree of autonomy, move out of the pivotal position to one more facilitative of the group's own mutual aid development. Depending on the type of group, the worker may or may not take up a more central role again in the final stages. Heap (1988) has suggested that there are two components of the worker as central person, a 'situational' position deriving from agency context, resource-provider etc., and an 'emotional' position deriving from use of self, values, and what they mean to the group members as a person. He goes on to say that whilst it would almost always be appropriate for the worker to move out of the 'situational' central position, in some groups he or she may continue in an 'emotional' central position, because group members need to use the worker in that role.

Groupings, by definition, do not normally reach the more cohesive stages of group development, so in the light of the above, what does this imply for the role of the worker? In those groupings initiated by staff, say an art class or a day-trip, we would agree with Sulman (1986) that, in lieu of the grouping being able to develop its own cohesion and autonomy, more structure is likely to be needed, and one way of doing this is by the worker quite deliberately and consciously retaining the central person role.

But what about user-generated groupings? What are the criteria for whether the workers get involved at all, and if they do, how? Explicit rules about who can go where in the centre (see Burton) may help, but often it will not be so straightforward. Heap's framework can be applied here in a different way. In any self-generated grouping in a centre, the staff, even if they are not physically present, will have emotional significance by virtue of their power and their roles in the centre as a whole. Staff have to try to judge whether users would like them to have some direct involvement with their grouping, even if they have not said so; if there appears to be an 'invitation', they need to work out sensitively what kind of role to take, and what kind of help to offer, whether 'situational' or 'emotional' or both. A worker, without intervening, can let a grouping know that he or she is aware of their existence. Brian and Kate Cairns, who are clearly in the ultimate emotional central position as 'parents', describe how they try to be around but unobtrusive, so they are not interfering, but are there if wanted.

The most difficult judgement is whether to intervene when you are obviously not wanted, but when the grouping is perceived as being oppositional to the centre's ethos, and potentially (or actually) destructive to individuals and the whole centre and what it is trying to achieve. Sapsed gives an example of the 'delinquent' sub-group which sometimes forms in the probation hostel, and the dilemmas this poses for staff. There can be no simple prescription for action, but, as a general guideline, potentially destructive groupings cannot be left to their own devices, because the interests of the whole community are at stake. However, as we saw when considering intervention in formed groups in centres, there will often be choices: some actions are direct, others indirect; some explicit, others implicit.

What is important is that staff, individually and collectively, are consistent in their responses to user-generated groupings of different kinds. This consistency of approach, in attitude and action, based on shared values in the staff group, mutual trust and understanding of how other colleagues actually work, is crucial. It also applies to responses to critical incidents. Day and residential groupworkers are likely to face many more unpredictable happenings than their fieldworker equivalent, and have to be able to respond with 'planned spontaneity' to these unplanned opportunities, to be able to intervene episodically, as seems right, and in the process role-modelling for users.

Timing and pacing are significant in relation to groupings. The first of these refers to choosing the moment at which to comment or intervene in what is going on. There is a tendency for day and residential workers to deal with things as they happen: this leads to insufficient consideration of whether this particular moment is the best time to deal with all aspects of an event. For example, staff may be confronted with a group of young people returning later than agreed to a hostel, in a belligerent, alcoholic state. The temptation is to deal with the anger and frustration at the broken agreement, even though a moment's reflection would lead to the realisation that there is no chance of any sort of rational discussion. Therefore getting the young people to bed quietly, without disturbing others, should be the priority; working out what to do about return times and agreements should take place the next day.

Consideration of timing can provide relief for staff. While it may mean holding back initially, the fact that the worker learns not to tackle issues unnecessarily at particular moments, such as when exhausted or upset or when the young person is volatile, leads to far better management of work. It does not mean avoiding confrontation, it means choosing the ground on which the confrontation is to take place.

As well as deciding when and where to intervene, the *pacing* of intervention can also be crucial in groups and groupings. What stage has the grouping reached? How cohesive is the group? How much feedback can a particular individual take during one meeting? Is the prejudice being expressed in a group best tackled gradually or in a direct immediate way?

Mealtime groupings emerge as having a special significance in several of the centres described in this book (see Burton, Sapsed, Atkinson, Cairns, Ball and Sowa). Meals and eating represent so much that is fundamental about caring, sustenance, sharing, and relationships. They can be a routinised, regimented, functional occasion, or they can be a rich, enjoyable focal time of the day for exchange and sharing. There can be opportunities for informal interaction, both between users and between staff and users, not only at the meal itself, but also in the time available preceding it and especially afterwards. All this assumes that staff join in on as equal a basis as their role allows, that mealtimes take account of individual needs, and that the food is good and culturally appropriate. Of course, not all meals have the same significance. A particular evening meal once a week, preceded or followed by a group meeting, can be a special occasion; it is also important to have opportunities for visitors to join some meals. Whatever the pattern, the central point is that meals and their groupings are in some way an expression of values and what matters to people who live in/use the centre.

TRAINING

Good workers are not just born; they have discovered ways of doing things, or skills, which bring about the outcome they want. Some people have developed these skills on their own. However, the point being stressed here is that practice skills can be learnt and improved. This is true at many different levels: a parent, caught in an unproductive cycle of exchanges with a child, may benefit from seeing an alternative way in which someone else handles a situation; a worker, understanding the fears people may have about how they are seen by others in a group, may develop a different way of talking to someone in front of others. Training needs to combine increased understanding with skill-development.

Knowledge, understanding, analysis

The knowledge which staff should have to work with groups and groupings is not detailed here, nor do we repeat the core concepts from earlier in this book. Instead we outline three aspects: context, knowledge of group behaviour, and knowledge of self.

The more that staff can see the relationship between the actions of particular people and the *context* in which those actions take place, the more likely it is that they will be sensitive in their work. Attention should be given to the significance of societal factors: for example, deprivation, of money, housing, environment and education; social prejudice; the discriminatory, institutional responses to certain groups of people, because they are black, women, or have a disability.

The second aspect of context concerns the attitudes that are held about different types of centres. Unless both the place and the people who use it and work there are valued, there is less chance of good practice. This is an extension of processes which take place in small groups whereby people can achieve little when they are limited by roles which they take on or are ascribed.

Knowledge about group behaviour is essential background to decisions such as: Which children should do what activity? What combination of people is more likely to be cohesive? What sort of capacity have different individuals within a group or grouping to cope with pressure or manage different activities?

Finally, the more individual workers know about *themselves and their style*, the better they will be able to manage their behaviour. Staff should be more conscious of themselves, of the way they react to others in various types of groupings and of the reasons for their actions, than should unpaid carers in their own homes.

Developing practice skills

Preparing oneself. We have commented on the importance of workers learning about themselves, their style and their own behaviour in groups and groupings. This can be done either away from the job, in groups specially designed for that purpose, or on the job by monitoring actual feelings and behaviour in daily work with groups and groupings. Experience of this sort, focused on people's behaviour here-and-now, should be an integral part of training. There are two main ways in which this can be done. One is to take part in some type of sensitivity group which has no set agenda, and which concentrates on group process, with particular emphasis on the giving and receiving of feedback between individuals. The other is to allocate space in a task group, by agreement, to the regular examination of group process and how what is happening between people is affecting task-achievement.

An effective method of examining skills and style is to study, with the help of feedback from colleagues, one's feelings and actions in different groups and groupings. A good starting point is to list the range of groupings which take place in a centre in a week. It is helpful to think as widely as possible, perhaps using the typology developed in Chapter 2. A worker can then write down feelings about each of these groups: Which groupings do I enjoy being in and which am I less keen on? Which do I try to avoid? What are the reasons? What are my feelings about the groupings I do not go to? (Being at ease in a group does not necessarily mean that a person is effective, and conversely.)

Next it is useful to think about what the worker actually does in various groups: Which are the groups in which he or she talks a lot or little? What strategies does that individual use to manage difficulties? The task is to search for patterns: does the person manage better in formal or informal groups, when a leader or a member, with colleagues, with users or with outsiders? In order to identify this 'personal profile', help is needed from colleagues: a great advantage of working in a centre is the shared and visible nature of much of the work, enabling supervisors and others, including users, to offer feedback based on direct observation.

Having collected information on performance, the next task is to do something about it. Again with help, techniques can be developed for managing better in at least some of the situations in which a person is less effective. For example, a person who cannot both follow the conversation in a staff meeting *and* contribute at an appropriate time may find it useful to scribble brief notes of key points to introduce when thoughts are in order. Someone who does not talk readily in groups may find it useful to be given an early slot to say something for which he or she has prepared since people who speak in groups have remarks directed back to them and thus get drawn into the conversation.

Studying interaction. The views people hold about others in groups are often based on slender evidence. Moreover a 'group' picture of another person, in effect a stereotype, can easily develop. Staff have to find ways to build accurate pictures of the behaviour of others in groups. One method is to create a *context profile*, as described by Dockar-Drysdale (1968). Staff are asked to record their interaction with an individual at particular times during a set period (for example, getting up, meals, leisure). From this will emerge a series of pictures of that person in 'normal' situations. It then becomes possible to look at the varying perspectives of different people on the same individual. It would be possible to use a method like this to ensure that recording is not only of occurrences when things have gone wrong, but could also be focused on someone's behaviour in various groups and groupings.

Other styles of recording of group interaction can be used. A diagrammatic method used in 'field' groupwork is to chart people's location in a room with an 'x' and then, on each occasion when someone speaks, to draw an arrow from that person to the person addressed. Patterns of communication are clearly illustrated by the clustering of arrows, and qualitative aspects can be added. This technique could be used in centres to track an individual's patterns of interaction in various groups and groupings through the course of a day. Whatever method is used, there is no doubt that valuable learning comes from studying what actually happens.

Developing techniques at a distance from practice. There are various means of improving practice away from the centre. Values are bound to influence our performance and are a crucial part of the context in which techniques are implemented. One way to consider them is to ask people to complete a questionnaire asking them to check their own assumptions about day and residential centres. Typical questions might be: 'When your mother or father is old, would you (did you) want him/her to move into a residential centre?' 'Would you feel the same/different about his/her attendance at a day centre?' Clearly there are no right answers. The purpose is to stimulate discussion after the questionnaire has been completed.

Another way is to examine attitudes to a specific event such as a meal-time. What does each person think important about different meals? How much priority would he or she give to: nutrition, enjoyment, choice (of menu or time or people with whom one sits), finishing everything that one has chosen to put on the plate, meals where people have time to spend with one another? Again, the different expectations of staff members soon become apparent, developing from varying cultural experiences (of race, class, gender, family).

Techniques can be improved by the use of exercises and role-plays. There are many possible approaches. One is to set up a typical situation and ask the group to examine what actions they would take. Thus, people might be given notes of the circumstances of someone who is coming to the centre for the first time, and be asked to plan for that person's first day. This can be done through discussion or by asking members to act parts (role-play). A useful elaboration of this is to divide the group up and ask sub-groups to think about the event from various perspectives; that of the newcomer, the relatives, the existing members, and the staff. At a different level, people might be asked to draw up an admissions policy for a department.

Another strategy begins with people studying selected theoretical frameworks and methods which underpin practice in groups and groupings. Participants would then be asked to take it in turns to co-lead the study group and to practise some technique. There are many variations of the form this might take: managing an intrusive, talkative member or a silent one; devising ways for members in a newly established group to get to know one another; establishing the ground-rules with a group of people (in relation to boundaries or confidentiality); or evaluating what has happened in a group. It would be essential for members to develop techniques related to informal groupings as well as more structured groups. Thus the task of managing silent or dominant members might be located at a meal-time in a residential centre, while that of considering ground-rules could be set in a day centre at a coffee break where one person is saying hurtful or intimate things about someone else.

Developing techniques whilst at work in the centre (as a student or employee). Some of the techniques above could be adapted for direct application on the job. There are also other possibilities. One is to focus on a particular aspect of practice, such as listening to users. Individuals are then asked to examine their own work in this area and to test out what they do. A task might be set where the person is asked to find out what users think about the routines at the start of a day. Key questions for the worker to consider will be: How do I plan to do this? How will I test out whether I have really understood what was said to me? How sure am I of the validity of what is said? Is it what they think I or someone else wants to hear?

A second method is to ask the worker to keep a diary of his or her interaction with various groups and groupings. Feelings would be noted, perhaps about joining particular groupings of people, or of events that were enjoyable or arouse anger. People would move from description of what happened, to possible explanations and then would consider what they hope to achieve the next time they participate in a similar event. The process is one of recording what happens, of noting one's own response, of thinking about explanations (both for the event and for personal reaction) and planning.

It is vital that people learn not only about being in groups where they are staff members with users, but also about being members of their own staff team. There are many team-building exercises that can be used for the latter. (Dyer 1977, Woodcock 1979, Collins and Bruce 1984, Payne and Scott 1982). These exercises are often more effective when the whole team is able to get away from the centre. The shared experience is integral to the learning and therefore it is essential for as many of the team as possible to participate. Some places achieve this by closing a day centre for half a day or a day, or getting in outsiders to look after a residential centre (a combination, perhaps, of managers and relief team).

External consultants are useful for occasions when groups of staff are looking at their own functioning (Brown 1984, Ch. 5). If there is not sufficient money to hire someone from outside the agency, it may be possible to find a colleague who works in the same organisation, but not in the same establishment. Some agencies are developing panels of internal consultants for this purpose.

Models and methods of learning. In conclusion we want to stress some key points. First, it is valuable to find ways to see things from the perspective of the users. Second, it is often hard for staff (as well as users) to envisage alternative ways of doing things. People get hooked into the values or practices of their own place. A useful (and cheap!) way of overcoming this is for staff from different establishments to swap for a period. This might take the form of a direct exchange of staff between two establishments, or of a group of centres working out a rota, in which people each have a set period in a different place. The third point is that reliance on a new worker picking up objectives and methods by being around with others is not good enough (Clough 1988). This style of modelling has been shown to lead to workers developing bad practices as well as good. There has to be more structure to the process of learning.

Fourth, emphasis should be given to those methods which demand that evidence is produced in relation both to understanding and to techniques. We have already mentioned a range of written ways of gathering evidence. However, audio and video-recordings (both of the 'real thing' and of role-play) provide particularly good material. Whilst they cannot illustrate everything that happens (looks, gestures or whatever happens 'off camera') they are helpful as a means of studying both interaction in a group and the practice of a worker. Video-recording of role-plays, particularly those in which several different techniques are tried out in response to the same initial incident, allows people to see their own practice and develop skills in safe environments.

Matching of skills and aptitudes

In this chapter we have identified a formidable array of skills for working with groups and groupings in centres. There is, of course, no suggestion that any single worker will have the full repertoire! Studies on worker-style confirm that each individual has particular strengths and aptitudes in particular areas, and other things at which they are not so good (see Brown 1977). The range of competence can be extended and latent skills developed, but for most of us there are limits to this process. This is certainly true when thinking about the different skills in groups and groupings needed in day and residential settings. Individuals will have a special flair for working with different types of groups and groupings: large groups; structured, closed, small groups; 'untidy' small groupings with unclear boundaries; groupings formed around domestic tasks; affinity groups; staff groups; outside bodies; one-to-one relationships. Thus, one person will be able to relate to an affinity group of users in a way which is not experienced as intrusive by the members while another will be an effective facilitator in a staff group.

One implication of this range of ability is to think about matching staff to those kinds of group contexts for which their abilities are best suited. In practice, staff shortages, rotas, illness, and other practicalities restrict the potential for matching, but the fundamental principle of a collective way of working which makes the best possible, differential use of all the resources available is valid. This often happens in an ad hoc 'natural' way in many centres, but there is scope for a more conscious thought-out approach. Apart from anything else it can be a great relief for it to be officially recognised that one is not expected to be brilliant at everything!

This same principle applies to users. The probability is that they are considerably less experienced than staff in coping with being in groups and groupings with other people, many of whom are, initially, strangers. They too have their individual strengths and abilities, and some things that they find very difficult. Staff need to be aware of users' different feelings about the range of groups and groupings and the stress involved in moving between them. They will also need to consider what, realistically, an individual can be expected to cope with.

CONCLUSION

The real test of the 'grand' objectives of social agencies is to be found in the daily life of the people who live and work in the centres about which we have been writing. If those people are to have more say in what happens within the centre, the inevitable consequence is that there will be less control from management. However, the gains are startling: users are reassured when staff are able to share their own struggles to adapt and cope with all the different demands; people, whatever their position, can enjoy being with others, find ways to contribute to the life of the place and, in the process, begin to value what is going on. In working out what should happen in various clusterings of people, the *groups and groupings* of the title, users and staff will discover the satisfaction of having more control over their lives.

BIBLIOGRAPHY

Adamson, J. and Warren, C. (1983) *Welcome to St. Gabriel's Centre!* London: The Childrens' Society.

Ainsworth, F. and Fulcher, L.C. (eds) (1981) *Group Care for Children: Concepts and Issues*, London: Tavistock.

Alissi, A. and Casper, M. (eds) (1985) *Time as a Factor in Groupwork. Social Work with Groups*, New York: Howarth Press. Special Issue 8 (2).

Allen, I. (1983) *Short-stay Residential Care for the Elderly*, London: Policy Studies Institute.

Argyris, C. (1968) 'Conditions for competence acquisition and therapy', *Journal of Applied Behavioural Science* 4(2) 147–77.

Atherton, J.S. (1986) *Professional Supervision in Group Care*, London: Tavistock Publications.

Atkinson, D. (1982) 'Distress signals in the community', *Community Care, 22 July.*

Atkinson, D. (1983) 'The community – participation and social contacts', in O. Russell and L. Ward (eds) *Houses or Homes? Evaluating Ordinary Housing Schemes for People with Mental Handicap*, London: Centre on Environment for the Handicapped.

Atkinson, D. (1984) *Steps Towards Integration*, University of Southampton (unpublished), M.Phil. thesis.

Atkinson, D. (1985) 'The use of participant observation and respondent diaries in a study of ordinary living', *British Journal of Mental Subnormality* XXX1, Pt.1, No.60, 33–40.

Atkinson, D. (1986) 'Engaging competent others: a study of the support networks of people with mental handicap', *British Journal of Social Work* 16, Supplement, 83–101.

Atkinson, D. and Ward, L. (1987) 'Friends and neighbours: relationships and opportunities in the community for people with a mental handicap', in N. Malin (ed) *Reassessing Community Care*, London: Croom Helm.

Atkinson, D. (1988a) 'Residential care for children and adults with mental handicap', in I. Sinclair (ed) *Residential Care. The Research Reviewed.* (Vol 2 of the Wagner Report), London: HMSO.

Atkinson, D. (1988b) *Someone To Turn To*, Kidderminster: British Institute of Mental Handicap Publications.

Bales, R.F. and Borgatta, E.F. (1955) 'Size of group as a factor in the interaction profile', in P. Hare *et al.* (eds) *Small Groups: Studies in Social Interaction*, Glencoe: The Free Press.

Ball, L. and Sowa, T. (1985) *Groupwork and IT-a Practical Handbook*, London: Intermediate Treatment Association.

Bateson, G. (1976) *Steps to an Ecology of Mind*, London: Palladin.

Beedell, C. (1970) *Residential Life With Children*, London: Routledge and Kegan Paul.

Beedell, C. (1984) Personal communication.

Bertcher, H. and Maple, F.F. (1977) *Creating Groups*, London: Sage Publications.

Bettelheim, B. (1950) *Love is not Enough*, London: Collier-Macmillan.

Bettelheim, B. (1974) *A Home for the Heart*, London: Thames & Hudson.

Bion, W.R. (1968) *Experiences in Groups, and other papers*, London: Tavistock.

Brandes, D. and Phillips, H. (1978) *Gamesters' Handbook*, London: Hutchinson.

Brandon, D. (1987) 'Participation and choice, a worthwhile pilgrimage', in *Social Work Today* 21.12.87.

Brown, A. (1977) 'Worker-style in social-work', *Social Work Today*, 8(29).

Brown, A. (1984) *Consultation*, London: Heinemann.

Brown, A. (1986) *Groupwork*, Aldershot: Gower.

Cairns, B. (1984) 'The children's family trust: a unique approach to substitute family care?', *British Journal of Social Work*, 14, 457–73.

Carter, J. (1981) *Day Services for Adults: somewhere to go*, London: George Allen & Unwin.

Carter, J. (1988) *Creative Day-Care for Mentally Handicapped People*, Oxford: Blackwell.

Casburn, M. (1979) *Girls will be Girls: Sexism and Juvenile Justice in a London Borough*, London: Womens Research and Resources Centre Publications.

Clark, D.H. (1965) 'The therapeutic concept: practice and future', *British Journal of Psychology* 111, 947–54.

Clough, R. (1981) *Old Age Homes*, London: George Allen & Unwin.

Clough, R. (1982) *Residential Work*, Basingstoke: Macmillan.

Clough, R. (1988) *Living Away From Home*, Bristol Papers: University of Bristol.

Collins, T. and Bruce, T. (1984) *Staff Support and Staff Training*, London: Tavistock.

Daines, R. (1988) *A Study of the Ely Day Centre*, Barnardo's Partnership Research: Bristol University.

Dearling, A. and Armstrong, H. (1980) *The Youth Games Book*, Scottish IT Resource Centre.

De'Ath, E. (1985) *Self-Help and Family Centres*, London: National Children's Bureau.

DHSS (1975) *Better Services for the Mentally Ill*, Cmnd 6823:HMSO.

Dharamsi, F. *et al.* (1979) *Caring for Children. A diary of a local authority children's home*, Ilkley: Owen Wells.

Dockar-Drysdale, B. (1968) *Therapy in Child Care*, London: Longman.

Douglas, T. (1976) *Groupwork Practice*, London: Tavistock.

Douglas, T. (1978) *Basic Groupwork*, London: Tavistock.

Douglas, T. (1983) *Groups: Understanding People Gathered Together*, London: Tavistock Publications.

Douglas, T. (1986) *Group Living. The application of group dynamics in residential settings*, London: Tavistock.

Dyer, W.G. (1977) *Team-building: issues and alternatives*, Reading, Mass.: Addison-Wesley.

Evans, S., and Galloway, D. (1980) 'Staff and supervision in home residential setting', in R. Walton and D. Elliott (eds) (1980), *Residential Care: a reader in current theory and practice*, Oxford: Pergamon.

Fennell, G. *et al.* (1981) *Day Centres for the Elderly in East Anglia*, University of East Anglia.

Fisher, M., Marsh, P. and Phillips, D. with Sainsbury, E. (1986) *In and Out of Care*, London: Batsford/BAAF.

Fulcher, L.C. and Ainsworth, F. (1985) *Group Care Practice with Children*, London: Tavistock.

Galinsky, M. and Schopler, J.H. (1985) 'Patterns of entry and exit in open-ended groups', *Social Work With Groups* 8(2).

Garland, J.A., Jones, H.H. and Kolodny, R.L. (1985) 'A model for stages of development of social work groups', in S. Bernstein (ed.) *Explorations in Groupwork*, Boston University School of Social Work.

Garvin, C. (1981) *Contemporary Groupwork*, New Jersey: Prentice-Hall.

Genders, E. and Player, E. (1986) 'Womens' imprisonment: the effect of youth custody', *British Journal of Criminology* 26(4).

Glasser, P., Sarri, R., and Vinter, R. (eds) (1974) *Individual Change through Small Groups*, New York: The Free Press.

Goffman, E. (1968) *Asylums: essays on the social situation of mental patients and other inmates*, Harmondsworth: Penguin.

Hampden-Turner, C. (1970) *Radical Man*, London: Duckworths.

Harlesden Community Project (1979) *Community Work and Caring for Children*, Ilkley: Owen Wells.

Harrison, R. and Lubin, B. (1965) 'Personal style, group composition and learning', *Journal of Applied Behavioural Science* 1, 287–300.

Hartford, M. (1971) *Groups in Social Work*, New York: Columbia University Press.

Hasler, J. (1984) *Family Centres*, London: Children's Society.

Hawkins, P. (1979) 'Adapting or Being Adapted'. Paper given at the 2nd Anglo-Dutch Conference on Therapeutic Communities, Windsor.

Hawkins, P. (1986) 'Living the Learning', Ph.D. Thesis, University of Bath.

Heap, K. (1977) *Group Theory for Social Workers*, Oxford: Pergamon.

Heap, K. (1985) *The Practice of Social Work with Groups*, London: Allen & Unwin.

Heap, K. (1988) 'The worker and the group process: a dilemma revisited', *Groupwork* 1(1).

Hil, R. (1986) 'Centre 81: clients' and officers' views on the Southampton Day Centre', in J. Pointing (ed.) *Alternatives to Custody*, Oxford: Blackwell.

Hinshelwood, R.D. and Manning, N. (eds) (1979) *Therapeutic Communities*, London: Routledge & Kegan Paul.

Home Office Statistical Bulletins (1986, 1987) *The Ethnic Origins of Prisoners*, Home Office Statistical Department.

Illich, I. (1975) *Medical Nemesis*, London: Calder & Boyars.

Illich, I. (1977) *Disabling Professions*, London: Marion Boyars.

Jahoda, M., Lazarsfeld, P.F., and Zeisel, H. (1972) *Marienthal, the sociography of an unemployed community*, London: Tavistock.

Jansen, E. (ed.) (1980) *The Therapeutic Community*, London: Croom Helm.

Jones, M. (1952) *Social Psychiatry: a study of therapeutic communities*, London: Tavistock.

Jones, M. (1968) *Beyond the Therapeutic Community*, New Haven: Yale University Press.

Jones, M. (1979) 'The therapeutic community, social learning and social change', in R.D. Hinshelwood and N. Manning (eds), *Therapeutic Communities*, London: Routledge & Kegan Paul.

King, R.D., Raynes, N. and Tizard, J. (1971) *Patterns of Residential Care*, London: Routledge & Kegan Paul.

Konopka, G. (1983, 3rd edn) *Social Groupwork: a helping process*, New Jersey: Prentice-Hall.

Konopka, G. (1970) *Groupwork in the Institution* (revised edn), New York: Association Press.

Kreeger, L. (ed.) (1975) *The Large Group*, London: Constable, and Maresfield Reprints.

Landau, S.F. and Nathan, G. (1983) 'Selecting delinquents for cautioning in the London Metropolitan Area', *British Journal of Criminology*, 23(2).

Lang, N. (1972) 'A broad range model of practice in the social work group', *Social Service Review* 46(1) 76–89.

Lang, N. (1981) 'Some defining characteristics of the social work group: unique social form', in S. Abels and P. Abels (eds), *Social Work with Groups*, Proceedings, First Symposium on Social Work with Groups. Hebron, Connecticut: Practitioners Press.

Lang, N. (1986) 'Social work practice in small social forms', in N. Lang (ed.) *Collectivity in Social Groupwork: concept and practice; Social Work with Groups* Special Issue 9(4).

Leff, J., Kuipers, L., Berkowitz, R. and Sturgeon, D. (1985) 'A controlled study of social interaction in the families of schizophrenic patients: a two-year follow-up', *British Journal of Psychiatry* 146, 594–600.

Lennox, D. (1982) *Residential Group Therapy for Children*, London: Tavistock.

BIBLIOGRAPHY

Levinson, D. and Astrachan, B. (1976) 'Entry into the Mental Health Centre – a problem in organisational boundary regulation', in E. Miller, (ed) *Task and Organisation*, London: Wiley.

Lindenfield, G. and Adams, R. (1984) *Problem-Solving Through Self-Help Groups*, Ilkley: Self-Help Associates.

McCaughan, N. (ed.) (1978) *Groupwork: learning and practice*, London: George Allen & Unwin.

McLean, A. and Marshall, J. (1988) *Working with Cultures: a workbook for people in local government*, London: Local Government Training Board.

Maier, H.W. (ed.) (1965) *Group Work as Part of Residential Treatment*, New York: NASW.

Maier, H.W. (1981) 'Essential components in care and treatment environments for children', in F. Ainsworth and L.C. Fulcher (eds) *Group Care for Children*, London: Tavistock Publications.

Main, T. (1975) 'Some psychodynamics of large groups', in L. Kreeger (ed.) *The Large Group*, London: Constable, and Maresfield Reprints.

Main, T. (1980) 'Some basic concepts in therapeutic community work', in E. Jansen (ed.) (1980), *The Therapeutic Community*, London: Croom Helm.

Malin, N. (1983) *Group Homes for the Mentally Handicapped*, London: HMSO.

Marshall, M. (1983) *Social Work with Old People*, London: Macmillan.

Maslow, A. (1972) *The Farther Reaches of Human Nature*, New York: Viking.

Mason, K. (1983) *An Examination of Policy and Practice relating to Minimum Support Group Homes for the Mentally Handicapped in Avon*, Bristol: Avon SSD.

Menzies, I. (1960) 'A case-study in the functioning of social systems as a defence against anxiety', *Human Relations* 13: 95–121.

Miller, E. and Gwynne, C. (1972) *A Life Apart*, London: Tavistock.

MIND (1981) *New Directions for Psychiatric Day Services*, London: MIND.

Mittler, P. and Serpell, R. (1985) 'Services: an international perspective', in A.M. Clarke, A.B.B. Clarke and J.M. Berg (eds) *Mental Deficiency: the changing outlook* (4th edn), London: Methuen.

Moos, R.H. (1974) *Evaluating Treatment Environments*, New York: Wiley.

Moreno, J.L. (1972) *Sociometry and the Science of Man*, New York: Beacon House.

Mortimer, E. (1982) *Working with the Elderly*, London: Heinemann.

Mounsey, N. (1983) 'It's not what you do, it's the way you do it', *Community Care*, 20 Oct.

National IT Federation (1985) *Anti-Racist Practice for Intermediate Treatment*, Nat. IT Fed. Working Party on Racism in the Juvenile Justice System.

Parker, C. and Alcoe, J. (1984) 'Finding the right way out', *Social Work Today*, 16 April.

Payne, C. (1978) 'Working with groups in the residential setting', in N. McCaughan (ed.) *Groupwork: learning and practice*, London: George Allen & Unwin.

Payne, C. and Scott, T. (1982) *Developing Supervision of Teams in Field and Residential Work*, London: NISW.

Phelan, J. (1983) *Family Centres*, London: The Children's Society.

Pick, P. (1981) *Children at Tree Tops*, London: Residential Care Association.

Pointing, J. (ed.) (1986) *Alternatives to Custody*, Oxford: Blackwell.

Polsky, H. (1965) *Cottage Six*, New York: Wiley.

Race, D.G. and Race, D.M. (1979) *The Cherries Group Home: a beginning*, London: HMSO.

Redl, F. and Wineman, D. (1957) *The Aggressive Child*, New York: Free Press.

Rice, A.K. (1965) *Learning For Leadership*, London: Tavistock.

Ross, S. and Thorpe, A. (1988) 'Programming skills in social groupwork', *Groupwork* 1(2).

Rowlings, C. (1981) *Social Work with Elderly People*, London: George Allen & Unwin.

Salmon, P. (1985) *Living in Time*, London: J.M. Dent & Sons.

Schopler, J.H. and Galinsky, M. (1984) 'Meeting practice needs: conceptualising the open-ended group', *Social Work With Groups* 7(2).

Schutz, W.C. (1958) *FIRO: a three-dimensional theory of human behaviour*, New York: Rinehart.

Shands, M.C. (1960) *Thinking and Psychotherapy*, London: Tavistock.

Shepherd, G. (1981) 'Day care and the chronic patient', in MIND, *New Directions in Psychiatric Day Care*, London: MIND.

Sherif, M. and Sherif, C.W. (1969) *Social Psychology*, New York: Harper & Row.

Silverman, P. (1980) *Mutual Help Groups*, London: Sage.

Slater, R. and Lipman, A. (1980) 'Towards caring through design', in R. Walton and D. Elliott (eds) *Residential Care*, Oxford: Pergamon.

Smith, P.(ed.) (1980) *Group Processes and Personal Change*, London: Harper & Row.

Southwark (1987) *Report of the Inquiry into Nye Bevan Lodge*, London: Borough of Southwark.

Stephenson, R.M. and Scarpitti, F.R. (1974) *Group Interaction as Therapy*, USA: Greenwood Press.

Sulman, J. (1986) 'The worker's role in collectivity', in N. Lang (ed) *Collectivity in Social Groupwork : concept and practice. Social Work with Groups*, New York: Howarth Press. Special Issue 9(4).

Tajfel, H. (ed.) (1978) *Differentiation between Social Groups: studies of the social psychology of intergroup relations*, London: Academic Press.

Taylor, W. (1981) *Probation and After-Care in a Multi-Racial Society*, CRE and West Midlands Probation and After-Care Service.

Theodorson, G. and Theodorson, A. (eds) (1969) *A Modern Dictionary of Sociology*, New York: Cromwell.

Tuckman, B.W. (1965) 'Developmental sequence in small groups', *Psychological Bulletin*, 63(6).

Twelvetrees, A. (1982) *Community Work*, London: BASW/Macmillan.

Tyne, A. (1977) *Residential Provision for Adults who are Mentally Handicapped*, London: Campaign for People with Mental Handicaps.

Tyne, A. (1978) *Looking at life in a Hospital, Hostel, Home, or Unit*, London: Campaign for People with Mental Handicaps.

Vanstone, M. (1986) 'The Pontypridd Day Training Centre: diversion from prison in action', in J. Pointing (ed) *Alternatives to Custody*, Oxford: Blackwell.

Vorrath, H.H. and Brendtro, L.K. (1984 edn) *Positive Peer Culture*, Chicago: Aldine.

Wagner Report (1988) *A Positive Choice*, NISW: HMSO.

Walton, R. and Elliott, D. (eds) (1980) *Residential Care: a reader in current theory and practice*, Oxford: Pergamon.

Whitaker, D.S. (1985) *Using Groups to Help People*, London: Routledge & Kegan Paul.

Whitaker, D.S., Cook, J., Dunne, C., and Lunn-Rockliffe, S. (1984) 'The experience of residential care from the perspectives of children, parents and care-givers'. End of grant report to the ESRC, Unpublished.

Whitaker, D.S. and Lieberman, M.A. (1964) *Psychotherapy through the Group Process*, New York: Atherton Press; London: Tavistock.

Willcocks, D., Peace, S., and Kellaher, L. (1987) *Private Lives in Public Places*, London: Tavistock.

Willmott, P. and Mayne, S. (1983) *Families at the Centre*, London: Bedford Square Press.

Wills, W.D. (1960) *Throw Away Thy Rod*, London: Victor Gollancz.

Wing, J. and Brown, G. (1970) *Institutionalism and Schizophrenia: a comparative study of three mental hospitals, 1960-1968*, Cambridge: Cambridge University Press.

Wolfensberger, W. (1972) *The Principle of Normalisation in Human Services*, Toronto: National Institute of Mental Retardation.

Wolfensberger, W. (1980) *Normalisation: social integration and community services*, Baltimore: University Park Press.

Wolfensberger, W. (1983) 'Social role valorisation: a proposed new term for the principle of normalisation', *Mental Retardation*; 234–9.

Wolins, M. (1982) *Revitalising Residential Settings*, California: Jossey-Bass.

Woodcock, M. (1979) *Team Development Manual*, Aldershot: Gower

Yalom, I.D. (1975) *The Theory and Practice of Group Psychotherapy*, New York: Basic Books.

Zander, A. (1982) *Making Groups Effective*, California: Jossey-Bass.

NAME INDEX

Adams, R. 20
Adamson, J. 20
Ainsworth, F. 14, 16, 20
Alcoe, J. 150
Alissi, A. 36
Allen, I. 35
Argyris, C. 107, 112
Armstrong, H. 141
Astrachan, B. 105
Atherton, J. S. 189, 197
Atkinson, D. 25, 41, 150, 151, 153,
   162, 164, 167, 189, 197, 201, 205

Bales, R. F. 33
Ball, L. 141, 192, 195, 196, 205
Bano, B. 193, 194, 199, 203
Bateson, G. 149
Beedell, C. 20, 200
Berkowitz, R. 101
Bertcher, H. 31–2, 87
Bettelheim, B. 169, 194
Bion, W. R. 39, 45, 54, 109, 112
Blake 102
Borgatta, E. F. 33
Brandes, D. 141
Brandon, D. 110
Brendtro, L. K. 15
Brown, A. 20, 30, 53, 85, 106, 113, 149,
   151, 152, 161, 165, 202, 211, 212
Brown, G. 104
Burton 28, 188, 193, 194, 200, 204, 205
Bruce, T. 20, 211

Cairns, B. 25, 170, 189, 193, 194, 201,
   204, 205
Carter, J. 17, 18, 100, 104, 193
Casburn, M. 136

Caspar, M. 36
Clark, D.H. 46
Clough, R. 4, 20, 29, 106, 113, 149,
   151, 152, 161, 165, 211, 212
Collins, T. 20, 211

Daines, R. 193
Dearling, A. 141
De'Ath, E. 20
Dharamsi, F. 18
DHSS 100
Dockar-Drysdale, B. 16, 208
Douglas, T. 16–17, 20, 30, 152, 166,
   170, 172, 173, 175, 181, 187
Dyer, W. G. 211

Evans, S. 20

Fennel, G. 18
Fisher, M. 4
Foulkes, S.H. 45
Freud, S. 108
Fulcher, L. C. 14, 16, 20

Galinsky, M. 20
Galloway, D. 20
Garland, J. A. 39
Garvin, C. 20
Genders, E. 136
Glasser, P. 20
Goffman, E. 29, 104
Gwynne, C. 8

Hampden-Turner, C. 49
Harlesden Community Project 20, 35
Harrison, R. 113
Hartford, M. 20

SUBJECT INDEX

Editors' note: In the text we have tried to distinguish between *groups* and *groupings*, whilst recognising that they overlap and that there is not always consistency between authors. When using the index, therefore, the sections on *groupings*, *groups*, and *groups and groupings* should be used in conjunction with one another; further similar references will be found under *group homes* and *groupwork*.